FOL
$1,00

THE
ROBERT F. KENNEDY
ASSASSINATION

D0863667

New Revelations On The Conspiracy
And Cover-Up, 1968-1991

Philip H. Melanson

Foreword by Anthony Summers
Introuction by John H. Davis

SPi.
BOOKS
A Division of Shapolsky Publishers

The Robert F. Kennedy Assassination

S.P.I. BOOKS
A division of Shapolsky Publishers, Inc.

Previously published in hardcover by
S.P.I. Books, New York

ISBN 1-56171-324-4

For any additional information, contact:

S.P.I. BOOKS/Shapolsky Publishers, Inc.
136 West 22nd Street
New York, NY 10011
212/633-2022 / FAX 212/633-2123

Manufactured in Canada

10 9 8 7 6 5 4 3 2 1

To Greg Stone

Each time a man stands up for an ideal, or acts to improve the lot of others, or strikes out against injustice, he sends forth a tiny ripple of hope, and crossing each other from a million different centers of energy and daring, those ripples build a current that can sweep down the mightiest walls of oppression and resistance.

– Robert F. Kennedy, *To Seek a Newer World*, 1967

We've had difficult times in the past. We will have difficult times in the future. It is not the end of violence; it is not the end of lawlessness; it is not the end of disorder.

– Robert F. Kennedy, to a crowd in the Indianapolis black ghetto, on the evening of the assassination of Dr. Martin Luther King, Jr.

Acknowledgments

The author's acknowledgments of the numerous persons who provided varied assistance and support for the pursuit of truth in the RFK case and/or for this book are both extensive and important. They are too long to be included here. The interested reader will find them on page 345.

Contents

Photo/documents section follows page 180

FOREWORD

BY ANTHONY SUMMERS

"**Y**ou would be very angry," a veteran congressional investigator has said, "if someone with a gun stopped you from going into the voting booth and took away your freedom to choose. I think you should get very angry about that. If not, you might as well let go of your individual freedom. It will be gone soon enough anyway."

The reference was to the assassination of President Kennedy. Robert F. Kennedy, his younger brother, was cut down at the age of 42, minutes after winning the California primary, his spring-board to the Democratic nomination for the presidential contest of 1968. After the shambles of the Chicago Convention that year, Hubert Humphrey – with neither Bobby Kennedy's charisma nor his apppeal to young people and minorities – lost only narrowly to Richard Nixon. Had Senator Robert Kennedy not been shot, he would very likely have won the presidency. The bullets fired in a Los Angeles hotel kitchen prevented us from finding out what he would have done with it and how he might have changed the course of history.

The very fact of Robert Kennedy's assassination should make American citizens – including millions not born when he was murdered – very angry indeed. After getting angry, they should demand answers to a host of important questions – answers long withheld from the American people. Why? Because justice faltered and because misguided officialdom has been obsessed with cover-up and secrecy. Americans should be angry all over again when they discover that those who are supposed to be their safety valve – the nation's reporters and academics – have failed to effectively press for the answers.

There are many thousands of journalists, full-time historians, and political scientists in the United States. With shame for my profession, for I am myself a journalist, I must remind us all that no major newspaper or broadcast outlet – not one – has worked consistently to throw light on the assassinations that have blighted our time. In the academic field, Professor Philip Melanson stands virtually alone. Assassination, unfortunately, is thematic to our time, yet it is not seriously probed in our newsrooms, nor is it accepted as a subject for mainstream scholarship in our universities.

Ponder that fact. Meanwhile, be glad that there is, at least, this sturdy author. He has given the public important books on the murders of Martin Luther King, Jr., John F. Kennedy, and now Robert. His work is scholarly yet highly readable. More than anything, it is about the denial of democracy to a people whose leaders endlessly speak as though America was some paragon of democratic perfection, a proud beacon for a less fortunate world. The light of a beacon can flicker, and if it can flicker it can be extinguished altogether. That is why this book matters.

Ireland
1991

Anthony Summers, a former BBC journalist, is the
author of *Conspiracy*, on the assassination of
John F. Kennedy, *Goddess*, a biography of Marilyn
Monroe, and a forthcoming biography of J. Edgar Hoover.

INTRODUCTION

BY JOHN H. DAVIS

By 1968, the year in which he entered the race for the presidency, Robert Francis Kennedy had made many powerful enemies – both individuals and groups. Among the most powerful individuals who hated him were: ex-Teamsters boss Jimmy Hoffa, whom Kennedy had sent to prison; Louisiana Mafia boss Carlos Marcello, whom Kennedy had unsuccessfully tried to deport; FBI Director J. Edgar Hoover, who had grown to fear and detest Kennedy when the young Attorney General had been his boss; CIA agent William Harvey, former coordinator of the CIA-Mafia plots to assassinate Fidel Castro, who was banished to the CIA's Rome office by an angry Robert Kennedy after Harvey sent unauthorized commando teams into Cuba during the Cuban missile crisis; and, of course, Republican presidential candidate Richard M. Nixon, who regarded Robert Kennedy as the only Democratic candidate who could defeat him in the coming election.

The most powerful groups arrayed against Kennedy included the Teamsters Union, organized crime, the Southern California ranchers (resentful of Kennedy's support of migrant farm workers leader César Chávez), the big oil companies and oil magnates (Kennedy wanted to repeal the oil depletion allowance), the military-industrial complex (Kennedy wanted to pull out of the

Vietnam War), and the Southern white segregationists, who were violently opposed to Kennedy's ardent support for civil rights.

A Robert F. Kennedy presidency would have severely threatened all these individuals and groups. For Jimmy Hoffa, who had actively plotted against Kennedy's life in 1963, it probably would have meant serving out his entire thirteen-year prison sentence instead of receiving a presidential pardon upon Richard M. Nixon's election. For organized-crime boss Carlos Marcello it would have meant certain deportation. For Hoover it would have meant the dreaded netherworld of immediate retirement. And for the Southern California ranchers (who contributed to a $500,000 contract on Kennedy's life in June 1968*), the Southwestern oilmen, and the principal American defense contractors, an RFK administration would have meant sure losses in the many millions of dollars.

And yet, with this powerful array of domestic enemies, who turned out to be the suspected assassin of Robert F. Kennedy? A Palestinian Arab whose family had allegedly been forced out of West Jerusalem during the fighting that broke out after the expiration of the British mandate over Palestine, in 1948. With the range and power of Kennedy's known enemies there was something suspect about Sirhan Sirhan's assassinating Kennedy for relatively hazy and difficult-to-believe political reasons. On close scrutiny, Sirhan's role appeared more likely to have been a diversionary one, a decoy to distract investigators from the true forces behind the crime.

Who or what was behind the assassination of Robert F. Kennedy? In his meticulously researched and eminently responsible book on the crime, Philip Melanson does not give us a definite answer to that question. What he does present is convincing evidence that, whatever his role in the killing, Sirhan Sirhan did not act alone. The author also provides equally convincing indications that the official investigative authorities consistently covered up evidence that suggested others may have been involved in the crime.

In reviewing both the John F. Kennedy and Robert F. Kennedy assassination cases, remarkable similarities between the two emerge.

* According to an FBI report.

Both suspected assassins appeared to have had "legends" created for them in advance of the commission of their crime, in order to account for their motivation: Oswald the mad Marxist and Castro sympathizer; Sirhan the anti-Israel Palestinian avenger. Both were stationed in high-visibility crowded areas at the scene of the crime. The police and the FBI declared both men to be lone gunmen, unaffiliated with any accomplices – determining this within days of the two crimes, long before the official investigations had been completed. Both appeared to be patsies, set up by others to take the blame for the crime. And in both cases the local police and the FBI actively covered up evidence of conspiracy.

It is to Professor Melanson's credit that he refrains from indulging in wild speculation as to *who* was behind Robert F. Kennedy's murder. Rather, he largely limits his attention to the concrete, available evidence, which indicates that the Senator's suspected assassin, Sirhan Sirhan, could not have acted alone and that the Los Angeles Police Department, the office of the Los Angeles District Attorney, and the FBI all tried to suppress and discourage the notion that Sirhan had accomplices.

What new evidence has Professor Melanson uncovered, and how and where did he find it? First, it must be pointed out that Dr. Melanson is the first author of a re-analysis of the RFK assassination to have had access to most of the existing Los Angeles Police Department's files on the case. For almost 20 years, LAPD had inexcusably sat on its 50,000-page file of assassination documents, refusing to allow public access to it. Finally, after considerable pressure from independent investigators (including Melanson), concerned citizens, and the efforts of a few influential media figures, the files were finally released and shipped to the California State Archives at Sacramento, where they were redacted, organized, and finally made available to the public – two decades after the crime.

We are fortunate to have had a scholar of Philip Melanson's stature address the huge task of examining the long-withheld LAPD files. A professor with impeccable academic credentials and long-standing familiarity with the RFK assassination case, he is the ideal writer to come to grips with the tangled web of this unsolved murder. It took Melanson and his team of research assistants four months to sift through the 82,000-page mountain of RFK assassination documents (50,000 pages of LAPD files and 32,000 pages of FBI documents). By the time he and his assistants were through, it was abundantly clear that the Los Angeles Police Department had altered, suppressed, and destroyed vital evidence in the case.

Exactly what was destroyed? Twenty-four hundred photographs were committed to the flames in a medical-waste incinerator at Los Angeles County General Hospital. Among these casualties were three rolls of film confiscated by the police from an eyewitness to the shooting who took pictures of Senator Kennedy at the very crucial moments when the shots were being fired. Why weren't these importance pieces of evidence preserved for analysis by later investigators? Furthermore, of the 3,470 interviews LAPD conducted during its original investigation, tapes of only 301 of them survived. The other tapes were apparently incinerated. Moreover, of the 51 witnesses considered significant by the FBI and LAPD, somehow not one tape of their testimonies has survived. But that is not all. Among the items of material evidence missing were the following: at least five pantry ceiling tiles, two of which contained bullet holes, a pantry doorframe containing two bullet holes, X-rays and test results on these ceiling tiles and the doorframe, spectrographic test results (on bullets possibly recovered in the pantry), as well as the left sleeve of Senator Kennedy's jacket and shirt.

What else did Professor Melanson's examination of the LAPD RFK assassination files reveal? Melanson puts it bluntly when he writes that the files reveal that crucial evidence was "ignored, altered, destroyed or covered up."

Does conflict with the lone-gunman scenario accepted and promoted by the official investigators emerge from Melanson's investigation? Yes, Melanson's seemingly bizarre but, on close scrutiny, believable scenario posits a second gunman firing the fatal shot at Kennedy from almost point-blank range, while a hypnotically programmed Sirhan Sirhan, three to five feet away from the Senator, fired wildly on cue, wounding five people but not Kennedy. Melanson also develops substantial evidence on the existence of a female accomplice in a polka-dot dress. (She was seen repeatedly by numerous witnesses but, inexplicably, was ignored by the investigators.)

Who among Kennedy's most threatened enemies could have concocted and orchestrated such a complicated plot – one surpassing in imagination and daring anything James Bond ever attempted? On this issue Melanson refuses to speculate. He clearly believes, however, that some intelligence arm of the federal government, or intelligence expert under contract with the government, had to have had a hand in it. He concludes that a coalition of Kennedy's enemies – those who felt most at risk by his likely election to the presidency – decided that Kennedy had to be eliminated, and awarded the job to the most sophisticated assassination team available.

What, now, is to be done about this case? The release of the LAPD files was a valuable first step toward dispelling the disarray and misinformation that have marked the case from the outset. What should the next step be? Professor Melanson believes that an official federal investigative body with subpoena power, not from Los Angeles or Sacramento, but from Washington, D.C., must take up the task of pursuing the truth behind the still-unsolved murder of Robert F. Kennedy. Only such an impartial body could ever hope to uncover the conspiracy that ended Kennedy's life and thwarted the American democratic process. If such an investigation ever does finally come about, it will certainly owe much to the persistence of Philip Melanson and the contents of this breakthrough book.

New York
1991

John H. Davis is the author of *The Kennedys: Dynasty and Disaster, Mafia Kingfish: Carlos Marcello and the Assassination of John F. Kennedy, The Guggenheims,* and *The Bouviers.*

PROLOGUE

The assassination of Robert F. Kennedy was a wrenching event. It was the third such case in five and a half years.* To many Americans it seemed as if the very fabric of their democratic system was being shredded by gunfire, as a trio of the most charismatic political leaders of the era were felled by assassins' bullets.

But the Robert Kennedy case was different, or so it was perceived by most of the media and the public. This tragedy seemed not to be compounded by uncertainties about whether the law-enforcement system was willing and able to respond effectively, or about whether justice could be done. In the cases of John F. Kennedy and Martin Luther King, Jr., there was no "smoking gun" arrest. Lee Harvey Oswald never lived to stand trial, major questions subsequently arose as to whether he perpetrated the crime. No witness even claimed to have seen King's killer fire the fatal shot. After a fleeting glimpse of a fleeing suspect, it took what was described as the "greatest manhunt in law-enforcement history" – two months – to finally arrest James Earl Ray in London, almost 48 hours after Robert Kennedy had been shot.

Though it was no comfort in terms of the loss of Senator Kennedy, this case at least appeared to have been solved. To most, it was open and shut. Dozens of witnesses saw the assailant fire.

---

* President John F. Kennedy in November 1963, Martin Luther King, Jr., in April 1968.

Sirhan Sirhan, apprehended with smoking gun in hand, was kept alive to stand trial and was convicted. Finally, there was a case that seemed clearly to fit the mold of the politically motivated, psychologically disturbed lone assassin. The rumors and allegations of conspiracy seemed to the majority of the media and the public to be, for once, not only unfounded but easily refutable.

Video tapes of the traumatic event were repeated endlessly: Here was the jubilant Senator making his way through the small pantry of the Ambassador Hotel in Los Angeles, shaking hands. Then chaos and panic as gunfire erupted. Cameras captured the frenzied struggle to subdue the attacker. They showed us the terrible vision of Robert Kennedy lying on the floor and bleeding profusely. To this day, many people believe that these same cameras captured the actual shooting (as the Zapruder film had done in President Kennedy's assassination); some are insistent to the point of anger that it's all on film. Like so many elements of this case, however, this too is an illusion: No photographic record of the actual shooting is known to exist.

With the vivid footage just before and just after Kennedy was shot, and with such a seemingly clear mental picture of what allegedly transpired in between – a picture created by drawings, trial testimony and media accounts – the image of the crime seems to many to be real enough to have been viewed on film. As the following analysis will clearly demonstrate, this is a case dominated by false images generated by assumption, ignorance and official government disinformation.

This seemingly simplest to solve of the three 1960s assassinations turns out to be, in many ways, the most complex; certainly, the most bizarre. The apparent simplicity is but the largest illusion, resting on a foundation of smaller ones created by conspiratorial design and official malfeasance.

Another striking difference in the RFK case is that because of the illusion of simplicity and the extreme official secrecy (which strongly reinforced one another), the case did not enter its ''Warren Commission phase'' until 16 to 20 years after the crime. The

Warren Commission released its report and 26 volumes of hearings and exhibits in 1964, one year after President Kennedy's death. This fueled further questioning and controversy; the record eventually showed that the Commission's work was seriously flawed. With the passage of the Freedom of Information Act in 1966, researchers successfully (albeit slowly) pursued the release of case files from the FBI, CIA and the Secret Service, as well as voluminous Warren Commission records not published in the 26 volumes. Challenges to the official findings escalated with each new release.

In contrast, the official investigative agency in the RFK case, the Los Angeles Police Department (LAPD), steadfastly refused to release the *Summary Report* of its investigation (the analogue to the *Warren Commission Report*) until 1986, and the raw files were not released until 1988.

In 1985-86, the Los Angeles District Attorney's Office (LADA) processed its files for public disclosure. In response to a Freedom of Information Act request by political scientist and RFK researcher Gregory Stone and myself, 32,000 previously unreleased documents were gradually made public between 1986 and the present.* Finally the raw data behind the official conclusions was accessible. Questions could no longer be convincingly dismissed, by officials and the media, as being uninformed. The official conclusions could be judged on the basis of the case record rather than what officials claimed about the record. For nearly two decades Los Angeles authorities had defended their findings by referring to a mountain of data that they refused to release. By 1988, with the vast majority of the documents disclosed, public debate and discussion about the RFK case finally, belatedly entered its "Warren Commission era."

By integrating the released files with the energetic investigative efforts of a handful of journalists, scholars and citizens, and through my own RFK investigation, it is now possible to come much closer to the truth than official investigators have done.

This case is not an open-and-shut, one-man job: It is an

---

* The disclosure of LAPD, LADA and FBI files was due to the efforts of a rather small but dedicated group of people (journalists, scholars, politicians, concerned citizens) who exerted legal, political and administrative pressure. Gregory Stone and Paul Schrade (a friend of Senator Kennedy and a shooting victim in the assassination) played prominent roles in this process.

unsolved conspiracy (as many people have speculated early on, without benefit of official files or much of the data that follows). Moreover, the RFK assassination is a conspiracy that employed one of the most complex, sophisticated and chilling of methods, (one that surely has been refined by its practitioners since 1968) – the hypnotically programmed assassin. In 1968 the majority of experts, scholars and media analysts deemed this *modus operandi* impossible, a fictional scenario that grossly exaggerated the mind-control potential of hypnosis. Today we know better.

What follows is more than the story of a complex conspiracy. It is also a portrait of law enforcement at its worst. This crime was covered up more by the Los Angeles Police and District Attorney's Office than by the conspirators. The trail of suppressed or destroyed evidence and intimidated witnesses is a long one, manifesting a new outrageous twist for virtually every year in the more than two decades since the killing.

The impetus for the cover-up came mainly from political pressures, internal and external to those of law-enforcement agencies, to settle the case quickly and credibly. There were also bureaucracy/law-enforcement pressures to prevent the chosen solution from unraveling. For over 20 years Los Angeles authorities have behaved, in this case, more like totalitarian ministers of propaganda than publicly elected or appointed stewards of the criminal-justice system. In the process of defending officially defined truth, a bunker mentality developed. At times, as we shall hear in their own words, the authorities seemed to succumb to a paranoia in which their critics were viewed as the ultimate evil, and were pursued more zealously than possible conspirators.

The RFK case is touted by most Los Angeles officials as LA law's finest hour – a competent, thorough and efficient response to a national tragedy, a response that is a model for crisis management. Apparently having avoided the mistakes of the Dallas police in the JFK case, they claimed to have performed an exemplary national service. In reality, the performance of the LAPD and the DA's office is so stunningly deficient that the question leaps out as to whether this was caused by the unique pressures of the case or whether this was, or is, business as usual in Los Angeles. We should all hope that these agencies do not operate at anything approaching this dismal level of performance when dealing with the all-too-numerous homicides that plague the City of Angels in any given year.

The disarray of this case could not be more profound. Because there were too many bullets fired to be accounted for by Sirhan's gun and because the official trajectories are grossly in error, it is an open question as to whether it was Sirhan's bullets or someone else's that killed Robert F. Kennedy. That Sirhan was manipulated or assisted by an attractive young woman (who was also present at the scene of the crime), as yet unidentified, is now in the realm of probability rather than possibility. That Sirhan was hypnotically programmed to attack Kennedy seems certain, as you will soon see.

We must now discard the officially sanctioned illusions created by conspiracy and cover-up and proceed to the disconcerting reality of the truth behind the assassination of Senator Robert F. Kennedy.

Chapter 1

ASSASSINATION

"Is everybody all right?"
— Robert F. Kennedy to busboy Juan Romero,
as Kennedy lay mortally wounded

The year 1968 is arguably the most politically chaotic and violent year in the last quarter-century of American politics. A country bitterly divided over the Vietnam War had witnessed the "abdication" of the once-popular president Lyndon Johnson, the assassination of Dr. Martin Luther King, Jr., demonstrations and riots requiring the National Guard to enter dozens of American cities. Then Robert Kennedy was struck down in his moment of political triumph, shattering the hopes of millions of Americans.

The California primary, with its richest of prizes (174 delegates to the national convention, winner take all), was a make-or-break race for the RFK campaign. The week before the June 4 California contest, Kennedy had suffered his first electoral defeat, losing the Oregon primary to Senator Eugene McCarthy in a bitter fight. The loss ended the seemingly magical string of political victories by John, Robert and Ted Kennedy, at the local, state and national levels.

While Kennedy was racking up primary victories, appealing directly to the voters, Vice President Hubert Humphrey was locking up delegates the old-fashioned way – through caucuses and conventions controlled by state party organizations loyal to Johnson and Humphrey. It would be an uphill battle for Kennedy to pry loose enough delegates at the Chicago convention to win the nomination, but it was surely possible given the momentum of a victory in the nation's last and biggest primary. Many of Kennedy's friends and foes alike believed he would overtake Humphrey (who was saddled with the albatross of being closely identified with Johnson's unpopular Vietnam policy), and believed Kennedy would go on to beat Nixon in the general election, as his brother had done only eight years earlier.

The jubilant crowd of 1,800 Kennedy supporters – a crowd atypically youthful and glitzy, with disproportionate numbers of Hollywood celebrities and students – packed the Embassy Ballroom of the Ambassador Hotel. Robert Kennedy's charisma was very much in evidence as he looked out over the sea of straw hats, balloons and smiling faces. He flashed his boyish smile, gave a victory sign and urged, "On to Chicago and let's win there."

The exhausted candidate stepped away from the podium amidst a clamorous ovation. He had one more performance to give – a meeting with print reporters to be held in the Colonial Room. To get there, and to avoid the crush of the frenzied victory crowd, he was scheduled to take the back way, avoiding the main ballroom by going backstage through the food-preparation area – the "pantry" or "kitchen area."

As was typical of this presidential campaign, security was minimal, to say the least. There was no Secret Service protection for Robert Kennedy; this would not be legislated until after his death, when an assault on a presidential candidate was finally made a federal offense.

No Los Angeles Police were present at the hotel, even though three election-night parties involving several thousand people were being held. On duty were ten plainclothes hotel security personnel and eight armed, uniformed guards hired by the hotel from Ace Guard Service. There was also Kennedy's personal bodyguard, ex-

FBI agent Bill Barry. Burly celebrities Roosevelt Grier, a former Los Angeles Rams lineman, and Rafer Johnson, Olympic decathlon champ, functioned as unofficial bodyguards as well as campaigners.

Compared to the present, security was exceedingly lax. Entry badges were not effectively controlled; no metal detectors or cordons kept crowds back, no security personnel constantly surrounded the protectee while scanning for suspicious behavior or sudden movement. This was a campaign in which the candidate frequently waded into crowds with nothing or no one between him and them – no bulletproof vest, no phalanx of security men. Zealous admirers tore at his garments, tousled his hair, slapped his back and made off with his cuff links.

As he left the podium in the Embassy Room, Kennedy at first headed forward toward the crowd. Someone in his entourage could be heard to say, "This way, Senator." Despite subsequent speculation about conspiratorial manipulation or an unlucky, spontaneous change of route, the plan was for the Senator to exit via the pantry. Some persons in Kennedy's entourage may have been confused about the route, but hotel security had been informed earlier in the evening that the candidate would exit the stage as he had entered – the back way. Dozens of people (busboys, waiters, campaign workers) waited in the pantry and in the corridor leading to it, positioning themselves for a handshake or a close-up view.

One young man had been in the pantry on several occasions during the late evening (before the speech ended around midnight). He had been asked to leave by a Kennedy staffer, because he did not have a kitchen uniform or a campaign badge. But he had returned. According to busboy Jesus Perez, Sirhan Sirhan had asked, more than once, if Kennedy would be passing through the pantry. Now the thin, 5-foot 6-inch, dark-featured young man stood in a corner of the room near a stack of serving trays, a .22 pistol concealed under his shirt and jacket.

Kennedy's entourage spread out as it made its way down the corridor toward the fairly small, crowded pantry. Ethel Kennedy trailed some distance behind her husband.

Hotel maître d' Karl Uecker led the Senator through the crowd. Police would later estimate that 77 persons were jammed into the immediate area (the pantry and the adjoining corridors). Smiling and nodding, the tired victor worked his way through the room toward the exit. He stopped to shake hands with busboys Jesus Perez and Juan Romero, who stood near the edge of a steam table about two-thirds of the way toward the exit.

Balloons that had floated in or been carried in from the ballroom popped underfoot.

Radio and TV reporters navigated through the pantry with their equipment shut down, assuming that there would not be anything newsworthy to record in this small, dimly lit area that offered nothing more exciting than the campaign's 10,000th handshake.

Uniformed security guard Thane Eugene Cesar walked with Kennedy, slightly behind him and to his right. Cesar was close enough to touch the Senator's left arm. For reasons of political image, the Kennedy campaign had specifically requested of the hotel that no uniformed security personnel be near the Senator during his appearance.

Maître d' Uecker was leading Kennedy through the crowd. He glanced back at the Senator, who had just shaken hands with busboy Juan Romero. "Let's go, Senator," Uecker said in his thick German accent. He took Kennedy's right wrist and led him forward.

Paul Schrade of the United Auto Workers Union was Kennedy's friend and served as labor coordinator for the California campaign. Now Schrade followed a few feet behind Kennedy and watched him shaking hands with the kitchen workers. He remembers that this seemed symbolic of the campaign, and he recalls thinking to himself, "This is really what this campaign is all about. We're going to have a president, finally."[1]

San Diego high school student Lisa Urso had worked for Kennedy. Now, seeking escape from the heat in the crowded Embassy Room, she stood near the pantry exit and watched as the Senator came toward her. With an unobstructed view she saw

Kennedy shaking hands with the busboy. Suddenly, she felt a shove from behind. Urso noticed a young man "a lot shorter than me," she told this author, later. Sirhan Sirhan stepped in front of her and moved to her right.

"I thought it was gonna be a waiter and it looked like he was trying to get in there and shake the Senator's hand."[2] Then she saw his arm move quickly across his body and down. "And I froze." Instinctively, she had a feeling that this young man was going to shoot Kennedy.

Busboy Juan Romero and waiter Martin Patruski also saw Sirhan approach. They, too, at first thought he was going to shake hands in part because he was smiling.

The smile was betrayed by Sirhan's words: "Kennedy, you son of a bitch!"

In a horrible sequence of visions burned indelibly into her psyche, Urso saw Sirhan, who was now standing about five feet in front of Kennedy, raise the gun.

"I saw the flash [from the gun] and then I saw the Senator . . . He went forward, then moved backward . . . Grabbed his head and fell backward." It was a "jerking motion," forward about a foot, then backward onto the floor.

Paul Schrade was shot in the forehead (apparently very early in the erupting gunfire). He saw neither the gun nor Sirhan and "didn't know what had happened [that anyone had been shot]." In 1986 Schrade publicly described the traumatic event for the first time: "I . . . began violently shaking . . . I thought that I was being electrocuted. There were TV cameras, and wires on the floor and so I thought that's what had happened."[3]

Two shots went off very near Karl Uecker's face. He felt Kennedy's hand slip from his grasp. Immediately, Uecker grabbed the gun and forced it down and away from the Senator, toward the surface of the steam table.

"The shooting stopped for just a moment," Uecker testified at the trial, but then "I felt him shooting." Uecker was joined by a pile of flailing bodies attempting to wrestle the weapon from the assailant's hand. The struggle was successful but not before the gun was emptied, wounding four other people besides Kennedy and Schrade. All would recover, except Kennedy. The Senator was shot three times; one bullet entered his head behind his right ear.

According to several witnesses, Kennedy reeled backward and put his hands up toward his head as if to protect himself. Now he lay on his back, limbs awkwardly spread-eagled, a widening pool of blood near his right ear.

A cacophony of screams, tearful cries, obscenities and pleas for help engulfed the room as pandemonium took over. The assailant was being held by bystanders who were waiting for police to arrive. Numerous persons rushed out to find medical help. Juan Romero cradled Kennedy's head in his right hand. "Come on, Mr. Kennedy. You can make it."

Kennedy's lips moved: "Is everybody all right?" he asked.

A young man gave rosary beads to Romero who wrapped them in Kennedy's left hand. The Senator clutched them to his chest. Ethel Kennedy appeared. She pushed Romero aside and talked soothingly to her wounded husband.

The confusion at the crime scene has typically been understated. This was not an event witnessed by 70 people who were watching Kennedy at center stage and suddenly saw him attacked. Many people did not see the shooting at all. Many thought, at first, that there was a harmless eruption of bursting balloons or firecrackers. Some saw Kennedy reel or fall but had no view of the gun or the assailant; some saw Sirhan but not his gun and vice versa. Some bystanders knew there was gunfire not by seeing Sirhan or Kennedy but by seeing one of the other five victims falling or bleeding. Some tried to rush out to avoid being gunned down; some, to find help; others, to chase persons they thought were escaping suspects. The uneven quantity and quality of eyewitness observations of this crime would contribute to its scrambled image. And there would be no video or photographic record of the actual shooting to clarify that image.

Dr. Stanley Abo, a medical practioner who had been in the

crowd at the hotel, now entered the kitchen and knelt beside Kennedy; he found the victim's breathing quite shallow. He probed the head wound with his finger in order to relieve "cranial pressure" by making it bleed. Kennedy spoke to Ethel.

The Senator was taken to Good Samaritan Hospital where he fought for his life as a team of six surgeons labored to remove the bullet lodged in his brain. Had he survived, nerve and motor-function damage to his vision, hearing and muscular control would have left him severely impaired. At 1:44 p.m. on June 6, Robert F. Kennedy died. Press Secretary Frank Mankiewicz announced the news to a nation benumbed by political violence.

Kennedy's death had a profound impact on the presidential race of 1968, and, quite probably, on several races beyond. For one, it profoundly altered the internal alignment of the Democratic party and its issue positions. It also had a more subtle yet equally profound effect on the psyches of millions of Americans. For them, this trilogy of tragedy in the 1960s was a dominant influence on their political thinking for the decades that followed.

As Jack Newfield poignantly described in the last paragraph of his book *Robert F. Kennedy: A Memoir:*[4]

> Now I realized what makes our generation unique, what defines us apart from those who came before the hopeful winter of 1961, and those who came after the murderous spring of 1968. We are the first generation that learned from experience, in our innocent twenties, that things were not really gettting better, that we shall not overcome. We felt, by the time we reached thirty, that we had already glimpsed the most compassionate leaders our nation could produce, and they had all been assassinated. And from this time forward, things would get worse: our best political leaders were part of memory now, not hope.
>
> The stone was at the bottom of the hill and we were alone.

Chapter 2

OPEN-AND-SHUT

It was an open-and-shut murder case. We were probably more cautious than with any other case in the history of the department.

— Former L.A. Police Chief Ed Davis, 1988

My feeling is that when they found Sirhan's diary and they read it, I think that everybody was ready to hang their hat on that and say, "O.K., it was only one guy alone, by himself, for whatever his reasons might have been, and let's quit beating the bushes and wrap things up" . . . *They probably should not have done that. They should have continued to resolve all matters and issues.*

— Retired FBI Agent William Bailey
(asssigned to the RFK case), 1977[1]

L os Angeles law enforcement's rallying cry for this investigation was not "search for conspirators" or "pursue every lead" but "not another Dallas." This meant keeping the suspect alive, getting a conviction, and presenting a credible public image. To handle the case, the department created Special Unit Senator (SUS), a task force with its own personnel and command structure. According to press releases, LAPD's SUS investigators conducted nearly 4,000 interviews. Data and "progress reports" flowed into the DA's office, building a solid case against Sirhan. The investigation, whose flaws and cover-ups will be analyzed in subsequent chapters, concluded that there was no second gun, no female accomplice – and no conspiracy.

As we shall see, LAPD worked hard to debunk every lead to a possible conspiracy, through a process that often resembled a political campaign more than an orthodox police investigation. Except for a handful of skeptical journalists and citizens, there was no one to challenge the department's methods or findings. The vast majority of the press and public assumed Sirhan was guilty, that he acted for political reasons, that he was mentally unstable, and (as the investigation and trial unfolded) that he acted alone.

The police were wedded to the lone-assassin conclusion almost instantly.* Sirhan's lawyers had no interest in challenging that finding. It would be much harder to successfully plead diminished capacity and lack of premeditation if he had been involved with others. Since the police told the prosecutors that no one else was involved, they could concentrate on their main goal of sending Sirhan to the gas chamber and not have to worry about the legal complexities of a conspiracy.

At a press conference following a pre-trial hearing, defense lawyer Russell Parsons pronounced, "We have seen no evidence of a conspiracy." An *L.A. Herald* headline the following day announced: "Both Sides Agree Sirhan Acted Alone."

One of the widely misunderstood aspects of this case is the scope of Sirhan's trial. It is generally assumed that all of the evidentiary conflicts and issues – the possibility of a second gun, the eyewitness accounts that challenged whether it was physically possible for Sirhan to have inflicted Kennedy's wounds – were addressed at the trial. Surely, the point goes, Sirhan's lawyers would have pounced at any chance to create doubt in the minds of the jurors – à la Perry Mason.

Instead, most of the evidence was stipulated by both the defense

* 24 hrs. after the crime, LAPD Chief Tom Reddin told the world: "As near as we can tell there was only one person and this information has been gleaned from dozens of interviews...." Reddin dismissed a police All Points Bulletin for additional suspects as the meaningless product of "great pandemonium."

and prosecution. Evidentiary conflicts that raised doubts about the lone-gun conclusion or about Sirhan's role were either excluded from the courtroom or ignored, floating over the heads of jurors without discussion or debate. The defense stipulated that Sirhan Sirhan killed Robert F. Kennedy. Virtually the only area of contention was the perpetrator's state of mind. Was this a premeditated, first-degree crime punishable by death, as the prosecution contended; or was it the spontaneous act of a psychologically disturbed young man who was not responsible for his actions? The trial was not about the number of shots fired or whether Sirhan could have shot Kennedy behind the right ear while standing in front of him: It was about Sirhan's psyche. Fittingly, it was not a battle of ballistics experts or conflicting eyewitnesses but of dueling psychiatrists armed with ink-blot tests and psychological profiles.

Thus, when prosecution star-witness Karl Uecker testified that he grabbed Sirhan's gun and forced it away from Kennedy after the second shot – Kennedy was wounded three times and a fourth shot passed through his coat – it caused not a ripple. When LAPD criminologist DeWayne Wolfer introduced the wrong gun into evidence as the murder weapon instead of Sirhan's gun, and proceeded to testify that all recovered bullets could be matched to that gun, to the exclusion of every other gun in the world, no one noticed. When dozens of witness reports and trial testimonies placed Sirhan's gun several feet in front of Kennedy while Coroner Thomas Noguchi testified that RFK was shot behind the right ear with the weapon as close as one inch away, the discrepancy slid by unexplored. In fact, it was the defense that cut Noguchi's testimony short, contending that the Coroner did not have to get into the "gory details" about the precise location of wounds and the angle and distance of firing.

This trial was adversarial only within very narrowly defined limits involving motive and mentality. LAPD's conclusions, its methods and its competence were not tested in an adversarial proceeding before the judge and jury.

Even with what seemed like a rather tame defense for Sirhan and with a police department that covered up or neglected troublesome areas of the case, even with all the stipulations about the hard evidence and about guilt, the police and DA's office still played hardball with Sirhan's lawyers, not wanting anything to jeopardize a murder-one verdict.

Chief defense attorney Grant Cooper and his assistant Russell Parsons decided on a diminished-capacity plea in order to avoid the death penalty. The defense tried, apparently not very forcefully, to obtain crucial audio tapes of Sirhan's interrogation sessions with police during the early-morning hours following his arrest. The defense hoped the tapes would reveal a spaced-out, disoriented prisoner exhibiting mental incoherence. LAPD was vague in its responses to the defense about where the tapes resided. The defense apparently never obtained them but instead had to settle for interviews with interrogating officers, who described Sirhan's behavior and demeanor. Assistant DA John Howard sat in on these interviews and challenged the defense investigator's right to ask certain questions concerning Sirhan's appearance, thereby effectively limiting the scope of the inquiry. Police inaccurately characterized Sirhan's behavior, ignoring his bizarre breathing, strange speech pattern and the near-incoherence manifested during his first interrogation session.

The defense enlisted Manhattan attorney Emile Zola Berman, who argued the diminished-capacity defense to the jury: "The killing was unplanned, undeliberate, impulsive," Berman asserted, "and without premeditation or malice, totally the product of a sick obsessed mind and personality."

The prosecution rebutted with evidence of premeditation. Fifteen witnesses had seen Sirhan at the San Gabriel Valley Gun Club on the morning and afternoon of June 4. He was rapid-firing his .22 pistol – target practicing for the kill, the prosecution implied.

Sirhan was seen at the Ambassador Hotel on June 2 when Kennedy made an appearance there. He admitted being there. It seemed as if he might be stalking his target, although Sirhan denied it. When arrested after the shooting, he had in his pocket a newspaper clipping criticizing RFK for opposing the Vietnam War while favoring military aid to Israel. In the minds of jurors this reinforced both political motive and premeditation.

But the coup de grâce of premeditation was the notebook found by police in Sirhan's bedroom at his mother's house in Pasadena. The authorities would label this item his "diary." While its mysterious origin and content will be discussed later, its impact on the trial is not in doubt. There were two pages containing repetitive, scrawled references to killing RFK. The most damning read, "May 18 9:45 AM-68 My determination to eliminate RFK is becoming more the more [sic] of an unshakable obsession . . . RFK must die."

Sirhan admitted writing the diary and shooting Kennedy, but he claimed he could not remember doing either. Even under hypnosis his memory blacked out when it came to both writing and shooting. Sirhan had practiced self-hypnosis and was keenly interested in mind control and mental projection. Defense psychiatrist Dr. Bernard Diamond argued that the accused was in a trance during the shooting, a trance accidentally self-induced. Sirhan, Diamond argued, had become mesmerized by the sparkling chandeliers and huge mirrors in the crowded hotel; fitting the profile of an excellent hypnotic subject, he had slipped into a trance and become disassociated from reality.

However, Diamond's soliloquy to the jury on diminished capacity triggered by an accidental trance seemed to imply a strange form of premeditation: Sirhan had "programmed himself" for the assassination:

I see Sirhan as small and helpless, pitifully ill, with a demented, psychotic rage, out of control of his own consciousness and his own actions, subject to some bizarre, disassociated trances in some of which he programmed himself to be the instrument of assassination, and then, in an *almost* [emphasis added] accidentally induced twilight state, he actually executed the crime, knowing next to nothing as to what was happening.

Sirhan was not at all helpful to his own defense. He took on the role of a political prisoner at a show trial – the Arab hero who killed Kennedy on behalf of oppressed Palestinians. He lectured from the witness stand on the violence and exploitation visited on his homeland, Palestine, by the Israelis. Before his family immigrated to the United States, he had witnessed Middle Eastern violence first hand: massacres and bombings; his younger brother was crushed by a truck in a gun battle between Arabs and Israelis.

Sirhan testified that "anything that has to do with Israel or Zionists or support of Israel, that is enough cause for me, sir, to hate him [RFK]." The alleged flash point came when Kennedy endorsed the sale of 50 U.S. Phantom jets to Israel.

At one point in the trial the rather defiant Arab hero attempted to fire his lawyers, take over his own case and withdraw his plea of diminished capacity.

"I will ask to be executed," Sirhan told the court. Judge Herbert V. Walker demanded a reason.

"I killed Robert Kennedy willfully, premeditatedly, with 20 years of forethought. That's why."

Judge Walker refused to accept Sirhan's new plea, but the jury refused to accept his old one of diminished capacity. Sirhan Sirhan was found guilty of first-degree murder and sentenced to death. The California Supreme Court upheld the conviction, but the U.S. Supreme Court voided the constitutionality of the death penalty before Sirhan could be executed. He is now eligible for parole.

It was all so straightforward – a legal exercise in which the crime and the evidence were stipulated by everyone involved including the defendant, who seemed compelled to make the prosecutors' case for them. The open-and-shut investigation led to an open-and-shut trial. The only door that did not shut on cue was that of the gas chamber at San Quentin Prison.

The profound discrepancies and conflicts in the evidence were suppressed or ignored by LAPD and were never addressed by the judicial process, but they did not go away. They surfaced unevenly over the coming months and years. Still, Los Angeles authorities would have it both ways. Having avoided dealing with the conflicting evidence during the investigation and trial, they would, for over two decades, staunchly insist that the investigation and trial had resolved everything. Worst of all, the ploy was largely successful and the public still does not have satisfactory answers to the glaring conflicts in the physical evidence.

Chapter 3

CONFLICTING EVIDENCE

Eyewitnesses are notoriously unreliable, but this time the sheer unanimity was too phenomenal to dismiss. Not a single witness in that crowded kitchen had seen him [Sirhan] fire behind Kennedy's ear at point-blank range.

– Coroner Thomas Noguchi
(from his book *Coroner*, 1983)

For a case allegedly so simple, the conflicts in the evidence were indeed glaring (although ignored by the authorities and the media). Prosecution "star witness" Karl Uecker offered grand jury testimony consistent with what he had told police and the FBI: He grabbed Sirhan's gun after the second shot, moving it away from Kennedy. Yet the Senator was wounded three times and a fourth shot passed through the right sleeve of his suit coat. Another close-up eyewitness, assistant maître d' Edward Manasian, confirmed that Uecker had deflected the gun before a third shot was fired. Manasian told LAPD within hours of the shooting, "I saw the first two shots fired . . . At that time Uecker hit his arm and grabbed his . . . neck, hold around his neck, and then I grabbed him from the left side."

In addition, there was the "distance problem," as it came to be known, constituting one of the most fundamental conflicts in the evidence – a conflict between what the eyewitnesses saw and the data provided by the autopsy and powder-burn tests. On June 11, LAPD test-fired a gun identical to Sirhan's into clothing similar to Kennedy's and into pigs' ears used to simulate human flesh. The dark, well-defined burn (a "tattooing" effect) found on Kennedy's head and clothing could only be replicated if the gun was fired nearly point blank. LAPD concluded that "the bullet which entered behind Senator Kennedy's right ear was fired at a muzzle distance of approximately one inch."

This confirmed the findings from Coroner Thomas Noguchi's autopsy. The nitrite deposits and powder burns on the body indicated conclusively that the shots were fired from very close range. Dr. Noguchi testified that the fatal bullet entered between "one to one and a half inches" from the edge of the ear and that the other wounds were inflicted from a distance of "contact" to "one inch." According to a 1974 article in the *Los Angeles Herald Examiner* (which quoted Noguchi), he was approached by an unnamed assistant DA before entering the grand jury room and was asked to change his distance finding from one to three inches to one to three feet. It is easy to understand the reason for such a request.

The powder-burn test and autopsy findings sharply conflict with the accounts of virtually every eyewitness, including those who, according to the FBI, were described by LAPD as the prosecution's "five best" witnesses: Uecker, Patruski, Burns, Romero, Perez. The witnesses placed the gun one and a half to six feet from Kennedy, not point blank as the technical physical evidence had concluded.

Frank Burns, now a successful Los Angeles attorney, worked for the Kennedy campaign, in his capacity as an aide to the politically powerful Jesse Unruh. Unruh, nicknamed "Big Daddy," was Speaker of the California Assembly and a staunch Kennedy backer. Burns was within several feet of Kennedy when the shots were fired. In a 1987 interview with the author, he vividly recalled the tragedy that was still painful for him to talk about. He was certain that Sirhan's gun was never anywhere near contact with Kennedy's head. It was several feet away, he adamantly asserted. "We're talking several . . . several feet." Burns said it might have been as many as six feet, but he would have to see a diagram to clarify his estimate. Later he reconstructed the crime in his spacious and richly appointed office, using this author and chairs as stand-ins for the principals. He positioned "the gun" approximately three to four feet from "Kennedy's head." Burns was extremely confident that his positioning of the stand-ins and the distance it created was accurate. It is one of the elements of the shooting that the guarded, precision-oriented barrister told me he is most certain of.

Waiter Martin Patruski, who said he was three to four feet from Kennedy, asserted that the gun never got closer than three feet. And busboy Juan Romero told authorities the weapon was "approximately one yard from the Senator's head."

Karl Uecker is perhaps the best witness because of his consistency and credibility and because his visual estimate of the distance is bolstered by his sense of touch. He testified that the gun was one and a half to two feet away. Uecker had reached behind him and grasped the Senator's right wrist, leading him forward, when the gun was fired near the maître d's face. In 1971 Uecker asserted, "There's no way that the shots described in the autopsy could have come from Sirhan's gun . . . Sirhan never got close enough for a point blank shot. Never!"

Beyond the "five best" witnesses, newspaper reporter Pete Hamill, who was present during the shooting, placed the gun at least two feet from the Senator. Coed campaigner Valeria Shulte said it was three yards away; security guard Thane Cesar, two feet. Assistant maître d' Edward Manasian placed the barrel approximately three feet from Kennedy. Vincent DiPierro, who got Kennedy's blood sprayed on his glasses, told the grand jury the gun was four to six feet away.[2] TV producer Richard Lubic was walking behind and to the right of Uecker. When he knelt to the floor after Kennedy went down, he got the Senator's blood on his pants. "Sirhan's gun was two to three feet from Kennedy's head," Lubic insisted in a 1975 interview.

Lisa Urso, a key witness whose vivid account of her unobstructed view of the shooting was suppressed by Los Angeles authorities, reported to me that the gun was "three to six feet" from Kennedy when she saw the "first flash" (a flash from the barrel of Sirhan's gun that seemed to come from the first shot).*

Grand jury or trial testimony never placed the gun closer than one and a half to six feet. The only witness to do so was *L.A. Times* photographer Boris Yaro, who said it was "inside a foot." But Yaro was viewing the shooting through his camera lens – although not taking pictures – which may have distorted the distances.

In his original interviews and testimonies in 1968 and in subsequent interviews with authorities and journalists during the next few years, Karl Uecker clearly asserted that Sirhan did not get around him or past him to reach Kennedy at point blank range. Sirhan was trapped between the steam table on his right and Uecker on his front left. Uecker told LAPD just hours after the shooting:

LAPD: Did he [Sirhan] get past you?
UECKER: He was right in front of me.

The best evidence is that Sirhan's gun never got farther than the forward edge of the steam table on which his gun hand was later bashed by Uecker.

Frank Burns told me in 1987, "I remember precisely where the gun was when I first saw it [as the first shots went off]. It was at the edge of the steam table." Even the official LAPD crime-scene diagrams place Kennedy's forward progress at no more than two to three feet from the forward edge of the steam table.

Had the autopsy and powder-burn data conflicted with only some of the witnesses rather than virtually all, or had the discrepancy been two feet compared to three feet instead of contact to one and a half inches versus one and a half feet to six feet, the problem would not be as glaring and serious. But officials dealt with the big flaw in their case by ignoring it. When L.A. District Attorney Evelle Younger was asked about this important discrepancy he gave

---

* Ms. Urso's bizarre treatment as a witness is described in Chapter 8.

the following incredible reply: "If somebody says one inch and somebody else says two inches, that's a discrepancy. But the jury didn't think it was a significant discrepancy and neither did I." [3]

In addition to problems concerning distance and whether Sirhan could get off more than two shots at Kennedy, there were problems regarding the angle, the front-rear dimension and the pattern of the wounds. The autopsy revealed three wounds: one behind the right ear, a second near the right armpit, a third one and a half inches below the second. A fourth bullet pierced the right rear shoulder area of Kennedy's suit coat. All bullets entered at fairly steep upward angles and their direction was slightly right to left; all also entered from the right rear of Kennedy's body – not the front or side.

This is clearly illustrated in the accompanying LAPD photos. A detective is wearing Kennedy's coat, and metal wires have been placed through the bullet holes in order to show the trajectories of two of the four shots.

Witnesses disagree on whether Sirhan shot at Kennedy while the Senator was turned to his left shaking hands (with "a busboy") or after the handshake had finished and he was walking forward. For example, Lisa Urso, a very credible witness, believes that Kennedy was turned toward his left and shaking hands when Sirhan fired the first shots. In contrast, Uecker insists that he had taken Kennedy's wrist and looked back to see him moving forward. "I heard the first shot and the second shot right after that," Uecker told the grand jury, "and Mr. Kennedy fell out of my hand. I lost his hand."

Juan Romero told the FBI and LAPD that the handshake had finished and Kennedy had then taken two or three steps forward when the shooting started. Romero also asserted during his June 5 LAPD interview that he was the last one to shake the Senator's hand.

ROMERO: . . . I was right next to Kennedy when . . . he just finished shaking my hand.
LAPD: You are the one that he shook hands with just before he was shot?
ROMERO: Yes, sir.

Corroborating Romero, waiter Martin Patruski told the FBI that, "After Senator Kennedy shook hands with Juan Romero, I noticed a man [Sirhan] pushing his way toward the Senator and Karl Uecker."

In any event, we know that Sirhan approached from in front of Kennedy. The Senator was either facing primarily forward, walking toward Sirhan, or had turned leftward to shake hands. Sirhan attacked from Uecker's front left. Kennedy never turned his back to Sirhan nor did the assailant have a path to Kennedy's right rear side, even if Kennedy was shaking hands. The best that an RFK turn to the left can accomplish for the official version is to allow Sirhan to inflict a wound in the Senator's right temple or the side of his ear (discounting, for the moment, the distance problem), but this turn could not account for a bullet entering the head from behind the right ear.

There are also problems concerning the angle and pattern of the wounds. To inflict the damage discovered by the autopsy, Sirhan would have had to move the gun and fire at Kennedy from two different levels (to account for the bullet behind the right ear and the lower shoulder or armpit), which none of the witnesses saw. Absent this latter movement of the gun, Kennedy would have had to be changing position while Sirhan was firing. Since the Senator apparently fell backward (with his back away from Sirhan) and the angle of the wounds was upward, it would be impossible for Sirhan to have inflicted them unless he fired from his knees and somehow got access to Kennedy's back. In addition, there is the further complication created by Uecker's undisputed deflection of the gun away from Kennedy, after two shots.

Though perspectives vary, witnesses are nearly unanimous in their agreement that Sirhan fired with an outstretched arm, with the gun generally parallel to the floor and perpendicular to Sirhan's face, not pointed downward or upward or moving up or down before Uecker forced it away from Kennedy.*

---

* Frank Burns is an exception to this agreement in testimonies. Burns told LAPD on June 5 that Sirhan was "shooting downward," "slightly downward" as Kennedy was falling, and that the gun was at his (Burns) eye level. He told this author the same thing in 1987.

One selective use of evidentiary logic employed by government officials has been to insist that there couldn't have been a second gun fired because someone would have seen it (ignoring that at least three witnesses did see another gun, which I will elaborate on later). LAPD officials used the fiction writer's prerogative of inventing something that no one saw – describing Sirhan, in their *Summary Report,* as "lunging" at Kennedy to get the gun at point-blank range. This distinctive "lunge" went unreported in eyewitness accounts.

The previously described conflicts in the evidence would not be as disturbing if it weren't for a related problem, which is addressed in the next chapter: the overwhelming circumstantial evidence of too many bullets fired to be accounted for by one gun. This growing body of data supporting a second gun means that the various conflicts between the witnesses and the autopsy need not be resolved by determining whether the coroner or the bystanders are wrong. It is quite likely that both are correct, except for the specific issue over the distance of the gun when it was fired behind Kennedy's right ear. Despite the massaging and obfuscation of the coroner's report, the bullet to the Senator's head was scientifically proven, by powder burn analysis, to have been fired inches or less away from the wound.

Chapter 4

NINE BULLETS = TWO GUNS

There were eight bullets fired, seven recovered and there were never any more shots fired. That's a fact.
– Los Angeles District Attorney Joseph P. Bush, 1974

Seven bullets were recovered from the bodies of Senator Kennedy and the five surviving shooting victims; one was allegedly lost in the ceiling interspace. Sirhan's gun held eight shots, and he had no opportunity to reload. Thus, with all of Sirhan's eight bullets otherwise accounted for, if but one bullet was recovered from the crime scene, it constitutes a ninth bullet – too many for one gun. That much is agreed: The disagreement is whether the doorframe in the west end of the pantry did, in fact, contain a bullet or bullets.

Before focusing on the extensive evidence of a ninth bullet, it should be recalled that even if we exclude this possibility, the official version is hard pressed to provide a valid one-gun accounting. It requires three bullets to perform double duty via trajectories that range from surprising to virtually impossible.

According to LAPD criminologist DeWayne Wolfer, one bullet passed through Kennedy's suit coat, traveled upward at approximately an 80-degree angle, and struck Paul Schrade in the head. But the bullet passed back to front, and all eyewitnesses place Kennedy with his back or side to Schrade. Witnesses, including Schrade, place him four to five feet behind Kennedy. To fulfill Wolfer's scenario, Schrade would, in his words, have had "to be nine feet tall or have my head on Kennedy's shoulder."

Another bullet is supposed to have gone cleanly through Ira Goldstein's pant leg, hit the cement floor, then deflected upward to lodge in Erwin Stroll's leg. But Goldstein testified to the grand jury that when the bullet passed through his pant leg, Stroll had already reacted to being hit and fallen to the floor.

Elizabeth Evans is alleged by LAPD to have been wounded by a bullet that pierced a one-inch-thick ceiling tile, ricocheted off the inner ceiling, re-entered through the tile, and struck her in the head (15 feet from the point of re-entry from the ceiling). But the medical report on Mrs. Evans described the bullet as entering "just below the hairline" and traveling "upward." She testified that when she was wounded, she was kneeling down to tie her shoe. Moreover, the hollow-point bullet retained three-fourths of its original weight and did not fragment or mushroom. Thus it is at least a distant cousin of the "magic bullet" described by the Warren Commission as wounding both President Kennedy and Governor Connolly.

Further pressure was placed on the official accounting by the author's 1987 interview with Vincent Di Pierro. The young hotel waiter had been standing only a few feet from Kennedy, near Schrade, when the shooting took place. Kennedy's blood splattered Di Pierro's sweatshirt. When he washed the garment, which he showed to me, he discovered two small, well-defined holes in the upper left sleeve, holes which he asserts were not there previously. Indeed, their size, shape and alignment appear consistent with a .22 caliber slug having passed cleanly through. If it is a bullet hole, it constitutes yet a third through-and-through shot in addition to Kennedy's suit coat and Goldstein's pants.

To Di Pierro this was simply a graphic reminder of how close he came to being shot. But it also puts further strain on LAPD's

ballistics accounting. While Di Pierro's precise position and alignment can only be estimated, he was standing up and in Sirhan's line
of fire. In order to avoid lodging in the wall or door frame, a Di
Pierro through-and-through shot must end up in either of two
shooting victims – in William Weisel's stomach or Goldstein's hip.
Otherwise, there were two guns. While such a trajectory cannot be
discounted, it further illustrates the fragility of LAPD's one-gun
scenario. One also wonders if the left sleeve of Kennedy's coat,
inexplicably missing, was purposely destroyed by those running the
investigation because it contained yet another hole or holes, which
even Wolfer's logically tortured trajectories could not account for
with one gun.

Before considering the door frame evidence, there is the
question of how many bullet holes were in the ceiling tiles. LAPD
admits there were three holes. Three is the limit that is possible for
a single-gun scenario, given the rest of the known damage that must
be accounted for. In his book *Special Unit Senator*, LAPD Deputy
Chief Robert Houghton quotes Wolfer as saying, "It's unbelievable
how many holes there are in the kitchen ceiling." If there are more
than three then it is the one-gun conclusion that becomes unbelievable. A police property report, curiously dated 22 days after the
property was booked into evidence, describes "two" ceiling tiles
removed; LAPD crime-scene photos show that *numerous* ceiling
tiles were removed, including several which are outside of Sirhan's
officially defined range of fire (outside of Wolfer's trajectory reconstructions).

At the crime scene most witnesses were removed from the
pantry area and put in holding rooms to await interview. But
eyewitness Lisa Urso was wandering around the hotel and was not
discovered by authorities until later in the morning. She described
to the author what she saw in the pantry when she returned there
within three hours after the crime.

Urso recalled that just after the shooting, before she left the
pantry and went upstairs, she looked up at the ceiling and was
surprised to see what appeared to be "bullet holes." She doesn't
remember how many.

When she returned to the pantry several hours later there was still blood on the floor, and the room was bustling with activity "all over the place." She noticed that tiles had been "removed from the ceiling and placed on the floor – five or six, she estimates. A uniformed police officer stood guard while another was kneeling, "poking around" – poking the tiles for bullets, she thought.

She looked down at two of the panels that were nearest her and saw several holes in one (three, she thinks) and a single hole in the other. She does not recall seeing the doorframe, located at the other end of the pantry, being dismantled or probed, but she does recall that there was activity in virtually every area of the room.

Said Urso: "I don't know how many rounds a gun holds but it sounded like there were more people shot than there were bullets to go around. And they [police] kept saying about ricochets."

From 1969 to the present, a cumulative and extensive body of evidence indicates that one or more bullets were found in the doorframe. Recall that since all eight bullets from Sirhan's eight-shot revolver are otherwise accounted for, by being found in the victims' bodies (with one allegedly being lost in the ceiling), any bullet in the doorframe is proof that two guns were fired. Three photos of holes in the doorframe, released by the FBI in 1976 under a Freedom of Information Act request, describe "bullet holes"; one describes a "bullet mark." There are four separate holes labeled as "bullet holes."

LAPD crime scene photos show Wolfer pointing to a spot on the upper doorframe. In a 1971 deposition he stated: "We wouldn't photograph just any hole. I mean, there were too many holes to photograph." He also asserted that he was "in charge of the crime scene and I recovered the bullets that were recovered."

Los Angeles Coroner Dr. Thomas Noguchi is shown in a police photo pointing to two holes in the doorframe. The holes are circled. Inside one circle is what appears to be a law officer's badge number. In a 1975 affidavit given to Attorney Vincent Bugliosi, the Charles Manson prosecutor who was independently re-investigating the RFK case, Noguchi described the context of the photo: "I asked

Mr. Wolfer where he had found bullet holes at the scene. I forget what he said, but when I asked him this question, he pointed, as I recall, to one hole in a ceiling panel above, and an indentation in the cement ceiling. He also pointed to several holes in the door frames of the swinging doors leading into the pantry. I directed that photographs be taken of me pointing to these holes.''[1]

Los Angeles police officers Robert Rozzi and Charles Wright are shown in an AP photo kneeling near a hole in the doorframe, pointing to the hole and illuminating it with flashlights (see photo/documents section). The caption reads: ''Police technician inspects a bullet hole discovered in a doorframe . . . Bullet is still in the wood.''

In 1975 Bugliosi obtained an affidavit from Rozzi:

Sometime during the evening when we were looking for evidence, someone discovered what appeared to be a bullet a foot and a half or so from the bottom of the floor [sic] in a door jamb on the door behind the stage. I also personally observed what I believed to be a bullet in the place just mentioned. What I observed was a hole in the door jamb, and the base of what appeared to be a small caliber bullet was lodged in the hole.

Bugliosi then telephoned Rozzi's partner, officer Charles Wright, who confirmed that the hole contained a bullet. According to Bugliosi, Wright said that ''It [the bullet] was definitely removed from the hole, but I don't know who did it.''[2] Bugliosi asserts that Wright subsequently refused to confirm the telephone conversation or to provide a statement and insisted that a city attorney be present during their meeting.

Another Bugliosi-obtained affidavit came from Ambassador waiter and crime-scene witness Martin Patruski: ''. . . one of the officers pointed to two circled holes on the center divider of the swinging doors and told us that they had dug two bullets out of the center divide. The two circled holes are shown in a photograph shown to me by Mr. Bugliosi . . . I am absolutely sure that the police told us that two bullets were dug out of these holes.''

On the morning of June 5, 1968, two amateur photographers, John Shirley and John R. Clemente, took pictures of the pantry that included the door frame. In March 1969, Shirley provided a statement to the late Lillian Castellano, the courageous and energetic force behind the Kennedy Assassination Truth Committee (a small band of citizens seeking answers to the questions and conflicts raised in the unsupportable official conclusions).

Said Shirley:

> In the wooden jamb of the center divider were two bullet holes surrounded by inked circles which contained some numbers and letters.
>
> I remember a manager pointing out those particular marked bullet holes to another person, who appeared to be a press photographer.
>
> It appeared that an attempt had been made to dig the bullets out from the surface. However, the center divider jamb was loose, and it appeared to have been removed from the framework so that the bullets might be extracted from behind.
>
> It also appeared to me that there was evidence that another bullet had hit one of the padded swinging doors.

The men who helped authorities remove the wood were two carpenters employed by the hotel, Dale Poore and Wesley Harrington. In 1975 interviews conducted by the DA's office, the men described what they saw. Poore stated: "It looked like the bullet had went [sic] in at sort of an angle as it was travelling this way. So it made a bit of an oblong hole and the fiber of the board had closed in some after it went in. And that's the only reason I thought it had been a bullet went in there because you put any kind of a metal instrument, punch nail sets, anything in the hole, it won't have a fiber around the edge."

Harrington answered:

Q: Would you be comfortable with using language that said they actually were bullet holes?

A: Yes. Yes. I would. During my teenage years . . . we had use of
air rifles and .22 rifles and we had fired into old buildings and trees,
and this looked like a hole similar to a small caliber bullet.
Q: And both holes appeared to be of that nature. Is that a fair
statement?
A: Yes. Yes.

L.A. law's response to the question of extra bullets was to
conduct a continuous, systematic cover-up, engaging in destruction
of evidence, conspiracy of silence, and disinformation. Early in
1969 Lillian Castellano and Floyd Nelson, both of the Kennedy
Assassination Truth Committee, wrote an article in the *L.A. Free
Press* highlighting circumstantial evidence of door frame bullets.
Subsequently, on June 27, 1969, LAPD destroyed the ceiling tiles
and doorframe wood, in flagrant violation of the public's trust. This
unbelievable destruction of evidence occurred while Sirhan's case
was being appealed in the courts.

The destruction was not revealed until 1975 during hearings
conducted by the Los Angeles Police Commission regarding public
disclosure of police files. A police spokesman informed the nation
that the material was destroyed because it was "too large to fit into
a card file." This raises the question of whether LAPD also trashed
all of the assorted rifles, bales of marijuana, or vehicles that
constituted bulky material evidence in all of its cases on appeal
in 1969, or was there some special reason that they wished this
evidence to disappear?

LAPD's subsequent, equally preposterous position, articulated
by then Assistant Chief Daryl Gates, was that the destruction didn't
matter because the artifacts contained no bullets and therefore were
not evidence. (This is the same Daryl Gates who was in charge of
LAPD when the notorious brutal beating of the black motorist took
place in March 1991.) One would expect that any department whose
publicly and privately pronounced goal was to "avoid another Dallas" should have been overjoyed to preserve and release evidence
that would refute critcs and "conspiracy nuts."

Having destroyed the physical evidence, Los Angeles authorities proceeded to exercise damage control and to discredit the circumstantial evidence. Carpenters Harrington and Poore were referred to as laymen, not trained experts, and the Associated Press was making an erroneous assumption when it labeled the Rozzi-Wright photo (of the two officers and the "hole in the door jamb") as showing a bullet hole.

In a 1985 conversation with this author, former FBI agent Roger LaJeunesse put forth a new explanation for the confusion over extra bullets in the door jamb: mistaken photo-labeling by his FBI colleagues. LaJeunesse, who served as liaison between LAPD and the Bureau during the Kennedy case, is a staunch defender of the department's performance and conclusions. He still maintains close ties with LAPD and runs a private security firm in Los Angeles. He contends that Agent Alfred Greiner, whose captions on crime scene photos refer to "bullet holes" in the door frame, was "only a labeler" and did no analysis.* Greiner refused to respond to this author's requests for an interview.

In February 1985, I wrote to then-FBI Director William Webster seeking clarification of the apparent conflict between Bureau photo descriptions and LAPD conclusions. Assistant Director William M. Baker responded: "Neither the photographic log nor the photographs were ever purported to be a ballistics report." The descriptions were generated "for the convenience of the photographic team in recording information." One would think that random captioning of photos would be a major inconvenience for the case analysts at the nation's most sophisticated law-enforcement agency.

I again asked the Bureau for clarification of its substantive conclusion about bullets at the crime scene, rather than about its cataloguing procedures. Baker replied, "The results of the FBI's crime-scene examination concerning that assassination were fur-

---

* Over drinks in a Los Angeles restaurant, LaJeunesse told me about "The Sirhan Society," comprised of "cops, prosecutors, even the defense team. We get together at a good restaurant every year . . . Hell, it's our place in history." FBI RFK-case supervisor Amadee O. Richards told me in 1986 that he gets a telephone call from LaJeunesse "now and then" and they "get together" with the Sirhan prosecutors and others.

nished to the Office of the District Attorney in Los Angeles and to the Los Angeles Police Department . . . It was the responsibility of the FBI to assist that agency however possible, not to draw conclusions from the investigation the LAPD conducted.''

The FBI ''assistance'' must have been less than helpful if its crime-scene examination reached no conclusions about whether the pantry was bullet-riddled or had simply been originally decorated with distressed pinewood. Moreover, Baker's unbelievable contention was directly refuted by a more knowledgeable FBI source, RFK-case supervisor Amadee O. Richards. I talked with Richards at his fashionable home in Pasadena where he now collects rare antiques. He emphasized emphatically, no fewer than three times during the two and a half hour discussion, that the Bureau conducted a ''parallel investigation.'' It did its own, ''independent'' evaluation of data, Richards asserted, and reached its own conclusions about the case and the evidence.

In 1988, I came across a letter in declassified LAPD files that indicates that the FBI had received a similar request for clarification in 1977 – from the chief administrative officer of Los Angeles County. In a letter co-signed by one of his investigators, Harry L. Hufford wrote: ''If more bullets were fired within the pantry than Sirhan Sirhan's gun was capable of holding, we should certainly find out who else was firing. If, in fact, the FBI has no evidence that the questioned holes were bullet holes, we should know that so that the air may be cleared.'' I have found no response to this letter either in LAPD files or FBI files.

The Bureau's closed-mouth and contradictory posture on the substance of its investigation seems to have translated into extraordinary secrecy, even as public disclosure was being required. In December 1984, I joined political scientist Greg Stone in a Freedom of Information Act request for FBI case files. With the help of some of the nation's leading experts on FBI files and the expertise of Washington attorney James H. Lesar, our detailed request produced more than 32,000 pages of previously unreleased documents.

Unlike similar FBI releases, such as the files on the assassinations of President Kennedy and Dr. King, these documents arrived purged of the names of FBI personnel, save J. Edgar Hoover and case supervisor Amadee O. Richards. The Bureau stated that agents' privacy outweighed "historical" research. We responded that with the names of more than 100 RFK-case agents in hand, disclosed in previously released files and publications, the secrecy was unnecessary. Agents still had a right to refuse to talk but the public deserved to know who did what in this controversial case. The FBI responded that it would only disclose an agent's name within the precise context in which it was previously disclosed, and no other. If, for example, we could provide documentation that an agent had conducted a particular interview, we could have the agent's name restored to the released interview. We refused this less-than-generous offer to officially give us what we already had. The FBI's position seemed aimed more at concealing who did what than protecting privacy of agents whose identities are already a matter of public record.

In federal court in Washington, D.C., Attorney James Lesar challenged the Bureau's secrecy on behalf of Stone and myself. He presented 19 supporting affidavits attesting to the public-interest importance of not deleting the names of agents – affidavits from academics, journalists, authors of major books about the FBI and even one from the Bureau's former Freedom of Information Office Directors, as well as a retired agent. The FBI presented not one affidavit. But in January 1989, Judge Charles Richey ruled in favor of the Bureau's continued secrecy, stating, in part, that the agents' expectations of privacy and freedom from possible harassment outweighed the value of public disclosure. This, even though the unresolved evidentiary controversies manifested in the Bureau's own files were clearly presented to the court. A three-judge federal appeals court unanimously upheld Judge Richey's decision.

Returning to our reseach in LAPD files, we found that in 1974 the department generated a further "explanation" of how officers Rozzi and Wright came to be photographed examining a hole in the doorframe. The memo is to then-Assistant Chief, today Chief,

Daryl Gates, and is written by four of the officers who, according to LAPD logs, played a major role in developing the evidence. This additional explanation to support the nonexistence of bullet holes in the now-famous photo went as follows: Officers Rozzi and Wright were interviewed by LAPD in 1974, and they revealed that the photo resulted because they were merely complying with Chief Thomas Reddin's policy of "full press cooperation." The press asked them to point to holes, and they did. According to the memo, the photographers then asked "if the holes were bullet holes." They (Rozzi and Wright) replied, "I don't know, could be."

There is no record of these alleged interviews of Rozzi and Wright with LAPD officials anywhere in the police files, apart from the 1974 memo, which purports to quote them. The story attributed to the two officers conflicts so sharply with Rozzi's 1975 affidavit to Bugliosi (in which he stated that he personally obverved what he thought to be a bullet) that it raises the question of whether these contradictory, self-serving 1974 LAPD interviews ever truly took place.

In 1975, Congressman Allard K. Lowenstein and Greg Stone obtained from the L.A. DA's office three LAPD photos – one of Wolfer and two of other officers besides Rozzi and Wright – pointing to particular locations on the doorframe. Were these also a product of the willingness to pose anywhere for the press, spawned by Chief Reddin's policy of press cooperation? Was this policy in the forefront of everyone's mind during the crime-scene search? Could the shock of a second major American political assassination within two months (Dr. King in April 1968 and Senator Kennedy in June) have caused this *Glasnost* on the part of LAPD?

The 1974 memo to Assistant Chief Gates shows the down side of this policy. It contends: "Due to the Associated Press photo, the door frame was later removed and examined. It was determined that there were no bullet holes in the doorframe." In this preposterous new version of the official history of the case, the very booking into evidence of the wood was caused by a mislabeled photographic mock-up that quickly circled back on LAPD to shape its crime-scene search.

In 1975, then-Los Angeles District Attorney John Van de Kamp sought to refute the mounting public suspicion concerning excess bullets. Court order in hand, the DA's investigators executed what critics would dub "the great pantry raid": searching after the seven-years-cold trail of the missing bullets. Descending upon the crime scene armed with an array of instruments and video cameras and followed by a small army of press, the authorities, including Assistant Chief Daryl Gates, conducted a meticulous search for bullets and bullet holes. The press had to wait outside, which could only have enhanced their sense of drama. The searchers stoically ignored the fact that the most relevant holes had been removed and destroyed seven years before – those in the original door jamb and ceiling tiles. They concluded that one supposedly surviving hole, which in 1968 had allegedly been labeled as a bullet hole, could now be determined to be a nail hole. The day after the raid, an official spokesman dramatically announced that "No other bullets were found last night."

In subsequent correspondence and press releases, Van de Kamp and his office would tout this bizarre exercise as a manifestation of "our continuing interest in making sure that no significant stone remains unturned in this matter."[3] Rather than focusing its attention on where the destroyed physical evidence used to be, the case would have been better served had Van de Kamp's office conducted a new, thorough investigation of existing files and witnesses – especially FBI and LAPD personnel.

In the same year as the pantry raid, retired 15-year FBI veteran William Bailey was teaching criminology at a New Jersey college. He attended a lecture by Vincent Bugliosi and, afterward, told the attorney that he had worked at the RFK crime scene and definitely saw what appeared to be bullets lodged in the doorframe.

It was not until two years later that Van de Kamp's office contacted Bailey after somehow receiving a copy of an affidavit that Bailey had given Bugliosi. Apparently, it was more important to debrief hotel carpenters via detailed, transcribed interviews than to talk with veteran investigators from other law-enforcement agencies. In 1977, the District Attorney's Office investigator, William R. Burnett, telephoned William Bailey.

BAILEY: There were at least two bullet holes in the center post.

Burnett asks how Bailey knows this.

BAILEY: Short of actually taking the wood off myself and examining it, I would say that I'm reasonably certain they were bullet holes. I've seen bullet holes in wood before. I looked into these holes . . . They were definitely not nail holes. There appeared to be objects inside.

Burnett did not ask Bailey to elaborate on the "objects" but asked if any other agents could corroborate this. Bailey replied that Agent Robert Pickard could.

The tape recording of this conversation was released to researchers like myself in 1986 during the first public access to the DA's RFK case files. It was not in the main file but in a separate box located at another DA branch office in Los Angeles. It was brought to the downtown office by an official who never assessed its contents. It was processed for disclosure by a young intern who had no knowledge of the case and did not screen the tapes prior to release. The box contained considerable data that was in conflict with the official version and may have been purposely segregated from all of the other case files by officials.

In May 1990, former FBI agent William Bailey appeared at a Los Angeles press conference demanding a re-opening of the case.* Having seen the close-up photo of the center divider that the FBI had labeled as manifesting two bullet holes, he could now correlate the sight of the released photo with what he remembered physically observing at the crime scene: "I personally observed in that center divider, depicted in that photograph E-3, two bullet holes . . . I looked at them very closely. I did observe what appeared to be the

---

* Other participants were Paul Schrade (an RFK friend wounded during the assassination), journalist Dan Moldea, political scientist Greg Stone, media producer David Mendelsohn and this author.

base of a bullet in each hole.''

The DA's files contain no evidence of any follow-up on William Bailey's allegation of additional bullets, either with Bailey, other FBI agents or LAPD officers. Bailey could not be challenged for a lack of expertise or dismissed as only a photo labeler or as posing for a photo. So he was apparently ignored by the office that pledged to leave ''no stone unturned.''

L.A. law would seek to disarm the growing furor over destroyed evidence and sightings of extra bullets by putting the best possible spin on the 1975 findings of a court-appointed panel of seven independent firearms experts (the panel resulted from a lawsuit initiated by assassination shooting victim Paul Schrade and *CBS News*). With considerable help from superficial media coverage, L.A. authorities were successful in appearing to have put the questions and controversies to rest. Headlines from Los Angeles newspapers on October 6 and 7, 1975, cried out: "Only One Gun, 7 Experts Say," "RFK Slain by Single Firearm" and "RFK Second Gun Theory Ruled Out." While it is true that the panel found no evidence of a second gun, the headlines were very misleading. The experts could find no evidence that the bullets being tested came from two different guns, nor could they conclude that the bullets came from Sirhan's gun. Panel member Lowell Bradford, selected by *CBS News*, testified under oath that the panel's findings rendered the question of a second gun "more open" than previously.

Despite the destruction and distortion of evidence, the case for too many bullets has strengthened with each new public disclosure of files and with recent interviews conducted by the investigators and researchers. In 1987, I interviewed Angelo Di Pierro and his son Vincent. Both were waiters at the Ambassador and crime-scene witnesses. Both men are staunch believers in the official version and are effusive in their praise of LAPD's work and of the police officers who dealt with them during the investigation and trial. There were not two guns, they flatly assert. Ironically, both are actually strong witnesses for a second gun; they are positive that they saw a bullet in the doorframe.

Vincent Di Pierro told me: "I do know one of the bullets wound up in the wall. Actually it was either the door post or the wall . . . my father pointed out that there was . . . [that] it was in the doorframe. I remember them taking the whole doorframe off. They took that away. I don't know whatever happened to it."

Angelo Di Pierro asserted that there could not have been two guns in the pantry because someone would have seen it. Regarding bullets, he said: "We counted the next day the exact number of shots, where each one went. One hit the ceiling, then bounced back by the door, so that's the same bullet." Before the tape recorder was turned on, Angelo Di Pierro told me that a police officer explained to him that the bullet he saw in the doorframe was a "ricochet." Thus, in Di Pierro's mind, it created no problem concerning the number of guns fired.

MELANSON: The bullet in the door was the door at the west end, with the [center] post there?
A. DI PIERRO: Right.
MELANSON: The door or the jamb?
A. DI PIERRO: The post.
MELANSON: Did you help dig that [the bullet] out, find that, or . . .
A. DI PIERRO: They dug it out.*

In 1990, John Burns, head of the California State Archives, conducted an oral history interview with key witness Karl Uecker. For the first time in his numerous interviews over the years, Uecker revealed that he too had seen what appeared to be two bullet holes in the center divider of the pantry doorway. Incredibly, no one had previously asked him if he saw bullet holes and, not being cognizant of the significance of the controversy, he "didn't think it was important. . . ."

After being interviewed by police the morning of June 5, 1968, Uecker returned to the crime scene, which was being examined by law-enforcement personnel. He noticed two holes in the center

* He did not witness the actual removal but was told that the bullet was removed.

divider that he is positive were not there prior to the shooting. He passed through the door dozens of times each night and is sure he would have seen them if they existed previously: "Two holes, which were never there [previously]." Uecker recalls pointing the holes out to a man whom he thought to be plainclothes policeman. The man responded that everything would be checked out.

BURNS: How come you thought they were bullet holes?
UECKER: Because these holes never were there before and I knew where the shots were going to. I saw him [Sirhan] *shooting*, and I know it must have been this way.

In the spring of 1990, investigative journalist Dan Moldea conducted an extensive probe into the question of extra bullets. He did what Los Angeles officials had systematically failed to do: He attempted to talk to all of the law-enforcement personnel involved and succeeded in interviewing over 100 LAPD officers and sheriff's deputies. His May 13, 1990, article in the *Washington Post* ("RFK's Murder: A Second Gun?") provided strong new evidence of extra bullets, based on the statements of some of the law enforcement officers themselves:

- LAPD photographer Charles Collier was asked how sure he was that he took pictures of bullet holes in the pantry. He answered, "A bullet hole looks like a bullet hole if you've photographed enough of them." (Only 51 of 98 Collier photos apparently taken at the crime scene have been accounted for.)
- Patrolman Al Lamoreaux told Moldea, "I do recall seeing one or two holes in the door around wherever he had just shot him . . . it was just obvious. Just being a dumb cop you look and see where the bullets went."
- Sergeant James MacArthur, the senior police detective at the crime scene, told Moldea he had seen "quite a few" bullet holes, including one high on the wall to the left of the swinging doors.
- Kenneth E. Vogel stated that he was positive he saw two .22 bullet fragments on the pantry floor and he brought his discovery to the attention of an LAPD official. No such fragments were

ever reported or booked into evidence, according to released LAPD files.

- Sergeant Raymond Rolon told Moldea, "One of the investigators pointed to a hole in the doorframe and said, 'We just pulled a bullet out of here.'"
- Deputy Sheriff Thomas Beringer recalled a man in a tuxedo "trying to take a bullet out of the [doorframe] with a knife, a silver knife, for a souvenir."

In 1988, investigator Jonn Christian discovered a newspaper article from the *Chicago Tribune* buried in released LAPD files. Ironically, in its effort to keep a massive file of newspaper clippings concerning the case, LAPD had unknowingly provided yet further testimony to extra bullets. In 1968, Robert Weidrich was a veteran crime reporter for the *Tribune*. His editors dispatched him to Los Angeles after the shooting. Arriving at the crime scene in the early hours of the morning of June 5, he interviewed Karl Uecker and filed his story "Felt Him Fire Gun, Hotel Worker Says." The article contained the following corroborating revelation:

On a low table lay an 8-foot strip of molding, torn by police from the center post of the double doors leading from the ballroom. These were the doors through which Sen. Kennedy had walked, smiling in his moment of victory.

Now the molding bore the scars of a crime laboratory technician's probe as it had removed two .22-caliber bullets that had gone wild.

In December 1988, I contacted Weidrich at the *Chicago Tribune*. He was unaware of the controversy about extra bullets. He recalled for me his journalistic coup in the pantry. With 20 years' experience as a crime reporter he arrived at the scene not expecting that, as an out-of-town correspondent, he would not have much access to Los Angeles police in such a big case. He found two officers sitting at a table near the pantry drinking coffee. "Technicians" were still examining the crime scene. Weidrich began chatting with the officers and asked them questions. To his pleasant surprise they handed him a terrific story. "I've seen a lot of crime scenes," he recalled, "but they were very, very cooperative" – especially Detective Sergeant J.R. MacArthur, who pointed him to star witness Uecker: "MacArthur, God bless him, steered me to that fella [Uecker] . . . He told me no one else had interviewed [Uecker]." MacArthur vouched for the validity of Uecker's account.

Regarding the two bullets referred to in his article, Weidrich did not witness the actual removal, but he states, "I would have asked, 'What did you find?' [MacArthur would have replied] 'Oh, we found these two slugs.' "

"The molding had obviously been removed from the wall," Weidrich asserted; "they had recovered the two slugs."

"Now the removal of the bullets probably occurred prior to my getting there. But MacArthur would have told me about that or the crime lab guy would have. They were amazingly cooperative . . . Especially under these circumstances they tend to be very close-mouthed. But these guys were friendly as the dickens. I remember writing MacArthur a note when I got back, to thank him for his help."

Other supporting information includes a June 8, 1968, FBI memo that I discovered among recently released files, summarizing the state of LAPD's ballistics work.

It says: "[deleted] Detective division, Los Angeles Police Department, advised that the ballistics examination regarding the slugs recovered at the shooting at the Ambassador Hotel on the morning of June 5, 1968, has not been completed."

In LAPD files a property report significantly lists "2 pieces of wood from doorframe at crime scene." It goes on to say that "both contain numerous holes."

In terms of further disappearance of evidence, police "logs of work performed" describe tests done on doorframes and ceiling tiles. None of the results of these tests have ever surfaced. The log indicates that at 3:30 p.m. on June 5, Lt. D. W. Mann examined ceiling tiles both chemically and microscopically. On June 6 at 7:00

a.m., "examination of ceiling tiles X-ray" was conducted. A 1975 LAPD interview with Wolfer states that wood removed from the crime scene "was further examined by fluoroscope." The substantive results of these analyses are nowhere in police files. LAPD hasn't even been asked by Los Angeles officials or the press to explain why.

Included in LAPD files released in 1988 were three dozen crime-scene photos, some of which show Wolfer and the police examining the doorframe and the ceiling. It is, to say the least, highly suspicious that not one photo is captioned or labeled, except by number (there is no corresponding log to decipher the numbers). Standard police procedure requires the captioning of photos in the most routine auto accidents. Otherwise – as in the case of close-ups that could be anything from a moon crater to a hammer mark – the evidentiary value of the photos is drastically reduced. Did LAPD really forget rudimentary police procedure in the biggest case in its history? Does the department that has had so much trouble as a result of allegedly sloppy labeling – by the AP and the FBI – actually have no labels of its own?

Released LAPD files contain a summary of an interview with "C. Collier," a "photo lab civilian" who was assigned by "D.H.Q." (department headquarters) to take pictures of the crime scene and the Senator's autopsy. He arrived at the Ambassador at 2:00 a.m. and "he was assigned to photograph from all angles" the following:

- the podium in the Embassy Room
- kitchen area and the route taken by Senator Kennedy from the Embassy Room to the kitchen
- bullet holes
- blood
- route taken by Kennedy from his room to the podium

Obviously if there were not supposed to be any bullet holes, why was a photographer assigned to take pictures of "bullet holes"?

The paradox is that with all the systematic destruction and manipulation of the evidence and the case record, so many references that would appear to be to extra bullets survived in the released files. One hypothesis is that a complete purge and cover-up was not possible because the problem was not discovered until later, after a web-like paper trail of activities, evidence and analysis had already been generated. When the shooting victims were taken to the hospital, police at the crime scene had no way of knowing how many bullets had caused their wounds. For example, Senator Kennedy was generally believed to have been shot twice. Later it would be discovered that he was hit three times and a fourth bullet went through his coat. Within hours after the shooting, finding and/or removing one or more bullets from the doorframe would have been viewed as good news – a rich opportunity to build an airtight case against Sirhan. At a later point, when a total of seven bullets were sequentially recovered from the various surgeries and the autopsy - - and with one bullet lost in the ceiling – bullet(s) from the crime scene were transformed from helpful evidence to an instant crisis. They constituted proof of two guns and, except for the most bizarre of coincidences, conspiracy.

There was a strange, but not necessarily incidental, footnote to the findings of the 1975 special firearms panel. The panel discovered that two bullets allegedly found in the glove compartment of Sirhan's car contained traces of wood on both the base and tip. Were these bullets really found in Sirhan's car, or were they dug out of the pantry doorframe? The wood tracings were not microscopically compared to the surviving remnants of the original door frame at the Ambassador pantry. They obviously should have been. Absent such a definitive test, there are two possibilities. One is that Sirhan fired two rounds into a tree or board, dug them out, and put them in his glove compartment before he drove to the crime scene. The other is that the bullets were actually dug out of the wooden doorframe and were mistakenly switched or purposely falsely labeled. We already know that this case betrays one of the most glaring errors imaginable regarding the labeling of ballistics evidence: DeWayne Wolfer introduced into evidence at Sirhan's trial a test gun that he offered as the proven murder weapon, even though it clearly had a different serial number than Sirhan's gun.

Extreme secrecy served LAPD well. The department successfully resisted disclosure of its files in 1975, despite legal, political and administrative pressures. Had the documents been released then instead of 13 years later, the 1975 discovery of the destruction of the wood and tiles would have seemed all the more sinister, given the additional gaps and inconsistencies in the official record. As it was, LAPD could say that the destruction didn't matter, because its work was solid and its files proved that there were no extra bullets – while never having to accept responsibility for where crucial evidence in the murder of a presidential candidate disappeared to. Furthermore, to this day the LAPD has avoided being held accountable for this action.

Chapter 5

SECOND GUN

Kranz found no indication that there was more than one assassin, who may have fired more than one gun with more than eight bullets. Special Counsel Kranz is convinced, from all the evidence, that there was no second gun . . .

— Conclusion of the *Kranz Report*
(re-investigation by Special Counsel Thomas Kranz,
Los Angeles District Attorney's Office, March 1977)

L os Angeles officials like to argue that with more than 70 witnesses there could not have been a second gun or "someone" would have seen it. Actually, of course, someone did. Vincent Di Pierro, a witness who was within a few feet of Kennedy at the time of the shooting, became indignant about the possibility of a second gun during my 1987 interview with him. He insisted that the idea was nonsense: He would have seen it, and he hadn't. As previously described, however, witnesses saw different things, different segments of the tableau of violence and intrigue. Many failed to see the gun or Sirhan or both. We know Sirhan was there firing. Yet dozens of people failed to see this even though they were close to the action.

Lisa Urso had one of the few unobstructed views of both Sirhan and Kennedy (from behind Sirhan) and she saw the gun. Still, she did not see one of the most conspicuous figures in the group tightly surrounding Kennedy: the uniformed security guard, Thane Eugene Cesar, who was at the Senator's right elbow. Cesar was the only person in Kennedy's immediate vicinity wearing a uniform, complete with hat (discounting the drab "uniforms" of the kitchen help). Moreover, the majority of witnesses in Kennedy's area did not see or report Cesar drawing his gun, although he himself says that he did. The possibility of a second gun cannot be dismissed by the notion that it would have been in plain sight.

Beyond the limitations of eyewitness data, what about the hard evidence, the scientific data? Did ballistics analysis prove or disprove that Sirhan's was the only gun fired? Recall that in 1968, LAPD's chief criminologist DeWayne Wolfer stated that he had conclusively matched all of the testable victim bullets with test bullets fired from Sirhan's gun. In 1975, shooting victim Paul Schrade initiated legal action that resulted in a re-examination of ballistics data by a court-appointed panel of seven firearms experts. The panel was given a very limited mandate that inexplicably excluded the questions of whether more than eight rounds were fired or whether LAPD's trajectory analysis was valid. It was charged only with determining whether the bullets recovered from the victims came from Sirhan's gun.

The experts unanimously rejected Wolfer's findings: They could not match any of the four, testable bullets to Sirhan's gun (the other three were too fragmented to test). Neither could the panel prove that any of the bullets did not come from Sirhan's weapon. Authorities misrepresented the experts' inability to prove a second gun as conclusive proof that there was no second gun. This was not the only conclusion that should have been drawn, because the experts' more important finding was that the bullets could not be conclusively matched to Sirhan's gun either, refuting LAPD's findings of eight years earlier, in 1968. In fact, the second-gun theory had been given new validity, since Wolfer's allegedly conclusive one-gun findings had been refuted. Said panelist Lowell Bradford, ''The firearms examination simply closes one episode of evidence and should not constrain further efforts to resolve the possibility of the firing of a second gun at the assassination scene.''

But L.A. officials would continue to successfully cloak their flawed case in the alleged scientific proof of one gun. LAPD's press conferences and skillful manipulation of the media actually twisted the inconclusive results to support their original findings of one gun. This is an incredible public relations feat, given that the panel of experts actually found that Sirhan's gun could not be conclusively matched to the bullets. How did the truth become so obscured? The Teflon effect was measurable. Even the FBI conveniently adopted or believed the propaganda. The Bureau's RFK-case supervisor, Amadee O. Richards, told me that all questions regarding a second gun had been answered by the 1975 panel. When in 1985 I queried the FBI about its conclusion regarding the possibility of too many bullets for Sirhan's gun, Assistant Director William Baker responded, ''The panel members, working independently, examined all the firearms evidence available in the investigation and unanimously concluded that there was no substantive evidence to support any so-called second-gun theory.'' While Baker is literally correct, his response glosses over the fact that the issue remained unresolved according to the experts' findings.

One major obstacle to scientifically concluding what was the truth behind the second-gun question is the integrity of the evidence. If one or more bullets were removed from the crime scene but were lost, discarded or suppressed, then the validity of the ballistics evidence has obviously been severely compromised.

There is another test that could be performed and would be more conclusive than those conducted by the 1975 panel. In the neutron activation test, bullet samples are bombarded with neutrons, and this provides data on the precise quantities of trace elements that comprise the metal. By comparing the number and level of trace elements (copper, silver, sodium, chlorine, etc.) it is possible to determine if fragments came from the same bullet, or if bullets came from the same batch of manufacture. Again, however, even a high-tech analysis like this one is only as valid as the evidentiary integrity of the bullets under test.

With ballistic science inconclusive and seemingly thwarted by the limitations of the evidence, we will return to the best available data – the most credible eyewitness accounts. It must be understood that from the first round of police interviews within hours of the shooting, through the investigation and trial, to the subsequent "re-investigations," the one-gun theory so dominated the process that witnesses were not even questioned about other guns. On the morning of June 5 when LAPD interviewed dozens of witnesses, the primary interest was in whether they could identify Sirhan or "the gun." Audio tapes reveal that the witnesses simply were not asked if they saw anyone else fire or saw other guns drawn.

One might assume that a competent witness who saw any sort of gun at a shooting scene would volunteer this information, even if not asked. The questioning at all phases of this investigation was so completely preoccupied with Sirhan that witnesses must have thought everything else was superfluous. On the morning of June 5, the traumatized, fatigued bystanders wanted to get home as soon as possible.

Police obliged by providing "efficient" – as one officer described it to a witness – highly structured questioning that focused almost exclusively on Sirhan. Later, during re-interviews, most witnesses believed that the one-gun conclusion had been solidly established and that the case was open-and-shut. Authorities did nothing to disabuse them of this view. I was told by five significant witnesses that they did not volunteer certain observations that we now know to be important: The investigators seemed uninterested or downright hostile to such information, or the witnesses assumed the information was irrelevant because the case was sewed up or because the questioners didn't ask about it. We must also remember that the population of witnesses who saw particular occurrences tended to be much more finite than the group of 77 persons who were in the pantry area.

Many witnesses mistakenly thought Kennedy was guarded by the U.S. Secret Service. For them, the presence of other guns would tend to seem natural and appropriate. This author has found two witnesses who saw another gun in the pantry – sightings not recorded by official investigators. There may be more such persons, who perhaps thought they saw "police" or "Secret Service" drawing guns or even firing "back at Sirhan." There could also be witnesses who believe that the gun they saw was part of a conspiracy and are afraid to talk. The widely publicized allegations concerning numerous "mysterious deaths" of witnesses in President Kennedy's assassination have had a chilling effect on a number of witnesses in the King and Kennedy cases.

In addition to Sirhan's gun and that of security guard Cesar, Lisa Urso saw another one. During our interview she clearly recalled someone she assumed to be a "security guard" drawing a gun. But Urso's "guard" was not wearing a uniform. She sighted the gun immediately after the shooting, just as Sirhan's gun was wrestled from him.

"But the security guard had a gun and I think he went like this [drawing a gun] or he put it in a holster or something . . . Somebody [the "guard"] put it back into a holster." She described the man as blond and wearing a grey suit. He was located "by Kennedy." Urso said she had mentioned this "guard" to the authorities on a couple of occasions. They reacted with disinterest on one occasion; hostility, on another.

A second witness, whom we shall call Martha Raines, told the author of seeing a man fire a gun in the pantry. He was approximately 6-feet 2-inches tall, Caucasian, with dark, wavy hair and wearing a suit (not a uniform). Raines had seen the man standing near Sirhan earlier in the evening. She believed that the man constituted a sinister presence in the pantry and was not protecting the Senator.

According to Raines, the man fired a handgun of some kind. She recalled that the gunman "was not composed." He didn't shoot "more than once or twice" before running out of the pantry.

"And, as I recall," said Raines, "one of them [the shots] was high and should have gone into the ceiling. I don't know what these people found when they did their ballistics tests ... but it appeared to me there should have been a gunshot in the ceiling."

The most controversial and well-known of the second-gun witnesses did tell his story early on. Don Schulman was a runner for KNXT-TV in Los Angeles. Immediately following the shooting he was interviewed on radio by Jeff Brent of Continental News Service. He gave the following account:

BRENT: I'm talking to Don Schulman. Don can you give us a half-way decent report of what happened within all this chaos?
SCHULMAN: O.K. I was ... a ... standing behind ... a ... Kennedy as he was taking his assigned route into the kitchen. A Caucasian gentleman stepped out and fired three times ... the security guard ... hit Kennedy all three times. Mr. Kennedy slumped to the floor ... they carried him away ... the security guards fired back ... As I saw ... they shot the ... a ... man who shot Kennedy ... in the leg ... He ... a ... before they could get him he shot a ... it looked like to me ... he shot a woman ... and he shot two other men. They then proceeded to carry Kennedy into the kitchen and ... I don't know how his condition is now.
BRENT: Was he grazed or did it appear to be a direct hit? Was it very serious from what you saw?
SCHULMAN: Well ... from what I saw ... it looked ... fairly serious. He had ... he was definitely hit three times. Things happened so quickly that ... that ... there was another eyewitness standing next to me and she is in shock now and very fuzzy ... as I am ... because it happened so quickly.
BRENT: Right. I was about six people behind the Senator, I heard six or seven shots in succession ... Now ... is this the security guard firing back?
SCHULMAN: Yes ... a ... the man who stepped out fired three times at Kennedy ... hit him all three times ... and the security guard then fired back ... hitting ...
BRENT: Right.

SCHULMAN: Hitting him, and he [presumably Sirhan] is in apprehension.

In 1971, journalist Ted Charach interviewed Schulman for his film *The Second Gun*. Schulman stated that the uniformed "guard [Cesar] fired his gun." But in a lengthy 1971 interview with the DA's office, Schulman flatly denied that he saw the guard shoot Kennedy or that that's what he had said in his crime-scene interview with Brent. "I didn't even see *Sirhan* shoot Kennedy," he told the DA's men.

Despite the intense pressure exerted upon him during the lengthy 1971 interview – pressure to be "absolutely positive" about what he saw, pressure not to allow himself to be exploited by sensationalists, etc. – he insisted he saw the guard fire and also that he saw wounds erupting on Kennedy's body. But he refused to make a connection between these two events. His final response to the intimidating challenges from his questioners was that he was "pretty doggone sure" the guard fired a gun.

In his original radio interview with Brent, Schulman stated that Kennedy had been shot three times. The media, Kennedy's press secretary Frank Mankiewicz, and the crime-scene witnesses unanimously asserted that the Senator was hit only twice. Schulman recalled that the media tried to correct him during a couple of his interviews, but he stuck to his story. The autopsy proved Schulman right. This lends credibility to his claim that he actually saw bullets impact on Kennedy's body.

In October 1975, Schulman had his last official interview, with Special Counsel Tom Kranz who would author the *Kranz Report* re-affirming the official conclusions. During the lengthy, audio-taped session, Schulman reiterated that he saw "three blood splotches" on the Senator. Displaying a monumental ignorance of the basic evidence, Kranz later commented (on this same tape), "Well, actually he hadn't been shot three times; there were only two wounds . . . Well, there were three bullet holes but one didn't hit his wounds . . . just went through a coat." There were, of course, three wounds and a fourth shot that passed through Kennedy's coat. It is incredible that Special Counsel Tom Kranz did not even know the basic autopsy facts about the number of bullets that hit the Senator.

During the course of the interview, Schulman's relevant statements about a second gun were as follows:

"I thought I saw other guns pulled."

"I had thought I saw three guns."

"I saw other guns pulled and possibly fired."

To the latter statement an unidentified Los Angeles law-enforcement person sitting in on the interview responds, "No, there was no other guns."

"I thought I saw 'em," says Schulman.

"Nope, you didn't."

Later Schulman says, "I have said I thought I saw a security guard pull his gun and possibly fire." Still later, "I saw other guns pulled and possibly fired and I'm not sure about possibly fired."

After Schulman's departure Kranz and his colleague have a revealing discussion while the audio tape was still recording. The latter is putting down critics of the official version, describing one as an "assassination buff, old, old broad with nothing else to do [pejorative references directed at Lillian Castellano of the Kennedy Assassinations Truth Committee]." Kranz changes the subject back to Schulman, whom he had just interviewed . He concludes, "I never felt, particularly in light of the ballistics examination, that his statements about a security guard had that much weight."

His colleague says, "Yeah, but he really has not changed his [story]; he's still sticking with . . . he still sees guns and this kinda shit . . . I think if, if this thing is gonna go any place and he's gonna be a problem, I'd like to call him in and we'll interrogate him." Since Schulman had just been questioned for an hour and a half, the purpose of such an "interrogation" would seem to be information suppression and disposal rather than information gathering.

The author's efforts to locate and interview Schulman were unsuccessful. He surely was not a publicity seeker. He had given his original account before there was a second-gun controversy, before any of the evidentiary conflicts had surfaced. He insisted during his 1971 interview that he enjoyed his work as a drug counselor and that he did not want fame but only to continue his work. It may be that his apparent diminished certainty between 1971 and 1975 was due in part to the pressures of his status as the only officially recorded, second-gun witness in the RFK case. In his 1971 interview he was clearly upset with both sides – with what he perceived as pressure to declare himself a witness to conspiracy and with the often-demeaning, high-pressured interrogation by officials who were hostile to his story.

No record exists in either LAPD or FBI files of Schulman having been interviewed during the original 1968 investigation, despite the fact that his story appeared on radio and TV and in some newspapers. It is as if the authorities wanted to ignore this witness and hoped he would disappear. His name was left off the police list of "witnesses in the pantry," and authorities would later seek to dismiss him by claiming that he was not in the pantry. LAPD's Summary Report states that he was "unable to furnish information that materially affected the investigation.'" This was certainly true by definition since LAPD had apparently decided that Schulman was wrong about everything, even though there is no substantive record in the original investigation as to how they arrived at such a determination, since there is no record of an interview.

What Schulman didn't know was that he was not the only person who claimed to have seen another gun or to have seen another gun fired. But Don Schulman was forced into a controversial, high-visibility and high-pressured role that he never wanted – that of the "only" second-gun witness in L.A. law's otherwise open-and-shut, one-gun case.

Yet, the available evidence strongly suggests that at least ten shots were fired, quite possibly a dozen, requiring two guns. Three drawn guns were reported by witnesses: Sirhan's, uniformed security guard Thane Cesar's and that of an unidentified man wearing a suit. Moreover, Martha Raines asserts that a gun besides Sirhan's or Cesar's was fired. Schulman is no longer the only second-gun witness. And there may be more such witnesses like Urso and Raines whose sitings of second or third guns have not yet been recorded.

Chapter 6

THE CESAR
CONTROVERSY

*I have a very good friend who works for the FBI. And after
the FBI interview I called him up and he went and pulled the
files to see exactly what they reported on me. They gave me
the same conclusion the LAPD did [that I wasn't a suspect].*
– Thane Eugene Cesar to journalist Dan Moldea, 1987

Too often, persons who entertain the possibility of a second gun
leap to the conclusion that it had to have been Thane Cesar, the
uniformed security guard who stood close to Kennedy. As we saw in
the previous chapter, however, two witnesses reported seeing a gun
other than Sirhan's or Cesar's. One witness asserts a man in a suit
fired a weapon. In this author's opinion, the conflicting, inadequate
data surrounding Cesar simply does not support either the official
conclusion that all questions relating to him have been satisfactorily
answered or the conclusion implied by some – that he must be the
second gunman. As with most other areas of the RFK case, the
inadequate investigation by Los Angeles authorities and their
tendency to cover up conflicts in this case rather than attempt to
resolve them has left this controversial area extremely murky.[1]

In 1986, it came to my attention that Al Albergate of the Los Angeles District Attorney's Office had told two researchers that Cesar was dead. I phoned Albergate. He reiterated that he had heard – from reliable sources that he could not recall – that Cesar had died several years earlier in Arkansas. This, of course, was not true. The DA's office could easily have checked with Cesar's lawyer, whose name was known to them, and discovered his current status and location. Maybe someone in the DA's office reasoned that if Cesar was thought to be deceased the second-gun controversy would die out.

As far back as 1971 officials were dispensing misinformation about Cesar to the press. An August 16, 1971, article by Dave Smith of the *Los Angeles Times* entitled "Sirhan Case – Was There a 2nd Gunman?" quotes an unnamed "official" who tries to turn the Cesar problem into the solution, stating that the inconsistencies in Cesar's story were cause for writing him out of the case rather than investigating him further.

Said the official: "The guy's stories didn't jibe. He told conflicting accounts and it seemed obvious he hadn't really seen anything. He really had nothing to tell us."

"Because of the variances in his story," writes Smith, "the guard was dropped from any further questioning, his credibility questioned by officials who felt he was trying to inject himself into a sensational case he really knew little about."

Anyone who listens to the audio tapes of Cesar's lengthy interviews, which Dave Smith had apparently not been able to do, knows that the man who was close enough to touch Robert Kennedy as the shooting began had plenty to tell, and that his inconsistencies (about selling his .22, or about when he drew his gun) were cause for further interrogation, not dismissal. Other officials would tout Cesar as having forthrightly and satisfactorily answered all the questions put to him by investigators, as if he were a very good witness.

In 1968, when the 26-year-old guard held Robert Kennedy's right arm as they walked through the pantry, Cesar was employed by Lockheed Aircraft in a capacity he described as that of a plumbing-maintenance worker. The dark-featured young man moonlighted as a uniformed security guard for Ace Guard Service, which had been hired by the Ambassador Hotel to provide crowd control and security. Cesar's political views alone have caused some of the less discriminating students of the RFK case to leap to conspiratorial conclusions: There are people for whom the discovery of a right-wing ideology is as good as a smoking gun.

In his book *Special Unit Senator*, Chief Robert Houghton reassures readers that there were no "right wingers" in the pantry. Perhaps in the right-tilted spectrum of L.A. politics in 1968 Cesar came off as some kind of a centrist, or perhaps Houghton was not familiar with Cesar's politics. He supported George Wallace for president and claimed that he had done some work (passing handbills, getting donations) for Wallace's American Independent Party.*[2]

Regarding racial tension, Cesar told Ted Charach during a 1969 interview that a race war could be imminent: "And one of these days, at the rate they're goin, there's gonna be a civil war in this country. It's gonna be white against black. [Cesar predicted that blacks would lose] . . . Me as an individual, I'm fed up. It's just that we ain't had it shoved down our throats enough. But one of these days it's gonna be shoved too far and we're gonna fight back." [3]

Regarding the Kennedys, Cesar candidly told Charach, "I definitely wouldn't have voted for Bobby Kennedy 'cause he had the same ideas as John did and I think John sold the country down the road. He gave it to the commies; he gave it to whoever else he wanted to." [4]

However colorful such political background may be, it is the questions and conflicts in the foreground of Cesar's role that deserved resolution by the officials. One question that has arisen is why Cesar was where he was in the pantry walking close beside Kennedy.

---

* Cesar asserted this to Ted Charach in 1969. In a 1971 interview with the DA's Office, he said that he did not work for the Wallace campaign.

In 1987, Cesar told investigative journalist Dan Moldea,* "In fact, this is a matter of record, he didn't want any bodyguards around him." Therefore, said Cesar, he was not there as Kennedy's bodyguard but for "crowd control. Nothing else."[5]

Cesar said he was instructed by William Gardner, chief of security for the Ambassador Hotel, to accompany Kennedy through the pantry:"When he [RFK] came down there, through that area, he wanted to make sure I wasn't even there, that there was no guards in there. Well, I stayed anyway, because that's what I was told to do. I didn't give a shit whether it was Bobby or not. You know, they told me to stay there so I stayed."

William Gardner's FBI summary states that he moved the guards from place to place during the evening at the request of the fire department and some of Kennedy's aides. It further states:

> Senator Kennedy had been a guest at the hotel on previous occasions during the present campaign and during his previous visits to the hotel it was made clear to him [Gardner] that the Senator did not want any uniformed security guards in his presence nor did he want any armed individuals as guards. Mr. Gardner said that this is one of the reasons why he did not have any guard assigned to escort the Senator through the hotel during the visit.

Cesar told LAPD on June 5, "As far as the other security officers, they were behind me trying to keep most of the people from following, and I grabbed ahold of his right arm and sort of pushed all the way through the crowd . . . so we could get through."

Yet, it would seem to have been maître d' Karl Uecker who, according to his earlier testimony, was functioning as point man, leading Kennedy through the crowd with the Senator's arm in tow.

In 1969, when Cesar described to Charach his proximity to RFK while leading him through the crowded pantry, it seemed almost serendipitous: "As he walked through, for some reason I just . . . We started walking with him and I happened to wind up on his right side . . . Just as he passed me, I followed him." [6]

* The reader will find an Appendix containing excerpts, some previously unpublished, of Moldea's interview with Cesar.

Whatever the reason, Cesar's proximity is undeniable. Somehow during the shooting, his clip-on bow tie ended up on the floor near the right arm of the fallen Senator. It can be seen only a couple of feet away from Kennedy's outstretched hand (see photo, in photo/documents section).

Other conflicts concern when and how Cesar drew his gun and what happened to him during the shooting. Within hours of the event he told LAPD, "And I went for mine [gun] but it was too late. He had done [sic] fired five shots and when he did, I ducked because I was as close as Kennedy was. I fell against [the ice machine] and then the Senator fell right down in front of me."

Almost one week later Cesar told the FBI a different version: He got knocked over before drawing his gun and drew it as he scrambled to his feet. On June 24 he was re-interviewed by LAPD and he reiterated that he drew only after falling down.

Cesar's original interview (with LAPD on June 5) seemed to indicate that he fell on his own: "And from what I can remember from what I did, I grabbed for the Senator and fell back. When I ducked, I threw myself off balance and fell back . . . Then – I think it was Murphy, one of the security guards – helped, ah, grabbed, ah, helped me up, and he says 'Let's get out in front here and stop the pandemonium.' So I got up and went with him."

On June 24, Cesar told LAPD that "the maître d' which was in front of me, to my right, either jumped or something, but he knocked me down against the ice box." Uecker's most detailed accounts never mention colliding with anyone but Sirhan. In his testimony and interviews, Uecker indicated that he pushed Sirhan back and to the left, downward toward the steam table. Cesar was supposedly somewhere to Uecker's right and to Kennedy's right (which would place him several feet from Uecker). Cesar was allegedly holding Kennedy's right arm while Uecker was leading Kennedy from in front of the Senator, guiding him forward by holding the wrist of his outstretched right arm.

Another point of confusion involves Cesar's assignments at the Ambassador in the hours preceding the assassination. Late in the evening he was assigned to the pantry area. About a half hour before the shooting, busboy Jesus Perez saw Sirhan in the pantry. Perez claims that Sirhan inquired a total of three or four times: "Mr. Kennedy come through here?"

Judy Royer was the private secretary of former California Governor Edmund "Pat" Brown and was also a paid Kennedy press aide. She told the FBI that she encountered Sirhan "approximately one or two hours" before the shooting. He was standing in the passageway behind the Embassy Room stage that led to the Colonial Room, where Kennedy was to meet with newspaper reporters after his victory speech. Royer had been told by an L.A. marshal that too many staff people were entering the area behind the stage. She did not recognize Sirhan as being either a staffer or a member of the press, so she asked him to leave. He complied. Royer watched him leave the passageway and enter the crowded ballroom.

Dr. Marcus McBroom told the FBI that he saw Sirhan in the kitchen shortly after 10:30 p.m. He noticed him because he looked out of place: He was sitting on a table and had "dirty" clothes and was clearly not a kitchen employee.

Cesar may or may not have been in position to possibly see Sirhan's earlier visits to the pantry area. The available record is both conflicting and fuzzy. A summary of Cesar's June 11 FBI interview says that about 10:50 p.m. he was assigned "to the kitchen area" in order to prevent people from entering the overcrowded Embassy Room via the kitchen. He saw no one loitering, no one suspicious. Chief Robert Houghton stated that there was no security at the east-end door of the pantry (the "swinging door").[7] But an LAPD chart accompanying his June 24 interview places Cesar at that location from 9:30 to 11:15, as Cesar stated during the interview.

Cesar told Moldea, "It [the traffic in the pantry] was mostly political people that worked for him . . . And most of them had badges on. Otherwise, I wouldn't let them through." Somehow, Sirhan got through. Cesar has consistently asserted that he never saw Sirhan before the shooting.

Campaign worker Ellen German told the FBI that she and RFK

advance-man Jerry Bruno entered the deserted pantry at 11:00 and were ordered to leave by a uniformed security guard. Sirhan himself has a foggy recollection of seeing a "policeman" – which could be a fire marshall or a uniformed security guard* – when he had coffee with an attractive young woman.[8] It is unclear whether the coffee urn in question was inside or just outside the pantry. This occurred sometime late in the evening. Witness Vincent Di Pierro told the FBI that "later in the evening," a security guard was stationed at the kitchen entrance.

One fact is certain about a second gunman: He had to have a .22 handgun in the pantry. All of the victims were hit with this caliber of ammunition. Had it been possible to seal off the pantry after the shooting and systematically check for guns, we might know how many of what kinds of weapons were present. Cesar maintains that he carried only the .38 revolver required by his employers at Ace Guard.

Cesar told Moldea in their 1987 interview that he offered his .38 to police immediately after the shooting but they declined to inspect it. There is no reference to this in the audio tape of the interview or in any documents pertaining to it. According to a 1976 article in the *Los Angeles Times*, Special Counsel Thomas Kranz of the DA's Office said Cesar had told him that a policeman at Rampart station examined his .38 within hours of the shooting, but "did not keep it to be test fired."[9] In the final *Kranz Report* (1977) Kranz wrote, "Cesar states and LAPD orally verifies, but has no documents to substantiate, the fact that the .38 caliber weapon Cesar had on his person that night as part of his Ace Guard Service assignment was examined by LAPD officers." Kranz provides no names or specifics for this alleged "fact," which conflicts with what Cesar told Moldea.

The question is not whether Cesar fired his .38, since no bullets other than .22 caliber were found. The real question is whether he carried a .22 the night of the shooting. This matter is further complicated by the fact that Cesar did own a .22, and there is conflicting information about when he got rid of it.

* There were no LAPD personnel, either uniformed or plain-clothed, assigned to the Ambassador at this time.

In 1971 he told authorities that he had sold his .22 prior to the shooting. While researching his film, *The Second Gun*, Charach learned that Cesar had sold his .22 to fellow Lockheed employee Jim Yoder, who was retiring to Arkansas. Yoder produced a receipt for the transaction, signed by Cesar and dated September 1968. The gun itself was stolen from Yoder's Arkansas home. He reported the theft to local police.

Los Angeles authorities would deal with this inconsistency by trying to make it disappear. District Attorney Joe Bush flatly told reporters that Cesar had sold the gun before the assassination.

Another odd element in Cesar's account concerns his description of Kennedy's wounds. For days after the assassination the press and public assumed he was hit twice. Only Don Schulman correctly insisted Kennedy had been shot three times. In 1976 the late Congressman Allard Lowenstein retrieved a hoard of assassination-related radio broadcasts and sent them to researchers in California.

Floyd Nelson and the late Lillian Castellano came across an interesting item that had not previously been known to students of the case. Within minutes after the shooting, Cesar had been interviewed by John Marshall of KFWB radio in Los Angeles.

During the very brief broadcast Cesar was asked: ''And what sort of wound did the Senator receive?''

''Well,'' Cesar replied, ''from where I could see, it looked like he was shot in the head, the chest and the shoulder.''

''How many shots did you hear?''

''Four.''

This makes Cesar the only person besides Schulman to correctly state that Kennedy was hit three times. But Cesar even knew – or guessed – the approximate locations of the wounds. There were, of course, more than four shots fired, but four did impact on Kennedy (three wounds and the bullet that passed through his suit coat). How did Cesar come by this knowledge, or was it a lucky guess? Was he hearing another gun fired from a different direction than Sirhan's?

His story is that he ducked or was knocked down, apparently

early in the shooting. If so, Kennedy must have fallen either with Cesar or in close approximation to Cesar's fall. The Senator landed on his back. Nobody who looked down on Kennedy as he lay there reported the correct number of wounds.

Dr. Stanley Abo, the first doctor to Kennedy's side, saw and dealt with the head wound. No other wounds were mentioned in his FBI interview, which described his assessment of Kennedy's condition and his attempt to relieve the "cranial pressure" created by the head wound.

Whether Cesar had some clearer view of Kennedy's wounds while falling over or simply guessed their number and approximate location is problematic. It is simply another confusing dimension to the Cesar saga.

For all the questions, inconsistencies and political overtones, there exists an impressive list of items that argue against what Dan Moldea has termed a "more sinister scenario" involving Cesar. Why, for example, would anyone conspicuously sell a gun, complete with signed receipt, that was related to a murder? Moldea points out that he could not find any criminal record on Cesar, despite the unsubstantiated tales of criminal involvement spun by some assassination researchers and picked up and reprinted in several prominent works dealing with the case. Flatly stated assertions that Cesar had a criminal record, has known mob associates, was linked to Howard Hughes and did contract chores for the mob have no sources that I could discover beyond the as-yet-undocumented statements of several researchers – who tend to cross-cite each other. In contrast, Dan Moldea, a skilled investigator with excellent sources (both official and unofficial), could find no criminal record on Cesar nor any as-yet-demonstrable ties to organized crime, as some writers have insisted. Moldea is an organized-crime reporter who has risked life and limb exposing Mafia activities in his books and articles since 1974. Moldea points out that Cesar has not prospered in any significant fashion since the shooting.[10] He has been cooperative with the authorities during his interviews. He did not skip to some foreign country nor was he disposed of as excess baggage by conspirators.

His own story, as convoluted as it is, does not try to put Sirhan at point-blank range with the gun behind Kennedy (which is in Cesar's self-interest to do if he comprehends the conflicting evidence). Like other witnesses, he places the gun two feet away from Kennedy and "perpendicular," not at an upward angle. This, in his 1987 interview with Moldea, when the evidentiary conflicts were well publicized. He continues to be candid about his political views, telling Moldea, "I had no use for the Kennedy family . . . I've read a lot of books on the Kennedy family and I think they're the biggest bunch of crooks that ever walked the earth. And I'm not ashamed to say it today.''"

Whatever the reality of Cesar's role – whether he is, as Moldea put it, "a classic example of a man caught at the wrong time in the wrong place with a gun in his hand and powder burns on his face" – Los Angeles authorities tried to gloss over the matter without sufficiently investigating to establish what the reality was.

In 1970, when the second-gun issue was receiving considerable attention, LAPD demonstrated a strange curiosity about Cesar. Despite public statements that he had answered all questions satisfactorily and that his role had been thoroughly investigated, a recently released FBI memo (dated September 29, 1970) reveals that "the District Attorney's Office is interested in obtaining information regarding Thane Cesar, a security guard who was present at the Ambassador Hotel the night Kennedy was killed.'' What, if any, data was found has not appeared in released police or FBI files. The memo further states that John Howard of the DA's office was worried that Ted "Charach's public statements [about a second gun] might possibly jeopardize prosecution's opposition to Sirhan's appeal.''

In 1971 Cesar was handled very gingerly (compared to other witnesses) during and after his lengthy interview with L.A. law. He told his questioners from LAPD and the DA's office that he had sold his .22 to Yoder "somewhere around'' February 1968, when Yoder retired from Lockheed. A few minutes later he recounted that an

LAPD sergeant came to his home to interview him after the assassination.

"Now, that wasn't tape-recorded," said Cesar, "but I did mention to him – in fact, I don't remember if I showed it to him, but I mentioned I had a gun similar to the one that was used that night."

Picking up on the contradiction, Sgt. Charles Collins asked, "Did you own that .22 on the night of the Kennedy assassination?"

"No," Cesar replied.

"Well, how did you show it to the sergeant the night he came out to interview you?"

"No, I didn't. That's what I said. I just told him about it and I wanted, you know, I was telling him what it was. I wanted to show it to him, you know, what kind of gun it was."

"But you didn't have it available," said Collins, as if programming Cesar to get his story straight.

"No."

"To show it to him?"

"No, no. In fact, I don''t remember whether Jim Yolder [sic] had left the state or not for Arkansas, but I had already sold it to him for $10."

LAPD could easily have tracked down Yoder, as Charach did, and settled the matter of timing.

Near the end of this interview, LAPD and DA personnel take a break and go off the record, shutting down the recorder. Before doing so, they announce that they will discuss arranging a polygraph for Cesar, a possibility to which he readily agrees. When they go back on tape, the DA's man says, "I did indicate to you, Mr. Cesar, before we broke, we might be making some arrangements for the polygraph operator. We found that those arrangements won't be necessary, tonight at any rate. We would ask your cooperation."

Cesar responds that he has nothing to hide and will take one at any time. Having discovered a significant possible contradiction in his account, one wonders why the investigators decided not to administer the test that had been used so extensively during the original investigation (especially for conspiracy-related witnesses).

The transcript of Cesar's 1971 interview had been available for several years before the audio tape was released in 1986. The author's comparison of the two revealed some interesting discrepancies. For example, when Cesar was asked about the kind of gun he carried at the Ambassador, the rather jerky, blurting exchange between him and his questioner was edited into calm coherence.

The actual exchange (the tape):

INTERVIEWER: And the only gun you were carrying on you that night . . .
CESAR: Was a .38.
INTERVIEWER: .38 . . . ah . . . revolver that you carried on you . . .
CESAR: Possession.
INTERVIEWER: Moonlighting jobs, so to speak.

The transcript:

Q: And the only gun you were carrying on you that night was the .38 revolver that you carried on your possession on moonlight jobs?
CESAR: Yes.

Another question – "Did you ever tell anyone you fired a round at the Ambassador?" – was simply missing from the transcript, as was Cesar's flatly negative response. Perhaps authorities thought that their question raised more questions than Cesar's negative answer could quell – such as why did they ask the question?

When LAPD files were released in 1988, we found that the department had indeed finally become curious about Yoder and Cesar's .22 – not in 1971 when Cesar's account seemed self contradictory and was at odds with Yoder's bill of sale, but in 1974. Congressman Allard Lowenstein had posed a series of written evidentiary questions to LAPD. He never got responses, but police records under the rubric "Replies to Lowenstein" (replies seen only by LAPD) reveal a flurry of rather halfhearted investigative activity. Yoder's wife and Cesar's wife were queried about the .22, as were four Arkansas lawmen who investigated its theft from Yoder's home. Documents also claim that Cesar himself was re-interviewed in December of 1974 and that he "answered all questions put to him in a thorough, straightforward and honest manner." He was "unsure" about the date of sale of his .22. But no tape, transcript or summary of this alleged interview appeared in released LAPD files. Police had no luck in finding the stolen gun or in getting more than superficial information about it (according to released records). One document from the 1974 re-investigation concludes that Cesar was uncertain about whether he sold the gun before or after the assassination. It further states that "subsequent information" established that it was sold to Yoder Sept. 6, 1968. Finally LAPD obtained or heard about Yoder's receipt, three years after being confronted with conflicting information about the sale.

So far as the record indicates, police never bothered to check into another key facet of the Cesar story – how he got his assignment at the Ambassador. Was it totally spontaneous as he indicated? Cesar claims he was telephoned by Ace Guard's Tom Spangler, who convinced him on the afternoon of June 4 to work a shift at the Ambassador that night. Cesar says he was reluctant to take the job after putting in a full day at Lockheed, but Spangler promised to pay him for a full eight-hour shift and let him work less. The allegedly spontaneous nature of Cesar's assignment is often used to discount the possibility of some sinister planning. Yet, no official investigators, journalists or researchers have ever talked to Spangler during any of the various Cesar-related investigations from 1968 to the mid-1970s. The author learned from Ace Guard that Spangler departed the firm several years after the assassination.[12] Efforts to locate him, conducted independently by myself and also by my research assistant Steve Kissell, were unsuccessful. Kissell pointed out that the 1974 LAPD reinvestigative file states matter-of-factly that Cesar was summoned to work by Spangler on June 4; but, again, there is no record of any verification from Spangler.

In 1986, I visited the offices of Ace Guard, inquiring about their services and how their procedures had changed since the late 1960s. Ace is located in Sepulveda, twenty miles north of downtown Los Angeles, in a two-story office building that houses a mixed bag of commercial enterprises. It is headquartered in a small three-room suite – a waiting room, a business office for talking with clients, an inner office (or operations room). The layout is modern but rather austere and sparse.

Irv Slitsky, apparently second-in-command, had been with the firm for a number of years and gave me the history of the outfit and how it operates. Ace was basically the same kind of enterprise it was in 1968. It was not an elite firm with an exclusive client list of fat-cats, government agencies and defense contractors, like Wakenhut Security in Washington, D.C. Nor was it involved in high-tech surveillance and counter-surveillance as are many of the high-powered firms. Ace installs video monitors and alarm systems. But for counter-surveillance, the firm passes on its clients to another firm that has expertise in that area. Unlike some of the largest firms in the country, Ace has never been able to afford ex-federal agents, because its customers don't require the kind of services that could pay for such pricey personnel.*

In 1973, researcher Betsy Langman had interviewed Frank Hendrix, the firm's founder, in his office. The audio tape of this interview reveals yet another apparent conflict in the Cesar story, as well as some further data about Ace.

Hendrix told Langman that he had had the Ambassador account for two years prior to the assassination. While the hotel may have gone to other firms on occasion, said Hendrix, Ace got 90% of the private security action at the Ambassador. Moreover, the same was true of the Century Plaza and Hilton hotels. With what were arguably the three largest, most prestigious hotels on his client list, Hendrix's men could be predicted to guard most of the important politicians who held functions in downtown Los Angeles. The night of the assassination Ace Guards were assigned to the functions of

---

* This is not to suggest that Ace does not perform well in its field of endeavor but simply to establish for the reader that it is primarily a local-regional operation providing security for homes and businesses rather than one of the larger firms that function as private intelligence agencies for high-powered clients.

both Democratic candidates, also covering Senator Eugene Mc-
Carthy at the Hilton.

In 1987, Cesar told Moldea he had worked at Ace for six
months or more before the assassination and had worked at the
Ambassador "several times before the incident."[13] During her 1973
visit to Ace, researcher Langman asked about Cesar's employment
record. Hendrix's secretary retrieved the records while Hendrix and
Langman chatted. Then, apparently reading from the file, the
secretary stated, "He was hired in May of '68 and worked through
the year, and worked in January of '69."

"Did he work before that night [of the assassination]?"
Langman asked.

"I'd have to go to the records on that," the secretary replied.

Finally she returned with the data in hand. "O.K.," she said,
"the first time he worked was the week ending May 31."

On two less important points, what Hendrix read to Langman
closely approximated what Cesar told Moldea – the number of
hours he worked on June 4 and the amount of money he made.

On the basis of the available data, the gaps and conflicts
surrounding Cesar's presence in the pantry simply cannot be
resolved. Officials who professed to have answered all the important questions should have provided sufficient data, rather than
engaging in half-hearted, sporadic investigation and pretending to
have answers.

Cesar may be an innocent bystander plagued by bad luck and
conflicting recollections; but he cannot, in this analyst's mind, be
an unwitting, second gunman via a tragic accident. Many students
of the RFK case (including some reporters and law officers who
have privately expressed their opinions to the author) believe that
Cesar may have hit Kennedy by accident while trying to return
Sirhan's fire, a tragedy caused by his panic and minimal training as
a low-level rent-a-guard (compared to the training received by
Secret Service agents, for example).

First of all, for Cesar to have innocently shot Kennedy would
require a very major coincidence: He would have had to spontane-

ously decide to forsake his regulation .38 revolver and carry his .22 to work that night. Secondly, the pattern and distance of Kennedy's wounds strongly argue against an accidental shooting. Trying to shoot Sirhan and hitting Kennedy behind the right ear from one and a half inches away at an upward angle requires more than a combination of panic and professional ineptness: It would require someone with such deficient visual and motor skills that it is difficult to imagine him putting his uniform on.

Then, unless one posits some very complex scenario where Kennedy turns around in the midst of the gunfire and somehow gets shot by both Sirhan and Cesar, Cesar must accidentally pump two more shots into Kennedy's torso (with another one passing through the coat), at approximately the same point-blank distance. It is difficult to reconcile these wounds with any attempt to shoot Sirhan, no matter how confused the would-be protector might be.

One logical trap that has plagued this case is the simplistic notion that if there was a second gun, as the evidence of extra bullets suggests, it had to be Cesar. In fact, there seem to have been one or more plainclothes guns in the pantry, whose wielders' actions and backgrounds remain unknown to investigators, both official or unofficial.

Chapter 7

COVER-UP: LAPD

The first thing I said when Sen. Kennedy was killed, when he was shot, was that we are not going to have another Dallas here . . . Thus, they probably got one hundred times the case that the typical homicide would get.

— Los Angeles Police Chief Ed Davis

In the spring of 1984 I formally requested release of the Los Angeles Police files, on behalf of the Southeastern Massachusetts University Robert F. Kennedy Assassination Archives. It was to be a difficult four-year process. Gregory Stone, political scientist and aide to the late Congressman Allard K. Lowenstein, and Paul Schrade, a friend of Senator Kennedy who was wounded in the assassination, led the fight for disclosure. With the help of a small group of scholars, journalists and citizens, letters of support poured in to the Los Angeles Police Commission – from actor Martin Sheen, Arthur Schlesinger, Jr. (Kennedy's definitive biographer), Frank Mankiewicz, who served as Kennedy's press secretary in 1968, and others. Through a series of hearings, political confrontations and maneuvers that would take a chapter to describe, LAPD files were taken over by Mayor Tom Bradley's office and were eventually sent to the California State Archives in Sacramento for processing. Finally, on April 19, 1988, twenty years of official secrecy was ended.

The Los Angeles Police Department's rejection of the public right to know is rather unique by historical standards. In President John F. Kennedy's assassination, the Warren Commission's twenty-six volumes were published in 1964. Most commission files were gradually made public in the years that followed. FBI, CIA, Secret Service and some Dallas Police files were released. By 1986, the FBI and the Los Angeles District Attorney's office were in the process of releasing their files on the RFK case. Still, the primary investigative record of this national tragedy remained totally sealed. The only public glimpse was provided by Chief Robert Houghton's 1970 book *Special Unit Senator*, which was based on the files – a book whose primary purpose, Houghton told the author, was to refute conspiracy theories. The LAPD file was the primary case record: Assassination of a presidential candidate was not a federal crime in 1968, and local police had primary jurisdiction. The case was theirs to solve, with help from the FBI.

Prior to our 1984 request for release, the previous Armageddon in the battle for disclosure had occurred in 1975. CBS News led a group of petitioners who urged the California superior court to compel disclosure. Petitioners in part claimed that during the writing of the book *Special Unit Senator*, Chief Houghton's civilian co-author, Theodore Taylor, had apparently had access to LAPD case files. It was argued that this constituted prior public disclosure and the files could not now be withheld from other parties. Retired police Chief Edward M. Davis, then acting Chief Jack G. Collins, and Houghton provided affidavits to the court. They stated that, to the best of their knowledge, the case files had always been under lock and key at police headquarters. Access was strictly limited to a select group of law-enforcement officials on a "need to know" basis. No one else, they believed, had ever had access.

Houghton's affidavit stated:

> I did write a book with the assistance of Theodore Taylor.
> I had no recollection of having shown the 10-volume

Summary to Taylor, but I did show Taylor some items and some material from LAPD files. Much of the material I showed Taylor was material used in the trial of Sirhan, or held by the District Attorney. In showing this material to Taylor, it was not my intention or understanding that this amounted to any publication or release of confidential police information to the public, but was only shown him as my agent for the purpose of putting together the background material for the book. The book *Special Unit Senator* was published. At no time did Taylor ever come to Parker Center [LAPD headquarters] and go into the police investigative files. Generally, Taylor received whatever information he had regarding the investigation from me.

During my 1986 interview with Chief Houghton I asked him, "Did you have to provide any kind of security for those materials [that Taylor had access to]?"

He replied: "Oh yes, sure. There were all kinds of controls on anything that he used."

Also in 1986, being more enterprising than CBS's lawyers, I interviewed the man who would have first-hand knowledge concerning access to the files, the man never interviewed or deposed in 1975 – writer Theodore Taylor. As we sat in the living room of his comfortable seacoast home in Laguna Beach, California, he vividly described how he had taken possession of the files. Taylor says he picked up tapes and documents and transported them to his home, while the investigation was still ongoing: "My car was parked outside of Parker Center and I kept loading this crap in there. I don't know, the guy helped me with a cart; he had a big cart. And I thought Jesus Christ, what really do I have here [laughter]."

Taylor drove the files to his home and stored them in an office in his garage because there wasn't room for them in his study. As the investigation unfolded, said Taylor, Houghton would occasionally drive down from Los Angeles and provide new data.

I asked Taylor how complete his data was:

TAYLOR: I had access to some papers that I shouldn't have had access to.

MELANSON: In what sense, since they were giving you most everything? What do you mean 'you shouldn't have'?

TAYLOR: Well now, these papers were not involved [he chuckles], did not come from LAPD. They were FBI . . . Central Intelligence [CIA]. He [Houghton] said, "For Chrissakes, you know, you're looking at 'em and I'll give 'em to you for 48 hours and then you get 'em back up here [Parker Center] and don't copy anything down from 'em."

MELANSON: That's an example of how much he turned over.

TAYLOR: He just turned over everything he had.

Taylor has no reason to invent such a story. His possession of the files, despite the fact that two LAPD police chiefs said ño one had access, raises very serious questions. Were the strict security procedures described by LAPD officials adhered to over the years? Just who did have access? Was LAPD's handling and preservation of the records competent?

As the campaign for disclosure moved into high gear in the spring of 1985, official resistance stiffened. Los Angeles Police Chief Daryl Gates was clearly one of the main players. It was Gates who, as Assistant Chief, defended the destruction of the door frame wood and ceiling tiles on the grounds that they would not fit into a card file. Upon release of the files, we would learn that Gates received a confidential 1974 memo from his underlings on how to refute critics of LAPD's handling of the case. During a July 1985 hearing before the Los Angeles Police Commission regarding disclosure, Gates stated that release should come eventually at a "future date certain" when people could no longer be harmed by the information. Gates was presumably referring to the privacy of innocent people rooming at the Ambassador on June 5, 1968, and the protection of confidential sources rather than to himself and his department. When the hearing broke up a reporter asked the Chief what release date he had in mind. He replied, "Sometime in the 1990s." He nearly got his wish.

The flavor of the battle for the release of the files is captured by a February 12, 1986, incident in which I requested to speak before the Los Angeles Police Commision. The disclosure process had bogged down, nothing had been made public, and promised deadlines had been passed. It was no secret that I was going to be sharply critical: I had expressed my displeasure in numerous letters and telephone calls. But I wanted to express my criticisms publicly in the hopes of generating pressure on LAPD and the Police Commission.

The afternoon before my scheduled appearance I returned to my hotel to find an urgent message to call Commander Matthew Hunt of LAPD. I was impressed with the department's resourcefulness, since I was not in the habit of providing it with my local address when I arrived in town.

I telephoned Hunt at 5:30 p.m. Through his thick Irish accent, the gravel-voiced assistant to Chief Gates informed me that I could not appear before the Police Commission the next day. He explained that he had been "going through" the statutes and had discovered that my appearance would violate the law; it would constitute an illegal change of agenda. After rhetorically asking the Commander if he typically stayed this late scrubbing through law books, I informed him that I *was* on the agenda and that I would apppear no matter how many technicalities he unearthed. Hunt replied that when Police Commission President Robert Talcott learned of the error, he would change his mind about my being allowed to appear.

The next morning Greg Stone, Paul Schrade and I went to the offices of the Southern California American Civil Liberties Union seeking help. Attorney Joan Howarth agreed to accompany us to the hearing. She and her colleague Katherine Leslie asked what statute Hunt had quoted. I replied that it was something called the "Brown Act." The attorneys found this ironic: It was the California open meeting law.

At police headquarters, outside Police Commission offices, the ACLU attorneys, Schrade, Stone and I, confronted Commission President Talcott, several LAPD officers assigned to the Commission, and a representative from the city attorney's office. As Hunt predicted, Talcott had changed his mind. After a highly charged exchange between the two sides, Talcott offered to listen to us in executive session. We rejected the offer on the principle that a discussion of public disclosure should not be held in secret (and without the press, the Police Commission would be under no pressure to respond).

We were given permission to speak in public, but the victory was rendered hollow by the skillful maneuvering of the Los Angeles law-enforcement authorities. Inside the hearing room Talcott announced that the Police Commission would recess from the meeting to discuss another matter and the audience would be called back when business resumed. Press and spectators scurried for the exits, apparently under the mistaken impression that either nothing would be happening or they weren't supposed to be there. We vainly attempted to woo the press back, but most got away, chatting with Commission staff as they departed down the long corridor. A few minutes later, when we got to address the Commission, our protests played before a largely empty house. Press coverage was practically nonexistent.

Finally, however, there simply weren't enough legal technicalities, political maneuvers or red herrings about threats to "privacy" and "national security" to forestall the growing public indignation over LAPD's two decades of total secrecy.

When the RFK files were finally released on April 19, 1988, controversy was instant. California State Archivist John Burns announced to the packed press conference that 2,400 photographs had been destroyed by LAPD during the original investigation. The audience gasped. Researchers expressed their outrage to waiting microphones and cameras.

Besieged by press inquiries, LAPD responded that the photos were duplicates and of no evidentiary value. Roy Keene, the retired LAPD officer whose name was on the destruction order, told the press that he didn't recall the incident but added, "I guarantee you they were of no evidentiary value." The photos were taken to

County General Hospital in Los Angeles on August 21, 1968, where they were burned in a medical-waste incinerator.

The charges of cover-up, countered by official responses that nothing useful was destroyed, played themselves out in the media and disappeared from the newspapers after several days, with no resolution. The fact is, there are no known logs or inventories of photos precise enough to certify that the destroyed photos were duplicates of those existing in other files. LAPD's claim about the superfluous nature of the photos has yet to be verified and probably cannot be, because it's their word against the investigative researchers'.

The avid space-saving mentality exhibited by LAPD regarding its most politically sensitive and historically important case was a misguided priority, to say the least. Alleged "non-evidence" was destroyed to save space: Ceiling tiles and door frames would not fit into a card file, 2,400 photos presumably glutted the files. The "we can't save everything" paradigm appears to have been reversed when it came to files that were far more distant from the substance of the case. A pack rat mentality is almost at work in other areas of the files. Material preserved includes: biographical sketches and pictures of the officers who worked in Special Unit Senator, expense statements of police personnel, rosters of Kennedy campaign workers in the Los Angeles area, newspaper clippings from around the country, a log summarizing every incoming phone call received (no matter how frivolous or irrelevant). This same case file had the following items lost, missing or destroyed prior to disclosure: X-rays and test results on ceiling tiles and door frames, spectrographic test results (conducted on bullets), the left sleeve of Senator Kennedy's coat and shirt, the test gun used as a substitute for Sirhan's gun during ballistics tests, and results from the 1968 test firing of Sirhan's gun.

In 1988, retired Chief Houghton would dismiss the destruction of 2,400 photos as being "duplicates . . . and a flood of news photos from all over the U.S. and all over the world."

Within the surviving files is an August 20, 1968, memo from

Captain Hugh Brown to Chief Robert Houghton, who headed the investigation. It is entitled "Missing UPI Photographs," and it describes how an envelope containing photos was finally found in a closet after three unsuccessful searches of this same area. Brown states, "The five photographs were copies of pictures frequently used in newspapers and magazines published immediately after the shooting and are of no particular value to anyone outside the investigation."

The Brown memo, which is dated one day before the 2,400 photos were burned, clearly envisions saving photos even if they are not "evidence." Brown goes on to tell Houghton, "The following procedures have been adopted to prevent incidents of this nature in the future." The procedures were:

- All photographs received from outside sources should be dated and initialed by the person accepting.
- After screening by the case preparation team, selected photos shall be given numbers and properly filed.
- Pictures of no value at this time shall be filed alphabetically by contributor and shall be indexed in the master card file.

The five missing UPI photos were discovered on August 20. The above policy was adopted as a direct result of this incident. The question is, how could LAPD instantly become so well organized that it could burn 2,400 photos on August 21 and be certain they were all duplicates?

Moreover, it appears that some of the most potentially important photos in the entire case are unaccounted for. High school student Scott Enyart was following Senator Kennedy into the pantry taking pictures as he went.[1] Enyart asserts that he was snapping pictures when the shooting began and continued to do so.

The night of June 5, he told LAPD, "There was a table here about three and a half feet tall so I got up on it, so I was above everyone and I [inaudible] take pictures. And then the shots started to be fired and I took pictures and kept taking pictures."

"While the shots were being fired?" asked the interviewing officer.

"While the shots were being fired."

Enyart ran from the pantry and was followed by a security guard and detained outside the hotel. Police seized his three rolls of film. Within days he ventured to police headquarters to obtain a receipt for what he hoped would be his historically valuable film. At first, police denied having it. In response to several inquiries from Enyart's father and his lawyer, LAPD finally found some of Enyart's prints and returned them. There were no negatives.

According to a two-million-dollar lawsuit filed by Enyart in 1989 against LAPD and the FBI to recover financial damages for his missing photos, he was told (in 1968) that the FBI had the rest of his prints and that they would be needed as evidence at the trial, after which he could have them back. Periodic inquiries from Enyart produced no information regarding the whereabouts or disposition of the photos. In 1988, when LAPD files were finally made public by the California State Archives, Enyart discovered that there was no sign of his photos – no negatives, prints or references to them.

Most suspiciously, the eight to ten photos that Enyart claims to have taken in the pantry as the shooting unfolded have disappeared without a trace. The eighteen prints returned to him in 1968 were not taken in the pantry.

A picture of who was where when the first shots were fired would do much to unravel many of the evidentiary mysteries of the case. It might also totally unravel the official conclusions.

After the furor over the destroyed photos had faded from public view (without resolution), another episode of destruction was discovered in released LAPD files by journalist Jonn Christian.[2] It surfaced in one of the otherwise least interesting logs. In its lust for preservation of a detailed historical record, LAPD had documented every traffic accident – even the mildest fender bender – involving vehicles used in the Kennedy case. Within this somnambulistic chronicle of freeway failures is a July 18, 1968, accident involving two students who were working for Special Unit Senator.

Richard Groller and Thurston Best were using a police vehicle and decided to stop for lunch. Someone sideswiped the parked car.

Questions apparently arose as to how the two young men came to be driving a police vehicle and whether they were on official business. The students and their LAPD supervisor provided statements justifying their use of the car. The young men were "within the scope" of their assignment, which, according to both Groller and Thurston, was to drive to General Hospital "to burn important papers relating to my job."*

What documents were destroyed and why? How many burn runs were made to the General Hospital incinerator? Unlike the photo destruction, released files contain no official order pertaining to the burning of these documents. Had there not been a traffic accident, the destruction would never have surfaced. What the student workers meant by "important" and how the papers related to Special Unit Senator may never be known.

In 1988, Laren W. Metzer of the California State Archives wrote Commander William Booth of LAPD. On behalf of numerous researchers who had raised questions, Metzer asked for an explanation regarding destruction of documents, in terms of both general police policy and this particular instance. Booth's pompous and self-contradictory response asserted that, due to the passage of time, there was no one left in the department who: "from personal involvement [could] recite the meaning of a document beyond what the document says on its face. In other words, the records provided to the California State Archives contain all the information that the Los Angeles Police Department has to offer."

This total absence of departmental memory did not, however, prevent Booth from providing assurance that "what it [the burning incident] means is that materials superfluous to the investigation were disposed of in a manner that assured the investigation would not be compromised by falling into unauthorized hands." Since the available documents provide no such information, it is a mystery as to how Booth determined this.

Whatever documents were burned during this July 18 incident, it was on July 19 that Lieutenant Manuel Pena forwarded his second progress report to Captain Hugh Brown, detailing that 1,485

---

* Each used this exact same phrase in their separate statements.

interviews had been assigned and 838 completed. His report concluded, "To date no factual information has been developed that would in any way substantiate a conspiracy." Between July 5 and July 19, Night Watch personnel conducted 171 interviews. On July 18, the Case Prep Team delivered a major report to Lieutenant Pena. With all this important paper being shuffled around and with all this raw data being collated and reported, it would seem an odd time to be neatening up the files.

Other LAPD logs reveal conspicuous omissions. The record of overtime hours for police personnel begins on June 10; yet long hours were put in at the crime scene and at other locations on June 5 through 9, especially June 5th and 6th. One log reports the specific activities of Los Angeles Sheriff's Office personnel. There is no record of any work done in the pantry, although there is strong indication of such work. An LAPD crime-scene photo shows circles drawn around four holes, one of which the FBI labeled as a bullet hole. Inside the circle is the number 723 and the initials "LASO" as well as a name "W. Tew," apparently indicating that the circle was drawn by an officer Tew from the Sheriff's office with badge number 723.

In the spring of 1990, investigative reporter Dan Moldea set out to find Tew, only to discover that Walter Tew of the L.A. Sheriff's Office had died just a year earlier. A colleague of Tew's, who was in the Ambassador pantry with him, explained that Tew had indeed identified bullet holes: "That would be a typical way a deputy sheriff in that era would mark evidence." Yet Tew's name is nowhere to be found in LAPD's massive case file.

LAPD personnel were asked to provide statements of their duties and activities. Many are very detailed – three or four typed, single-spaced pages. Conspicuously, there is no substance regarding the search for bullets at the crime scene or the activities of removing the door frame and tiles.

Officers Robert Rozzi and Charles Wright, who were in the pantry and had their picture taken by the Associated Press as they pointed to a hole in the door frame (labeled a "bullet hole" by the

AP), have no first-person statements, only exceedingly brief summaries of their interviews. All that the Rozzi summary tells us is that he was "assigned to protect the crime scene" and that, "he did not make any statements to the press." Implicitly, this would seem to mean he did not tell the AP photographers there was a bullet hole in the door frame. We are told nothing more about his activities at the crime scene.

Wright's summary is a scant four lines. It says only that he responded to the shooting and guarded the front entrance to the hotel. His presence at the crime scene (the pantry) and his activities there are completely excluded from the report.

By contrast, officers stationed at the hospital with Kennedy describe in detail their security, sandwich breaks and communications setup. Personnel at the Ambassador give very specific descriptions of crowd control, rounding up witnesses, logistical and communications activities. Officer E. H. Hocking reports at length about the discovery and disposition of a key found in Sirhan's pocket. Officer L. D. Yant gives a meticulous description of a stakeout of Sirhan's car for several hours after the shooting and of finally recovering items from inside: "I observed 2 or 3 spent .22 calibre slugs on the right portion of the front seat which was covered by a newspaper." Yet, astoundingly, the search for bullets in the pantry is not substantively described. The special log "Activities at the Ambassador" is totally silent on crime-scene bullet holes and on the removal of artifacts from the pantry.

Instances of disappearing data abound. Another involves the All Points Bulletin on the polka-dot girl put out by Sergeant Paul Schraga. In 1968 Schraga was a 40-year-old veteran with an excellent record. He was in his patrol car one block from the Ambassador when his radio crackled with the report of a shooting. He quickly drove to the parking lot behind the hotel and, as the first supervising officer at the scene, set up a "command post" as required by departmental procedure. The "post" was the central point for communications and logistics at the crime scene. Therefore, Schraga played a pivotal role in LAPD activities and his name is writ large in the surviving record.

It is what Schraga did in the first few minutes of this long night's work that would forever change his status within LAPD. By his own account,[3] when he went to enter the hotel he encountered an older couple running into the parking lot. They were in a state of near-hysteria. The woman, in her early to late 50s, did most of the talking. The couple claimed they had been near the exit stairs when a young woman and man ran past blurting "We shot him! We shot him!" In response to the question "Who did you shoot?" the young woman in the polka-dot dress replied "Senator Kennedy." She seemed joyous. Unknown to Schraga, the couple was providing precise, spontaneous corroboration for the account of another key witness – Sandra Serrano.*

The sergeant took the names and address of the witnesses, then went to his car and put out an APB on two suspects – one a young woman in a polka-dot dress. That the APB did go out is verified by FBI documents that refer to, and reiterate, it. It is what happened after it went out that created controversy and charges of cover-up.

Within hours of the shooting, police interviewers were getting a collective ear full of polka-dot dress accounts from witnesses Serrano, McBroom, Griffin, DiPierro and others. How anyone could have validly decided that Schraga's APB was no longer needed is impossible to fathom. Schraga himself asserts that a senior officer requested that he cancel it. He refused; it was canceled anyway.

Police radio communications tapes (released in LAPD files) show that at 1:41 a.m. a patrol car radioed the dispatcher and asked for clarification: "Is there still an outstanding suspect and if so, can I have the descriptions?" After some cross talk, the dispatcher responded: "Disregard that broadcast. We got Rafer Johnson and Jesse Unruh who were right next to him [Kennedy] and they only have one man and don't want them to get anything started on a big conspiracy. This could be somebody that was getting out of the way so they wouldn't get shot. But the people that were right next to Kennedy say there was just one man."

*Ms. Serrano's story is discussed in Chapter 14.

Either the dispatcher – and perhaps some of his colleagues – had a peculiarly narrow view of how to solve crimes, or a decision had already been made that this case was not, could not, and would not be a "conspiracy." Schraga is now 63 years old and runs a repair shop in Missouri, after having been a small-town sheriff. Having fallen from grace, Schraga's efficiency ratings spiraled downward, and in 1969 he departed LAPD. This is all due, he believes, to his refusal to go along with the official history of the case as it pertained to him.

Schraga claims that after getting the name and address of the older couple – whom he remembers only as the "Bernsteins" – he gave his handwritten data to a courier who took it to headquarters. It disappeared, and he had no copy. He states that he later wrote up a report on the APB and the Bernsteins. Copies were filed with the watch commander and placed in a pigeonhole in the sergeant's office. When he went to retrieve his report, both copies were gone. Upon inquiring, he was told that investigators from Special Unit Senator had taken all such reports. Schraga's phone calls to SUS produced denials that the reports were gathered up.

An alleged summary of an LAPD interview with Schraga, dated September 26, 1969, does credit him with the APB and further states "names and addresses [of the Bernsteins] given to Rampart detectives." Yet, there is no record of this information anywhere in LAPD files.

Had the Bernsteins been pursued and interviewed, and had their story seemed as credible as Schraga's first impression of it, one can easily imagine the potential impact on the case, if only in terms of the increasingly awkward damage control LAPD would have been compelled to conduct. As will be described later, if the Bernsteins backed up Sandra Serrano and Serrano's account could not be discredited, then the witnesses who fell like dominoes might well have remained standing, and the polka-dot dress girl would be both real and at large.

This same LAPD summary of the alleged Schraga interview states that he "believes that due to the noise and confusion at the time, what was said was "they shot him." This is one of three standard LAPD dismissals of polka-dot witnesses: sartorial or syntactical confusion, or fabrication. LAPD insisted to Sandra Serrano that she too had mistaken "they" for "we."

Schraga found the Bernsteins very upset but able to recount their story clearly. What impressed him was that the account was so spontaneous, given within minutes after the shooting when there was no time for them to embellish or fabricate. Twenty years after the incident, Schraga told radio journalist Jack Thomas that he still placed "a great deal of credence" in their account.

Is it true that Schraga subsequently told LAPD that the whole incident was an innocent misunderstanding caused by a hysteria-generated mistake in pronouns? In 1988, journalist Jonn Christian showed him a copy of his supposed interview.[4] An angry Paul Schraga responded unequivocally: "Nobody from LAPD ever interviewed me, at any time. That interview is a phony, and many of the statements in it are just plain lies . . ." The retired officer provided Christian with a sworn statement that the document "contained false and deliberately misleading statements" and was "not based on any interview of me by anyone at LAPD . . ."

Apart from the Schraga story, there are other suspicious entries and omissions in released LAPD files. One group of six one-page documents purports to be "interviews" regarding the polka-dot-dress girl. All are dated June 6 or June 7 and are signed by Lt. Manuel Pena. According to Houghton's book, Pena was not on the case until June 10. These "interviews" are unique in that no interviewing officer is listed in the box provided on the document for that purpose. Pena signed off as the "approving" officer. The substance of each of these documents consists of one or two handwritten lines, apparently in Pena's handwriting and sometimes with his signature scrawled next to the entries as well as in the approval box. Moreover, every entry on these six documents is atypicallly handwritten when, in fact, typewritten documents are the rule in the case files.

The substance of the scrawlings is completely at odds with the known evidence on the dates shown. Either the dates are grossly in error, or the documents are premature, to say the least. Given the wealth of accumulating evidence, the conclusions put forth in these documents could not possibly be valid on June 6 and 7: "Girl in kitchen ID and int. [interviewed] by case prep team"; "Polka dot story of Serrano N. G."; and "Girl in kitchen ID and settled."

In 1974, Congressman Allard Lowenstein, who pressed for disclosure and for a re-examination of the evidence, sent a long series of evidentiary questions to LAPD. He never received a response. Thirteen years later when the files were released, we would learn that LAPD did indeed "answer" each and every question, but only for internal consumption. A 67-page, single-spaced memorandum entitled "Confidential Addenda to the Lowenstein Inquiry" was prepared for then Assistant Chief Daryl Gates by five of the officers who had worked on the original investigation. The cover page of the December 20, 1974, document suggests why it was not intended to be made public: "This separate addenda contains confidential information relative to the questions submitted by Allard Lowenstein. The information has not been revealed prior to this report and may conflict with previous statements made by the Chief of Police and other officials. Serious consideration should be given to the release of this information."

When a copy of the released LAPD files arrived at our archive, two days after they were first made public in Sacramento, we were startled by the paucity of audio tapes of witness interviews. I commissioned my research assistants Alyson Wihry and Deanna Perry to do an analysis of the apparent shortfall. Their discoveries are striking and point to a massive destruction of evidence. LAPD conducted 3,470 interviews during its original investigation, yet only 211 witnesses and 301 interviews* were preserved on tape and disclosed. As will become clear, this conflicts sharply with prior descriptions of the quantity and quality of tapes, descriptions provided by the most knowledgeable of sources. The use of audio tape to create a rich and thorough record was supposed to have been one of the unique strengths of this investigation, according to Chief Houghton and others.

* Some witnesses were interviewed more than once.

With less than one-tenth of the interviews preserved on tape, it was incumbent on LAPD to include the most important and controversial witnesses. It did not. My assistants and I conducted a survey, checking a list of significant witnesses (defined by FBI files, Los Angeles District Attorney's files, LAPD's interview summaries, and by the key questions defined by LAPD investigators). We discovered 51 people with important or potentially important information for whom no tapes were found.

Of these 51 persons, 29 had accounts that related directly or indirectly to questions of conspiracy. These included:

- twelve witnesses with information relating directly to whether Sirhan was accompanied by a female accomplice the night of the shooting
- an interview with Paul Schrade, wounded during Senator Kennedy's assassination (His estimated position at the time of the shooting is absolutely vital to the question of whether two guns were fired. No tape was found for another eyewitness who was near Schrade and Kennedy.)
- five witnesses at a pistol range where Sirhan was target practicing the day of the shooting, and where he was also allegedly interacting with an attractive young woman
- three associates of Sirhan's whose backgrounds or relationship to him required probing for possible conspiratorial involvement

The rest of the unrecorded interviews did not relate to conspiracy but were indeed important – more so than several dozen of the interviews that were preserved on tape. These 21 unpreserved interviews included people with information about the crime scene and about security arrangements for the Senator, as well as three close-up eyewitnesses to the shooting.

In contrast to the missing data, a significant amount of what remained was of lesser relevance or useless. Twenty-two of the preserved interviews are of virtually no importance: a woman who once gave Sirhan Bible lessons; a doctor who analyzed Sirhan's X-rays after Sirhan fell off a horse; crime-scene witnesses who saw neither the suspect nor the shooting.

Among the witnesses for whom we have no tape are several of the most controversial – controversial because their stories, if true, indicate that Sirhan may have had a female accomplice. Five of these witnesses were rejected by LAPD as lying, or not credible, or mistaken.

The rejections are terse and in some cases unsubstantiated by the available record. For example, Albert LeBeau is rejected in LAPD's investigative *Summary Report* because "he admitted he lied." But this appears nowhere in two FBI and two LAPD interviews. Four of these rejected witnesses were interviewed two or three times over a period of weeks or months, and still no tapes exist for them.

The absence of tape for these interviews is appalling. Anyone seeking to avoid the ghost of Dallas by building a detailed record to back up the official conclusions would presumably understand that the credibility of the investigation would not hinge on how Sirhan's Bible teacher was interviewed, but might, in part, depend on how witnesses whose stories implied conspiracy were handled, even if those witnesses turned out to be mistaken or not credible. Police officials acknowledged that they anticipated controversy about conspiracy. Indeed, this was a primary motivation for the alleged thoroughness of their files.

In an internal police memo dated June 12, 1968, Chief Houghton stated that the use of tape recordings to build a "graphic" case record would benefit LAPD, the city of Los Angeles and the "entire nation." In his book he informs readers that he told his second in command to equip field investigators with tape recorders because written reports would not be enough. During my 1986 interview with Houghton he said that tapes were used – more so than in any other investigation – not only to build a thorough record but to assess interview technique and to evaluate witness credibility.

When I asked him if witnesses were taped "across the board," he replied, "Yes . . . you can say it was used across the board. And I think it was used extensively. I agree with that."

Houghton's co-author Theodore Taylor wrote in a 1985 letter

to me that "every single interview was taped" (even discussions between investigating officers). During our interview, Taylor said Houghton wanted "everything" on tape.

> What he didn't wanna happen was a repeat of Dallas. And so he told all these detectives, all the people that went into the field that did the interviewing, he said, "I want you to be wired up and you use your own judgment as to whether it's gonna be an open, visible mike or not." But, he said, "Nonetheless, don't come back and tell me what you think somebody said. Don't come back and tell me that these notes are what you think somebody said. I wanna hear it . . . Everything has to be on tape." And it was.

Regarding Taylor's claim that police interviewers were instructed to use their own judgment as to whether the taping would be overt or covert, we found a document relating to the purchase of a hidden recorder built into an attaché case, equipped with a concealed on-off switch.

Taylor asserted that he personally had had access to "3,000 hours" of audio tape. There is no precise log of how many hours were preserved and released. The running times for 110 tapes were listed. Averaging and extrapolating, a good estimate is that, at most, 300 hours were disclosed – a mere one-tenth of what Taylor claims he had access to.

Houghton told his readers, "There was no way of predetermining the usefulness of any interview or the irrelevancy of any fact." This alone would certainly argue for taping all of the initial interviews. What is highly suspicious is the absence of tapes for some of the most controversial witnesses who were interviewed two and three times. By 1968 the Warren Commission was being roundly criticized for its mishandling of witnesses who had conspiracy stories. Yet this crucial use of tape to build a credible record was supposedly neglected by LAPD – in some cases two to three times over.

Houghton's book also asserts that the retrospective critiques of supervising officers were critical of the quality of note-taking by investigators. He quoted Lt. Roy Keene, an administrative officer in Special Unit Senator, as stating, "There is no place in an operation of this type for handwritten reports." Houghton himself said of such reports, "Something always gets lost." He then cites the obvious solution: "In short," he writes, "the modern ease of sound tape proved itself."

The gap between Taylor's estimate of 3,000 hours and the 300 hours available, as well as the gap between the stated purpose for taping and the achieved results, is so huge that it helps to define the possible explanations. It seems highly implausible that in an investigation whose avowed policy was to provide an audio record, investigators were so consistently incompetent (and administrators so lax) that only one-tenth of the case made it onto tape.

The logs indicate that officers typically took taping equipment to field locations. In some instances, they taped witness A at, for example, 10:00, then supposedly *didn't* tape witness B at 10:30, then taped witness C at 11:00.

In *Special Unit Senator*, Houghton provides a dramatic account of a taped interview with Kennedy's "personal bodyguard," William Barry:

> Meanwhile Sergeants Henderson and Chiquet had left Rampart at 5 a.m. to interrogate witnesses in the waiting room on the ninth floor of the hospital. At 5:12 they began taping the statements of William Barry, the senator's personal bodyguard.
>
> "I was abreast of the senator," Barry said, "about four feet away from him, when I heard the shots. We were in the corridor. I saw this man holding a small-caliber revolver in his hands. He had just shot the senator."

The quoted account goes on for another eight lines. But unbelievably, despite the above claim by Houghton, no taped interview with Barry exists in LAPD's released files.

That several thousand hours of tape – or 51 of the most important tapes – could be inadvertently lost hardly seems likely. The most logical explanation is that someone within LAPD purged the record because the substance of many tapes countered the official conclusions and/or tarnished the law-enforcement agency's professional image. One of the more interesting questions is whether the tapes met the same fate as some of the photos and documents – reduced to ashes at General Hospital – or whether, having once resided in a garage at Laguna Beach, they now reside in a garage or vault somewhere else.

The released RFK files were not nearly as rich or complete as advertised to the American people by officials, nor do they provide the kind of investigative record that enhances the credibility of the official findings. On the contrary, the quantity and quality of missing information leads inescapably to the most unsettling conclusion. Rather than providing a shining example of effective law enforcement, LAPD's case files reveal a massive and concerted cover-up.

Chapter 8

COVER-UP: LADA

District Attorney Van de Kamp stated in 1975, and again in 1976, that it is the purpose of the District Attorney's Office, as the prosecutorial agency, to continue to search for truth in this case.

— From the *Kranz Report*
(a 1977 re-investigation of the RFK case by District Attorney's Office Special Counsel Thomas Kranz)

In 1985, political scientist Greg Stone and I were successful in getting the DA's office to begin processing its RFK assassination case file for public disclosure. On May 29, of that year, I received a telephone call from William R. Burnett, the DA's chief investigator on the Kennedy case. The announced reason for the call was to determine whether my affiliation was with a public or private university because, said Burnett, this related to public disclosure. (This really made no sense and had not been mentioned by any of the government administrators with whom I had been dealing.) I gave him the answer during the first minute of the conversation. Forty minutes later, Burnett had softly but thoroughly debriefed me about what really concerned him: the status of the case and my role in it. It seemed odd that he would be so concerned about whether a professor or a university wanted the case re-opened. Soon, however, newly disclosed files from the DA's office clearly revealed that the Los Angeles District Attorney's office had more secrets to cover up than most investigative researchers had imagined.

One audio tape among released files captured a lamenting DA investigator Burnett during a telephone conversation in 1978: "I've been on this case since 1970. I'm still on it. It's a career case; it'll never go away. Every time something pops up on it, it always falls back in my lap."

What had popped up in 1985 was impending disclosure of the DA's file, the result of my and Greg Stone's numerous contacts with Burnett's superiors and, especially, then-Head Deputy DA Steven Sowders. Speaking as though he were in charge of the process, Burnett told me during his call that "no inter-office memo will be released," only work products sent to the trial. Burnett was wrong about us getting at the internal files.

In the summer of 1985, disclosure proceeded with a minimum of censorship. Stone obtained from officials at the DA's office key witness interviews from 1971 and 1977, in the form of both audio tapes and transcripts, as well as documents and photos. Meanwhile, a few blocks away at Parker Center, LAPD still refused to release a single scrap of paper.

Then there was a surprising development within the DA's office. At the Van Nuys branch someone discovered a box marked "Sirhan case," containing audio and video tapes and a few documents. It was promptly sent to the main office in Los Angeles to join the file then being processed.

Stone and his research assistant David Cross were engaged in a massive copying effort. Using their own equipment, they duplicated audio and video tapes under the watchful eye of the DA's office personnel. Copied at high speed, the audio tapes were not listened to by either Stone or Cross.

My colleagues then began mailing me the tapes. The labels provided by the DA's office were annoyingly sketchy, but the content was both self-evident and dramatic – telephone calls and meetings taped by official investigators between 1976 and 1978. Most of them involved William R. Burnett. The tapes provide an inner look at the activities of an office whose steward during that era, John Van de Kamp, had proclaimed: "It may not be possible to resolve every lingering doubt . . . but we'll try." Among the questions raised by the substance of these tapes are what Van de Kamp meant by "resolution," and just how did he instruct his charges to "try" to achieve it?

In June 1985, I visited the DA's office and met with Assistant Director of Operations Sheldon Brown. I had a list of high-priority items that should have been in the released files but had not turned up. Atop the list was the transcript of a 1977 interview with witness Lisa Urso. Brown told me that my list would be given to Burnett. In fact, Brown's office never provided any of the requested items, despite my follow-up calls.

The box of materials discovered in the District Attorney's Van Nuys branch office contained significant data that, for one reason or another, countered or challenged the official conclusions. To illustrate how sensitive this material was, one taped telephone conversation is between a man who was apparently with the DA's office and an L.A. County marshal. The marshal complains about phony test scores and patronage in the promotion process, which he describes as a "retreat to the spoils system" by a clique he dubs "The South Bay Drinking Club." This may have ended up in the "Sirhan" box because the marshal discusses the work he did for L.A. County Supervisor Baxter Ward, who in 1977 was himself conducting inquiries into the Kennedy case.

Another series of telephone calls among two to three participants plots the rigging of a bid on $18,000 of electronics equipment. A is the fixer who is putting the deal together, B is an executive in the firm getting paid under the table to bow out:

B: It would have to be cash.
A: Cash, and it would be taken care of at the time of withdrawal.
B: Yeah, but if we send in the withdrawal and they [the other company] don't pay us, we're fucked. It's as simple as that.

A then describes a fail safe *quid pro quo* (an exchange of cash for withdrawal from the bidding process) carried out by "a mutual acquaintance" that both sides trust.

These tapes probably ended up in the Sirhan box because the audio-video equipment in question was being purchased by the DA's office in 1977 for use in connection with the RFK case. The point is that important case evidence appears to have been purposely segregated from the main file. Perhaps this was done because the data was simply too troublesome for the official version. Important case evidence was put in the same box as the tape of a sleazy bid-rigging scheme. It would appear that someone may have intended for this material to remain secret in perpetuity.

Before discussing the data in the segregated box, among items released in the main file were audio tapes of witness interviews, the transcripts of which had been previously released. In comparing the original tapes to the transcripts, I found some significant differences involving key witnesses.

As previously described, Don Schulman is controversial because of his assertion that he saw a security guard fire shots during the assassination. His transcript contains several "off the record" pauses of unknown duration, for a variety of reasons. The tape reveals that one of these departures from the record lasted for 25 minutes (nearly one-fourth of the two-hour interview). During this "break," key elements of Schulman's story were discussed in detail under some of the session's most intense questioning:

SCHULMAN: My story is that I saw a guard pull a gun and fire. . . . If other people didn't see this, I don't know what they saw or didn't see. . . .
LADA: Don.
SCHULMAN: Yes, sir.
LADA: I don't wanna tell you what to do, but temper what you say. You say 'I saw a guard pull a gun.' But a minute ago you told me you only saw him with the gun out.
SCHULMAN: I assume he pulled it 'cause where else is he gonna get it?

LADA: Did you assume he fired it?
SCHULMAN: Ah, I'm pretty darn sure he fired it, but . . . I've . . .
LADA: Are you positive?
SCHULMAN: I'm pretty positive he fired it.

When they go back on the record the questions are posed differently: They "recap" those facts about which Schulman is "definite," He says he is "not a hundred percent sure" that the guard fired, and there is a greater impression of tentativeness than in his off-the-record remarks. It seems as though the interviewers wanted to explore Schulman's story off the record in order to put the best spin on the version in the released transcript.

Among items of particular significance found by Greg Stone in the segregated box are the much heralded video-taped 1968 and 1977 reconstructions of the crime. Previously, only selected stills had been released, although the re-enactments were touted by L.A. officials as yet another pillar in the solid foundation of their case.

It is easy to see why these "reconstructions" were not released after they were performed: They graphically illustrate the near impossibility of Sirhan being in a position to inflict Kennedy's wounds. To comply with the autopsy and powder-burn data, the authorities are supposed to demonstrate how Sirhan could get the gun one to three inches from the Senator and inflict four bullets (head, chest and shoulder, as well as the through-and-through shot in the suit coat) at an upward, leftward angle – all before the gun is grabbed and deflected by Karl Uecker.

The first series of simulations, done in 1968, uses Uecker, one of the prosecution's star witnesses. Uecker's account is that he was leading the Senator forward, holding his arm, before Sirhan fired. Uecker has consistently asserted that he was between Sirhan and Kennedy, that Sirhan never got past him, and that the gun was fired parallel with Uecker's face – approximately two outstretched arms' (Uecker's and Kennedy's) length from Kennedy's head.

Like his testimony and law-enforcement interviews, Uecker's reconstructions are damning to the official conclusion that Sirhan was in a position to inflict the Senator's wounds. The front-rear problem is never solved (Sirhan firing from the front, RFK hit in the back without turning around), nor does "Sirhan" gain access to inflict the chest and shoulder wounds. "Sirhan" is grabbed and turned away after firing shots that are level, not upward. They are usually aimed at the temple or the ear rather than behind the ear. In two of the takes, the Kennedy stand-in moves his head awkwardly backward and slightly downward toward the gun (something not reported by any witness viewing Kennedy). This inventive motion also succeeds in getting the gun behind the ear.

In the second series of six 1968 reconstructions, in which Uecker is not present, his testimony and re-enactments are totally disregarded. With L.A. law playing all the roles, "Uecker" stands aside and lets "Sirhan" rush past him to get to "Kennedy," sometimes failing to grab the gun at all. "Kennedy" turns slightly backward to shake hands, exposing the back of his head to the gun. Witnesses placed him either facing forward or sideways but never backward.

With all this distortion of the available evidence, the best the play actors can do is to solve the distance problem, getting the gun close up (most often to the temple but, on several occasions, behind the right ear). The proper angle is never achieved: The gun fires parallel or slightly downward. And nothing but a head wound, or wounds, is simulated.

The third series of five reconstructions, enacted in 1968, places "Sirhan" three to five feet in front of his target, firing parallel to his own nose. None of the problems (distance, front-rear, angle, location of wounds) is solved.

It is as if the goal of all these tapings was not to study, nor even try to re-create, the assassination of Senator Kennedy as it relates to the known evidence. Instead, it seems that the only thing the officials cared about was getting a still picture of a gun being fired close to someone's head in the midst of re-enactments that disregarded the established evidence. At no time was an attempt ever made to simulate anything except a head wound, or wounds. In 17 tries investigators never broach any variable except distance, while the controversies supposedly being addressed by the officials involved all four variables.

The crime being simulated is not Senator Kennedy's assassination but a murder in which the victim is shot only in the head, usually several times – sometimes three or four – and usually in the right temple or side of the head. Perhaps this is because getting ''Sirhan'' in position to inflict the known damage would be so awkward and distorted that everyone would recognize that it is utterly impossible to accept the official LAPD version of events.

These reconstructions offer further, solid data that the official findings were grossly inaccurate. Had the video tapes been released at the times they were made, surely any reasonable analyst would have concluded this. But in their Hollywood-like world of illusion, L.A. law's RFK investigators were able to skillfully select stills that became proof of the validity of official conclusions while the contrary data simply disappeared.

Another startling discovery in the segregated box of sensitive RFK data included audio tapes of interviews with two men who had served time in prison with Sirhan. Both gave testimony about him in 1977 that would, if true, render the question of parole moot for many years. Each claimed to have information about Sirhan's role in the assassination. One of these parolees, Carmen Falzone, would become the DA's primary source against Sirhan and would be run by the DA's office as a spy against Sirhan's family. The other, Daniel T. Estrada, would never surface. His story apparently was not followed up. Unlike Falzone, he was peddling the wrong stuff – conspiracy.

Estrada was in San Quentin with Sirhan from 1972 to 1973 and, in his taped interview with Burnett, claims to have occupied the cell next to the convicted assassin for a period of seven months. Estrada had taken his story to the FBI first. He asks the L.A. DA's chief investigator, Burnett, for a small amount of cash for providing the information. Burnett promises he'll see what can be done.

The story is that Sirhan was involved in the prison murder of inmate Ronald Woods. Says Estrada: ''He [Sirhan] did have someone killed. He says, 'Know what? This motherfucker's gonna get it. . . . It won't be long. Somebody's gonna take care of his ass.' ''

Estrada went on to assert that Sirhan's animosity stemmed from Woods telling stories about the assassination to the FBI. Sirhan allegedly said Woods was "trying to fuck him up" concerning the Kennedy case. In response, says Estrada, Sirhan solicited letters from inmates in the cell block stating that he never had any contact with Woods.

According to Estrada, Woods told him that Sirhan had confided "there were more people involved" in the assassination. Sirhan allegedly explained in detail "how it came down."

Burnett is audibly nonplussed. There is no hint of any follow-up investigation or of checking with the FBI about Woods. Instead, the DA's office would invest its resources in Carmen Falzone, the slick-talking burglar and security expert who would become the centerpiece of its 1977 counter-offensive against pressures to re-open the case.

Falzone had been convicted of robbing numerous wealthy homes in the L.A. area. Supposedly he became very close to Sirhan in "X-wing" of Soledad Prison before being released only a few days prior to his new stint as spy for the DA's office. His story was that while in prison he was recruited by Sirhan to provide expertise on penetrating security systems for an unfolding terrorist plot: Sirhan and his brothers were involved with Libyan terrorists in a plan to steal plutonium from the United States in order to build an A-bomb for Libyan leader Muammar Qaddafi. Falzone would also provide lone-assassin data on Sirhan.

Burnett believed Falzone's stories and defended him to *Playboy* magazine (which ran a piece on the alleged Libyan plot) and to the California Justice Department. Falzone would be used in numerous roles in the Kennedy case, including the bizarre re-interview of Lisa Urso. Ultimately, however, he burned the DA's office by skipping out before testifying at a Sirhan parole hearing. A warrant for his arrest was issued by the FBI in connection with the theft of a $750,000 coin collection from a bank safe-deposit box.

Before he skipped out, on August 11, 1977, Falzone met in a

Los Angeles motel with Burnett and California Justice Department Agent Bruce True. The tape-recorded session seemed designed to sell Falzone to True. Falzone was already working for Burnett, both on the RFK case and the Libyan matter.

The lawmen discuss the deal on tape with Falzone. He agrees to monitor the Sirhans, follow the terrorist plot to Libya, and come forward at the appropriate time and give his lone-assassin story. Burnett asks what he wants in return.

FALZONE: I do not want to be under the jurisdiction of a parole office where somebody can pull a couple of political strings and find out where the fuck I live . . . Make my records dead [for a North Carolina parole] and put me on conditional-type parole for the balance . . . I do not want to be accessible.

BURNETT: If you come forward [for both the Libyan plot and the RFK case], you wanna pull a vanishing act on us and disappear out of sight.

FALZONE: After it's over; yes, I do. . . . That's justified. I think it's fair. . . . A good conscience and a good night's sleep. And, naturally, I'd expect my expenses paid. That's all. I want nothing for myself.

As will be described shortly, Falzone was already working for Burnett and was conspicuously flush with cash. Another oddity is that Falzone had already met with Sirhan's brother Adel and, by all indications, had secretly recorded the meeting. True was never told about the tape of this "very very real" plot that Falzone painstakingly recounted in apocryphal tones, even though the three men discussed taping the Sirhans. Perhaps the taped conversation was not nearly as provocative and terroristic as Falzone's rendition of it. The possibility exists that he may have been concocting data about the Sirhans for his own benefit.

Burnett asks Falzone if he has any taping equipment. He responds that he does not because he has no money. Yet, in the two days prior to this meeting, Falzone had taped calls to Sirhan's mother and brother.

Falzone's tape-recorded calls to the Sirhans on August 9 and 10 provide an intriguing insight into this anti-terrorist operation. The first call originates from the same Holiday Inn room where the August 11 meeting would occur (with Falzone, Burnett and True). Burnett calls the hotel operator and has her put him through to the number that gives "the time at the tone," which he test records. Then he places a call to the Sirhan house.

A male voice answers. Falzone asks for Mrs. Sirhan. He emotes about the joy of being out of prison and tells her that he must speak with Adel Sirhan. Adel is not home. Falzone is very cryptic. Supposedly he is talking about moving the Libyan plan forward, but his comments, as well as those of Mrs. Sirhan (and later Adel), could just as easily refer to a prison friend of Sirhan's who wants to deliver a message or to chat, absent a terrorist plot.

MRS. SIRHAN: I want my son [Adel] to see you [perhaps because he's allegedly a friend of Sirhan's].
FALZONE: Right, well, I've got to see either him or you, ya know, and I'd rather . . . Ya know, I don't . . . I don't like telephones. I never did [especially when discussing international terrorist plots].
FALZONE: I'll stay here until we get it taken care of.
MRS. SIRHAN: Yeah.
FALZONE: Cause it's terribly important to me.
MRS. SIRHAN: Uh huh, thank you, yeah.

Falzone had talked with her before (no recording known). Perhaps he had set up the "it" at that point (possibly a personal message from Sirhan).

Falzone calls again the next day. On the tape, he first calls the time-information number and test-records. He then says, "For the record this is August 10," and places a call to the Sirhans. Burnett's voice does not appear on the tape of this call, so it is unclear whether or not he was present.

FALZONE: Adel?
ADEL: Yes.
FALZONE: Hi, I'm . . . My name's Carmen, a friend of your

brother's.

ADEL: Your name's who?

FALZONE: Carmen.

ADEL: Uh huh.

FALZONE: I'm a friend of your brother's.

ADEL: Right.

Then Falzone says: "I've really got to get together with you, and, ah, talk." The urgency seems entirely Falzone's. He suggests meeting that afternoon. Adel says "I won't be here." Adel suggests this morning. Falzone suggests tonight. Adel says he's working tonight and coming home late, so that's no good. Considering that they are supposed to be arranging a major international plot, he seems pretty relaxed. Falzone suggest 1:00 this afternoon. Adel says he would not have time to get to work. Finally, they agree on Adel's suggestion that they meet at midnight at the Ali Baba Club.

During the meeting the following day with Agent True, Falzone described the Ali Baba as a hotbed of political intrigue and the vortex of the Libyan plot. A group of Arabs sat at tables in the back. Adel Sirhan was their leader. All attention was focused on him. "They," the Arabs plotting the Libyan caper, have "operatives all over the country."

Falzone told True and Burnett that he discussed the Libyan plot with Adel and that Adel agreed (subject to visiting Sirhan in prison and touching base with him): "We'll do it. . . . I'll start moving on it right now."

Falzone's contact call to Adel, which was not played for True during the meeting, seems at odds with his story. The selection of the Ali Baba appeared to have been genuinely accidental. If it was Adel's headquarters for hatching plots, one would think he would have suggested it first, not last; or that he would have met Falzone elsewhere and then gone to the club, without announcing the meeting over the phone. Falzone also claimed that Adel viewed him as his friend. The bonding must have been very rapid. During Falzone's call earlier that same day, the tone and substance of Adel's conversation seemed less than enthusiastic.

The Libyan angle was only one facet of Falzone's usefulness to the DA's office. At the August 11 meeting with True, as the undercover operative began to lay out the seriousness and specifics of the impending plutonium heist, Burnett interrupted. There was something the DA's chief investigator may have perceived as more important than the alleged Tripoli-L.A. terrorist web.

On the tape Burnett then says, "All right, let me interrupt you here and let's get on to an area that I am very interested in." He asks about Sirhan's comments on the Kennedy assassination. Falzone asserts that only a month ago, when he achieved near blood-brotherhood with Sirhan, he had demanded that Sirhan *confide* in him about the assassination, as part of their mutual loyalty. Falzone says that Sirhan stated flatly: "I did it by myself."

According to Falzone, Sirhan believed that Kennedy would become President. Sirhan had to stop him. Falzone quotes Sirhan as saying that Kennedy always gave Israel "more and more arms. More this, more that. Anything they wanted." And Kennedy "made the mistake of talking bad, insulting, humiliating the Arab people in front of the world." Sirhan was prepared to die while killing Kennedy, says Falzone; but since he didn't, he would continue to help "his country" via the Libyan plot.

Falzone then recounts dramatically how Sirhan "re-enacted" the crime, with so much emotion that Falzone had to quiet him down. "He was enraged," says Falzone. "Always obscenities. The word Kennedy and fuck were synonymous."

True asks for "details." As will later be described, Sirhan's genuine inability to remember the crime, much less the specifics of its perpetration, presented a problem for the official conclusion of premeditated political murder. The absence of "details" in Sirhan's accounts were noted as being very strange by psychiatrists and investigators for years after the trial.

But Falzone's response concerning "details" could not have been very comforting for Burnett.

"Oh, he showed me how he brought the gun up with his left hand, 'cause I stopped him. I goes, whoa – you're left-handed? He says: 'I can shoot with either hand.' That's a direct quote.''

Then, says Falzone, as Sirhan emotionally described the struggle to subdue him he flew into a rage, laced with obscenities.

This was hardly the quality of confirming detail that True and Burnett were looking for. That Sirhan fired with his right hand is one of the few facts of the case stipulated by everyone (except, apparently, Sirhan).

Falzone then gets into an area of the case that, surprisingly, elicits not one question or comment from the two law men, only silence. In very animated fashion, punctuated with laughter as if he were telling a joke, Falzone relates on the tape that he asked Sirhan: ''Where'd you get all the bullets for your gun?'' Falzone laughs. No one else utters a word. Sirhan allegedly replied: ''All I had was one gun full of bullets. Where the fuck the other bullets came from . . . probably someone shoots at me trying to kill me and they kill someone else, and then shut up about it. They were scared then and they blew away some old lady across the room or something.''

Tasteless jokes about extra bullets and the wrong shooting hand aside, Falzone was still giving L.A. law an inside vision of clarity regarding Sirhan's motive, politics and hatred of Kennedy that could be very useful. In addition, Falzone could help the DA's office reject Sirhan's request to the court that he be allowed to return to the crime scene to jar his failed memory. According to Falzone, Sirhan confided that the request was merely a publicly stunt, a sympathy ploy; because, observes Falzone, Sirhan ''remembers every goddamn second of it [the assassination].''

Falzone's informant activities for Burnett would entwine him in one of the case's most bizarre re-investigative episodes – the 1977 re-interview of key witness Lisa Urso. As with other witnesses' case histories in this crime, the handling of Ms. Urso and her testimony reveals much about the prevailing mentality within the District Attorney's office.

Urso viewed the assassination from behind Sirhan, to his left. She had an unobstructed view of both the assailant and the victim as the shooting unfolded. This alone makes her a unique and important witness. Sirhan had pushed her aside just before drawing his gun and was close enough to touch when he fired at Kennedy.

In 1977, Urso became a focus of the DA's office primarily because of the unresolved distance problem – the conflict between the one- to three-inch muzzle distance described by the autopsy and powder-burn tests and the one and a half to six feet described by the witnesses.

In 1974, then-L.A. District Attorney Joseph P. Bush asserted on the *Tomorrow* show (NBC, December 19, 1974): "Every witness that you talk to – every witness . . . There's nobody that disputes that he [Sirhan] put that gun up to the Senator's ear and fired in there." The truth was that the DA's office was looking for one witness who would would be able to verify that the gun was against the Senator's head. In 1977, under the pressure of an impending inquiry by L.A. County Supervisor Baxter Ward and because of the renewed controversy about conspiracy, the DA's office believed it had a "point blank" witness. Lisa Urso's 1968 LAPD interview had described the shooting in those precise words.

After several frustrating calls to Lisa's relatives, recorded by Burnett, he finally located her in Hawaii. They discussed her returning to L.A. "to do a statement," as Burnett described it. She requested air fare since she was not planning to come to the mainland at any time soon. Burnett replied coolly: "Don't know because it's not really that important. What we wanted to do is to go back over your statement with . . . No big hurry on it. Has anybody else contacted you recently?"

URSO: Ah, no.
BURNETT: And that was point blank range that he . . . ah, that he fired.
URSO: Uh huh. Pretty much point blank.

But this was indeed important to the DA's office. Lisa had earned a ticket, a free, lengthy cocktail hour, dinner at one of L.A.'s finest restaurants for her and her girlfriend, a room at a high-security motel swarming with law officers, and an interview with no fewer than nine officials and investigators from L.A. law (armed with audio and video equipment). The problem was that in his attempt to be low key and disinterested with Urso, Burnett had neglected to ask precisely what she meant by "point blank."

Lisa Urso was interviewed on August 10, 1977. The audio tape reveals a calm, thoughtful, confident witness. Her answers are detailed; her recall vivid. Burnett and LAPD's Sergeant Phil Sartuche do most of the questioning. Unlike so many of the interviews in the RFK case conducted by L.A. law over the years, the tone is friendly, not challenging. As had been documented with so many others' interviews, no attempts are made to intimidate or confuse this witness, a friendly source who is potentially very useful.

She described how Sirhan pushed her right shoulder with his left hand – a "step aside" push. He extended his hand (for a handshake with the Senator, she thought). But instead he drew his gun and fired.

Now came match point for L.A. law. Urso's credibility and clear recall had been established. It was time for the big question.

SARTUCHE: When you saw the flash [from the gun] how far was the flash from the Senator? Or how far was this man from the Senator?
URSO: From where I was standing it looked maybe three to five feet.

Nothing but silence for several seconds; the dead air is thick with disappointment. Burnett, sounding nearly choked up, announces that they will do a video reconstruction.

In October 1987, I conducted a lengthy interview with Ms. Urso at her San Diego home. Her recollection of the assassination was still vivid. She is a thoughtful, very credible witness. Urso described to me her 1977 interview in Los Angeles and her accompanying video re-enactment of the crime. She also re-enacted for me what she had seen. As her 1977 interview would suggest, Lisa Urso is not a "point blank" witness – just the opposite.

The gun was "three to six feet from the Senator's head," she told me. "The first shot was not up against his head 'cause it was next to *my* head [closer to her head than to Kennedy's]." She reiterated that her view of Kennedy and Sirhan was unobstructed.

According to Urso, the Senator was walking forward but turned his head leftward toward a busboy who wanted to shake hands. When he was shot, Kennedy had not completely turned to face the busboy but was still facing slightly forward, about to shake hands.

Urso remains puzzled by the double-motion reaction she claims to have observed: Kennedy grabbed his head behind the right ear and jerked forward about six inches before moving in the opposite direction and falling backward. Why this motion, she wonders, if Sirhan fired from the direction the Senator first moved toward. She saw no other guns fired. She does not recall a uniformed security guard within her field of vision at the time of the shooting.

Ms. Urso also described the intrigue surrounding her 1977 interview. She and her girlfriend met in San Diego and drove to Los Angeles hoping to be treated by the city to a good hotel and to have some fun while attending to the minor chore of "going over her statement." Instead she underwent a strange and scary experience that she describes as "right out of James Bond."

As she recounts to the best of her recall, she was first taken to a downtown law-enforcement office (DA or California Justice Department). She was surprised that all that happened there was that she was perfunctorily introduced to one Carmen Falzone, who was constantly accompanied by "a Justice guy [Cal. Dept. of Justice]."

The next stop surprised her even more. She, her girlfriend, Burnett, his secretary and two other men (whom she thought were from the California Justice Department) adjourned to a bar for an extended period.

According to Urso, Burnett was not drinking. Lisa was allegedly offered free drinks several times, but declined because she did not drink alcohol. While she sat at a table with Burnett, her girlfriend and Burnett's secretary imbibed at the bar.

Soon her friend came and took Lisa to the bar because there was something she wanted her to hear. Urso chatted with Burnett's secretary. "She was pretty toasted," Urso recalls. "She told me this was not just a 'they needed to finish the file up.' She said that what I had to say was very, very important to the case and not to let them jerk me around." The secretary's warning was indeed prophetic.

Lisa and her girlfriend were taken to their accommodations – a "sleazy" motel in East L.A. with plainclothes law officers everywhere, the same motel that served as Falzone's headquarters. The young women were given a room next to Falzone's, with plainclothes law officers on the other side.

Falzone came to Urso's room, introduced himself and proffered a letter from Mrs. Sirhan as proof of his friendship with the convicted assassin. The weird occurrences that followed left both young women suspicious, confused and a bit frightened about what they had gotten into and how it would play out.

The uptight, highly animated Falzone flitted back and forth between rooms: "It was like Falzone would come over and talk with us, then he'd go back and they'd ask him questions about what we had talked about." On one visit he told the women that he was testing out his electronic equipment, and he revealed a recording device concealed under his coat. He told them he would use it to tape conversations with Sirhan's brother. After he chatted with them for a while, a man in a suit came to the room and told Falzone that the device worked.

When Falzone left, the women told me they put drinking glasses up against the wall and pressed their ears against them to try to hear what was being said by the men in suits. They heard little substance but knew that the conversation focused on how credible a witness Urso was.

Falzone re-appeared, announced that he needed a change of atmosphere, and invited them to dinner. The girls thought it was strange that there were no visible chaperones from L.A. law, as the three of them drove to one of the city's most fashionable and expensive restaurants, La Scala. Urso was surprised that someone recently out of prison would have so much cash. He tipped the maître d' $50 to get a table, then paid cash for the very high-priced dinners. He also seemed to be acquainted with some of the waiters and customers, which also seemed odd to Urso.

During dinner he regaled them with stories about Sirhan, including the Libyan plot, and Sirhan's confidentialities about the assassination. Urso remembers becoming ''very nervous'' at hearing all of this ''confidential'' Sirhan information.

Falzone told Urso she was an important witness. While his reasoning did not seem odd to her, it was indeed so. He said her answers matched what Sirhan had told him, contrary to what some other witnesses had seen. He asked her what hand Sirhan fired with. Other investigators asked her that question too. She thought it peculiar because the gun hand was so visible. It *was* peculiar.

She and her friend became deeply resentful and suspicious. ''They never let me know what was going on all day. . . . Obviously they set me up to go with him [Falzone] or him to talk to me.''

Apparently, after Lisa Urso gave an unwanted answer about distance (during her interview the next day), she instantly became a liability to police officials instead of a valuable asset. She was irked when someone suggested, ''Maybe you'll remember what happened'' by a re-enactment of the crime. She found this condescending; she already remembered exactly what happened. What they were obviously hoping for was that she would place the gun much closer.

The video-taped re-enactment was suppressed until 1985, when it was found in the box of sensitive, segregated materials disclosed to Stone and Cross. Urso reconstructed the crime as she had seen it from her unobstructed view. A calm, confident Ms. Urso positions the actors consistently in all five re-creations. Each time, the gun is clearly about five feet from ''Kennedy's'' head. ''Sirhan'' does not lunge or otherwise advance toward the Senator, once he gets past Urso and starts firing. The shots are fired with ''Sirhan's'' gun hand parallel to the floor and his arm does not move upward or downward during the shooting. All ''shots'' (clicks from an empty revolver) are fired at "Kennedy's" head – none to the shoulder or armpit area, where the actual wounds were located. The Urso tape is vivid, damning evidence of the impossibility of the official conclusions.

Some of her interviewers apparently wanted to assure that if she did talk to anyone in the future, her story would appear muddled. Strangely, turning their distance problem upside down, they told her she placed the gun the *closest* of any witness.

"They said that my testimony was not the same as everyone else's," she told me, and that "I was only one witness." She was informed that everyone else had said the gun was farther away. "All of 'em kept telling me that."

When I informed Urso that her testimony was not exceptional, that nearly all the witnesses placed the gun several feet away, she was surprised. Compartmentalizing and neutralizing witnesses by falsely telling them they were a lone exception to the established evidence was a tactic sometimes employed by the Los Angeles law-enforcement investigators on the RFK case. Ms. Urso was, incidentally, never again contacted by Los Angeles officials.

Following Joseph P. Bush's example of evidentiary newspeak, Los Angeles District Attorney John Van de Kamp wrote to authors Jonn Christian and William Turner (July 12, 1979), scathingly rejecting the evidentiary questions raised in their book *The Assassination of Robert F. Kennedy*.

"Moreover," wrote Van de Kamp, "you apparently (deliberately) ignore certain significant developments such as the re-examination by my office and the Los Angeles Police Department of the pantry area of the Ambassador Hotel . . . the re-enactment of Lisa Lynn Urso and her return to the pantry with our investigators on August 10, 1977 . . . statements made by Sirhan to his cell mate Carmen Falzone."

With the true details about Urso's testimony kept secret, the DA's office could turn the evidence upside down and get away with painting a rosy picture to the confused public. But there are several questions that remain to be answered concerning Van de Kamp, who would later be elected Attorney General of California. Was he truly ignorant of Urso's real account? Did he comprehend its sub-stantive implications? Or would he say anything to defend the official version?

Chapter 9

CRITIC BASHING

It's like opening up a collection of pornography to a bunch of sex-hungry pornography addicts. They're going to fondle the gun, touch the wood, stick their fingers in the bullet holes and read the reports.*

– Retired LAPD Chief Ed Davis,
on release of the RFK police files in 1988

I n contrast to the supreme confidence publicly displayed by Los Angeles officials and investigators over the years, the long-suppressed law-enforcement files reveal a very different mindset – an almost paranoiac fear of critics and a preoccupation with controlling the potential fallout from their efforts. This would seem to indicate that key people in LAPD and the District Attorney's office were all too aware of the glaring flaws in the case they touted as their greatest achievement. This insecurity spawned a continuing effort not only to refute criticisms and critics but, in at least some cases, to gather discrediting information against those who would criticize them as well.

Evidence suggesting conspiracy was more often dealt with through damage control rather than substantive re-investigation. Criticisms of the official version were viewed as political attacks.

---

* Presuming that "the wood" refers to the pieces of the pantry doorframe removed by LAPD, they can't be touched by anyone since police destroyed them.

While officials proclaimed publicly that they expected challenges and would pursue every avenue of evidence no matter where it led, the operative response was highly political, concerned with tarnishing critics before they could tarnish the credibility of the official conclusions.

One indication of this bunker mentality is the conspicuous dichotomy in how witnesses were handled during the various flash points of the case: late in the original investigation, in 1971 (when questions of a second gun surfaced prominently), in 1975 (when the court-appointed firearms panel re-examined the bullets), and in 1977 (when the DA's office launched a flurry of re-investigative efforts). Witnesses whose stories countered the officially defined truth were typically quizzed in torturous detail about whom they had talked to – what journalists, critics or other investigative agencies – and what they had said, as if L.A. law was tracking the spread of an infectious virus. Witnesses with "friendly" stories were almost never asked such questions. For them the exclusive focus by officials was on the substance of their statement, not whom they talked to and how much. For troublesome witnesses, such as Karl Uecker and Don Schulman, investigators seemed at times to be more concerned with mapping information flow than analyzing case substance.

Following a 1971 interview with eyewitness Don Schulman, LAPD and DA investigators erupted into a frenzy – preserved on tape – after Schulman left the room. They wanted a copy of his original interview with radio newsman Jeff Brent, recorded minutes after the shooting, in which he asserts that he observed a security guard fire a gun. Their main concern is not the substance of the tape but how to get the copy that Schulman has, without spooking him, and before investigative journalist Ted Charach (producer of the film *The Second Gun,* implying an RFK conspiracy) can have access to it. One investigator goes so far as to posit that Charach and Brent have somehow conspired to alter the tape, undoubtedly to discredit the official version:

A.: You want that tape now? [Chaos, several voices at once.]

B.: You bet your life I want that tape now. What the hell are you doin'? It's the only goddamn tape in the world of that original conversation.

The female stenographer interjects: "It is not. He [Schulman] got it from Brent. He copied it from Brent."

B.: Brent has altered that fuckin' thing with Charach. That's how it comes out the way we [unintelligible].

Several people talk at once. Someone says the LAPD sound man will go out tomorrow and copy the tape.

C.: Hey, Charach's right on his [Schulman's] ass – Charach and Isaacs [Charach's lawyer Godfrey Isaacs] . . .
B.: Ah . . . I'd advise you not to . . . Where are you goin', calling his [Charach's] office to find out whether he's there or not? . . . As soon as he [Schulman] gets back they're gonna be right on his ass to find out what happened, and they're gonna want to know about that tape. They're gonna wanna hear the tape; he's gonna let 'em hear the tape [unintelligible] . . .

The female stenographer speaks: "All this swearing . . . you can . . . you know . . . delete."

Someone suggests that Schulman is not playing games and will be "a lot more comfortable if he's given a little bit of yardage."

B.: Yeah but then Monday you're gonna say, "Did anybody else see this tape?" "Oh yeah, Charach borrowed it for a few hours over the weekend." And then what the hell do ya do?
A.: He's not gonna loan that tape to Charach.
B.: How do you know?

The recorder is shut off as the discussion continues.

This was not the only instance in which L.A. law viewed critics as a sinister force conspiring to manipulate evidence to discredit their case despite the fact that there was absolutely nothing to substantiate such fears. In 1975, a panel of independent firearms experts discovered that the inside of the barrel of Sirhan's gun was coated with lead deposits. Since the copper bullets used by Sirhan and employed by officials during authorized test firing would clean out such deposits, this finding implied that there had been an unauthorized firing of the alleged murder weapon by someone using lead bullets.

According to the *L. A. Times*, Los Angeles DA Special Counsel Tom Kranz raised the question of whether "someone may have tried to discredit LAPD or intelligence agencies by creating doubt about the case."

Since the weapon never left official custody, Kranz's hypothesis implies one of two possibilities: A critic penetrated property-room security and was able to fire the gun; or the critics had a mole, or at least a sympathizer, inside L.A. law. In either case, a serious question of evidence custody was dismissed as some sort of disinformation ploy by critics.

High on LAPD's list of troublesome journalists was Peter Noyes, who in 1991 was news director at KNBC-TV in Los Angeles, and who had conducted extensive investigations into organized crime and right-wing extremist groups. Noyes alerted police to a man allegedly having ties to organized crime who had been arrested in Dealy Plaza, Dallas in the aftermath of President Kennedy's assassination in 1963 and was, according to Noyes, staying near the Ambassador Hotel during Robert Kennedy's assassination. Noyes provided other leads and data on what he hypothesized to be a right-wing-Mafia assassination conspiracy.

LAPD's *Summary Report*[1] devotes ten pages to glibly dispensing with Noyes and "the complicated hypotheses which he created." The section is as much a personal attack on the professional credibility of the journalist as a summary of a possible avenue for investigation.

His data was condescendingly referred to as "speculation", and his logic and motives were repeatedly questioned, as follows: "At another point in the investigation of the allegations made by Noyes, he constructed another set of circumstances" . . . He "provided investigators with a great deal of information, most of which was conjectural and nebulous." And worst of all was this unfounded attack: "His intentions cannot be wholly evaluated."

During a May 16, 1964, meeting held in the chambers of Judge Charles A. Loring, Deputy Chief Robert Houghton, Deputy DA David Fitts and Judge Herbert Walker discussed restricting public access to case photographs. Judge Walker asserted that he was "willing to seal those [photos], subject to order of the court, and I think I can put it on some kind of ground. I'm going to look at it and find myself some ground and do it. If the Appellate Court wants to upset us, that is fine."

Deputy DA Fitts opined that this would not be a problem, and the discussion manifests a rather cynical view of the public right to know and of the legitimacy of public interest in the case evidence.

MR. FITTS: Well, I don't think there is going to be too much demand to see these. The only people that could do anything are going to be cranks in the first place.
JUDGE WALKER: Well, those are the people I am worried about.
MR. FITTS: Well, I sort of thought these people would be the cranks and they want to see them so they can start cranking.
DEPUTY CHIEF HOUGHTON: I will agree with that.

One critic of the official findings who was hard to dismiss as a crank was William W. Harper, who had logged 35 years as a consulting criminologist in over 300 homicide cases and was a qualified expert witness in seven states including California. In the summer of 1969, LADA Evelle Younger announced that evidence and trial exhibits could be made available for public inspection. What at first appeared to be a boon to critics of the investigation turned out to be a legal nightmare. Harper scientifically examined the ballistics evidence in 1970, after obtaining a letter of authorization from one of Sirhan's attorney's. On December 28, 1970, he issued a seven-page sworn affidavit that a second .22 weapon was involved in the assassination. He had also criticized LAPD criminologist DeWayne Wolfer in the sharpest terms, directly challenging his professional competence.

Rather than confront the substance of Harper's findings or the questions raised by other researchers, L.A. law decided to launch an outrageous legal attack against them. As surprising as it sounds, Los Angeles law-enforcement authorities had such unchallengeable power in 1971 that they were able to act with total impunity, brushing aside all leads of evidence that contradicted their findings on the RFK case. In August 1971, the DA's office responded to the criticism and findings of Harper by going before a Los Angeles County grand jury and accusing him of tampering with the ballistics evidence. In addition, researchers who had availed themselves of the opportunity to examine portions of the case record and exhibits – Kennedy Assassination Truth Committee members Lillian Castellano and Floyd Nelson among them – were also hauled into court and grilled about what they had done and seen.

While the initiation of the grand jury's seeking indictments against Harper and others received extensive press coverage, its final conclusion, one year later, was barely reported. Not a single indictment was returned. The final report merely suggested some changes in procedure at the County Clerk's Office, which had custody of the material. But the critics of the official RFK investigation had been severely punished by the legal ordeal. All persons put through the legal procedure in the grand jury hearings had to pay for their own lawyers, take time off from work and prepare a defense against what turned out to be unfounded charges brought by a vindictive, powerful Los Angeles legal system. Now L.A. law had made it clear: If you are a researcher or critic of the official investigation, you too could find yourself before a grand jury. In addition, the notion had been created by the Los Angeles DA's Office that if the case record or evidence was deficient or distorted, it was the fault not of the original investigators or the official custodians, but of the assassination buffs who had gained access to the material and tampered with it.

Keeping track of critics was a major preoccupation of LAPD. A July 1, 1968, FBI memo reports that Lt. Manuel Pena requested that the Bureau report "any attempts to write stories regarding the assassination which might tend to suggest a conspiratorial aspect.'' This paranoid official tracking of conspiracy writings is in sharp contrast to LAPD's lack of investigative curiosity – prematurely canceling APBs on additional suspects, refusing to follow up leads, ignoring important evidence, refusing to investigate security guard Cesar. There was, however, an additional reason for LAPD's desire to know who was spinning out conspiratorial prose: damage control and counter-attack.

One conspiracy-theory journalist was Ted Charach, who was well known to L.A. law because he interviewed so many witnesses for his documentary film *The Second Gun*. Among released LAPD files is a four-page, single-spaced memo written by Sergeant D.O. Varney, dated August 2, 1969, concerning an interview with Charach conducted at police headquarters the previous day. The document was tucked away in the file on LAPD's dead-end conspiracy investigation of a man named David Kasaab, yet it has nothing to do with the Kasaab investigation. In fact, it is an intelligence report on who was doing what in the assassination-investigation community, based on a debriefing of Charach.

Sergeant Varney provides a potpourri of snide observations, sociological data and reports on investigative activities of critics. He names seven people who met at the ''Hollywood Franklin Apartments'' to form a team to re-investigate the case for *Ramparts* magazine. ''Prior to the meeting, Mark Lane [Warren Commission critic] was at the Pickwick Bookstore autographing books.'' RFK assassination witness Richard Lubic had been publicly critical of LAPD's investigation. The memo states: ''Steve Jaffe is working for Lubic (Also been interviewed by SUS and shown a liar),* who in turn, is a friend of Robert Buek (Of the Jet Set). Buek just returned from Washington with a story that his wife is a friend of Ted Kennedy's wife, and he learned that Ted Kennedy thinks there is a plot against all the Kennedys.''

Journalist Fernando Faura's hunt for the polka-dot-dress girl is described, and it is reported that he had developed a composite sketch that he was showing to witnesses. No suggestion is made,

---

* I am aware of no substantiation for this claim and presume this innuendo to be completely false.

however, that police should avail themselves of a copy: This memo is clearly concerned with mapping activities rather than exploring potential data. The names of members of Faura's investigative team are provided, with snippets of background data on each. Faura and Charach are described as "rounding up" witnesses, including a reported "19 witnesses to the RFK assassination that can prove conspiracy."

Charach's effort is called a "caper." Channel 9 TV personality Stan Borreman, who hosted programs raising questions about the case, is labeled as having a "leftist axe to grind."

By 1970, Charach was talking publicly about the conflicting evidence and the possibility of a second gun. A September 29, 1970, FBI memo, among Bureau files released to myself and Greg Stone in 1988, reports that the Los Angeles District Attorney's Office "is interested in obtaining information" regarding Charach. The DA's office had contacted the FBI ten days earlier. The memo asserts: ". . . one Ted Charach has recently been making public statements concerning the assassination. Howard [Assistant DA John Howard] is of the opinion that Charach's conduct might possibly jeopardize prosecution's opposition to Sirhan's appeal."

The document concludes that the DA's office should be recontacted "when the indices are reviewed so that his [DA official making the request, name deleted] office may be furnished with information necessary in opposing the appeal of Sirhan." This author has found no further reference to what, if anything, the Bureau might have discovered and passed on concerning Charach.

In 1974, forensic expert Herbert Leon MacDonell surfaced to challenge LAPD's ballistics work relating to the one-gun conclusion. Released documents show that the department's response was to have its robbery-homicide division conduct a "criminal record and background check" on the New York based-scientist. The division queried "FBI criminal files." With what seemed like thinly veiled disappointment it reported that he had no record and was known to the FBI as outstanding in his field. LAPD evidently asked the Bureau to check his *bona fides* as well: An FBI official "verified the authenticity of MacDonnell's biographical sketch." One LAPD document's contained unsubstantiated, gossipy challenges to MacDonnell's expertise put forth by someone in the Los Angeles Sheriff's Office. A second report reveals that a state police laboratory scientist telephoned colleagues in three eastern states as to MacDonnell's professional standing, then reported back to LAPD.

The files on MacDonnell and others apparently were not closed in 1974. A 1977 audio tape of telephone conversations between a Los Angeles DA investigator and an out-of-state attorney captures venomous attacks on three expert critics. The three were: Dr. Robert Joling, former president of the American Academy of Forensic Sciences, who pressed for an independent review of case evidence; Dr. Cyril H. Wecht, a nationally reputed forensic expert; and MacDonnell.

The attorney apparently wrote the DA's office after Joling's name surfaced in the RFK case. The DA's investigator telephoned the attorney regarding "our good friend Dr. Joling" and cheerily proceeded to record the virulent personal and professional attack on the critics proffered by this source. Absent were the kinds of questions relating to motive or validity that one might expect of an investigator evaluating a potential source. There is no indication that the extreme nature of the attorney's comments gave the investigator pause. Said the attorney: "I can't sock this guy [Joling] up and put him in the penitentiary where he belongs."

The attorney continued: "Now this cocksucker Joling wrote an article in the *Saturday Evening Post* that I didn't read because when I saw his name on the front of that thing I almost puked."

Of Wecht, the attorney says: "Can't think of the bastard's name. . . . Went?" . . . "A coroner in Pittsburgh." . . . "That bastard is a pal of Joling and MacDonnell."

The investigator asks for any "documents" the attorney might have in his files.

The investigator's statement that he might fly out to conduct an interview with this attorney provides a telling insight into the priorities of the DA's office: It would not follow up on the question of whether there were too many bullets for Sirhan's gun by interviewing the relevant LAPD and FBI personnel.

On another front, it seems that the DA's office could be very gracious with journalists who seemed inclined to report the right stuff. In 1978, James McKinley, *Playboy* magazine's resident "assassination expert," was doing a piece entitled "Inside Sirhan." The article resulted from "a tip" to *Playboy* and drew very heavily upon an interview with Carmen Falzone, the former fellow prisoner of Sirhan's who was also LADA's star undercover operative against Sirhan and his family. Recall that in addition to linking Sirhan to the putative Libyan terrorist plot, Falzone claimed Sirhan had confided that he acted entirely alone in the assassination.

William Burnett's (the chief RFK case investigator for the DA's office) taped telephone conversation with McKinley seems, to this author, to be extremely candid for an investigator who is discussing a former undercover informant in a terrorist investigation only a year earlier. It also contrasts sharply with Burnett's pronouncement to me, nearly eight years later, in 1985, that nothing on the RFK case relating to the inner workings of the DA's office (17 years earlier, in 1968) could be released because of its sensitivity.

Burnett told the *Playboy* author that Falzone had passed the polygraph and was "what he says he is."

McKinley concludes: "Tell 'em [the original investigators] that . . . ah . . . as a student of assassinations – I've been through 'em all in this country – this was by far the tightest and best investigation ever done."

BURNETT: Well I'm sure LAPD would appreciate hearing that.
McKINLEY: Of course, people are always gonna carp and trot out nonsense. I think it's nonsense about a second gun.

Floyd Nelson, an original member of the Kennedy Assassination Truth Committee who has researched this case since its inception, told me that Los Angeles authorities seemed very interested in the committee's work. According to Nelson, plainclothes men would suddenly pop up and boldly photograph some committee members as they walked about the city. There was never any indication that the photographers were from the press, and the pictures never appeared in the media. Nelson speculates that this may have been L.A. law's way of letting the committee know it was being watched.

In July 1971, Burnett interviewed Floyd Nelson and Lillian Castellano at Nelson's apartment. These two charter members of the Kennedy Assassination Truth Committee were being questioned about what access they had obtained to case records and exhibits housed in the county clerk's office. The DA's office was investigating alleged mishandling of the case records by the evidence custodians. But in the process of extensively debriefing the two researchers as to what documents they had requested, seen or copied, the investigator managed to elicit a good deal of strategic data on RFK assassination critics.

BURNETT: If I may ask, when you went to view these exhibits I take it this committee had already formed.
CASTELLANO: Oh lord, yes.
BURNETT: How many people, let me ask, are on that committee here in L.A.?
NELSON: About 2,000 [he laughs].
CASTELLANO: We have a mailing list. We don't have formal meetings and all that.

Burnett would mine data on the sociological composition of the critical community: "Do you know of anyone else, Mr. Nelson, who has been to the clerk's office?" Nelson mentions another critic. Burnett asks what the man does for a living and where he's located. Burnett is interested in what data Nelson and Castellano have exchanged with journalist Ted Charach. He asks them if they know three people: Two names are inaudible, but one is reporter Fernando Faura, who wrote about the polka-dot-dress angle and held a press conference criticizing LAPD. Burnett garnered a 1969 conspiracy article that had appeared in the underground press.

Surely these examples of monitoring and gathering information on critics are not exhaustive. They constitute the surviving record, if not the tip of the iceberg. They add credence to allegations of official surveillance and harassment discussed with the author by journalist Jonn Christian and others.[2]

Apart from the use of its investigative powers, LAPD is still capable of spontaneously putting down its critics in public. The syndicated television show *PM* magazine ran an April 2, 1987, piece featuring an interview with shooting victim Paul Schrade. He criticized the police department for destroying evidence and raised questions about the official accounting of the bullets. When Tami Sanders Lowen of *PM* asked LAPD for comment, a spokesman said: "For heaven's sake I wish kooks like Paul Schrade would get off of this. Hell, it's been 18 years."

"So you have no comment?" asked Lowen.

"No, because there's none to make."

One would have to have access to current LAPD and DA's office files to know the extent of their contemporary interest in RFK-case critics and researchers.

Chapter 10

MOTIVE AND MEMORY

I've known the man since 1969 and its rather clear that Sirhan acted alone, and he's acknowledged that. . . . Although Sirhan, I must admit, does not have a distinct recollection of everything that happened that evening. His memory is somewhat clouded.

— Sirhan's attorney Luke McKissak, 1988

With means and opportunity provided by the smoking gun, the "smoking gun" for motive was discovered very quickly. Sirhan was Palestinian and embittered against both Israel and the American politicians who supported her. His notebook contained numerous references to killing RFK – prima facie evidence of premeditation and fanaticism. It was all so simple, so straightforward. Like the smoking gun itself, however, the apparent motive was only a caricature of the complex labyrinth that was Sirhan's psyche. However, since the official version was being drawn in caricature, *Sirhan the political fanatic* fit right in.

Sirhan Sirhan differs from the two other notorious assassination suspects of the turbulent 1960s, Lee Harvey Oswald and James Earl Ray. Oswald was not arrested at the crime scene. He was silenced by Jack Ruby before protracted interrogation and trial could prove his guilt or innocence or his possible motive.

Ray, the convicted assassin of Martin Luther King, Jr., successfully eluded authorities for two months and, to this day, professes to being an innocent patsy. No one saw him pull the trigger. By contrast, Sirhan maintains that he did assassinate Robert F. Kennedy, acting entirely alone, for political reasons; that he is sorry for what he did, knows how and why he did it, is rehabilitated, and deserves parole.

Most of the media and the public take the position that this confession and conviction alone suffice to close the case. In reality, the facts are that Sirhan's motive is far from obvious. Despite the extended efforts of lawyers and psychiatrists to come up with a clear-cut version, his memory of the crime and its perpetration was largely nonexistent.

It should be noted that Sirhan's current status as the strongest spokesman for the official version is rooted in the politics of parole. His quest for freedom has been a pitched political battle fought out through a series of maneuvers that have surely had a profound impact on his assertions of remembrance and of an introspective understanding of the crime.

Having escaped the gas chamber because of the Supreme Court ruling against capital punishment, Sirhan was, under California law, automatically scheduled for release in 1984. Then the 36-year-old convicted assassin would have served 16 years –three years longer than the average time served for first-degree murder in California. The California Board of Prison Terms canceled the scheduled 1984 release in 1975.

In 1981, Sirhan's lawyers asked the Board to overturn its cancellation so that Sirhan would be automatically released in 1984. Also in 1981, the New York-based Arab-American Relations Committee launched a campaign to win early release for Sirhan before 1984. The group charged that if he were held any longer he "must be regarded as a political prisoner." It contended that he had paid his debt to society and the only reason for continued incarceration was the fame of his victim – an unjust reason.

Los Angeles District Attorney John Van de Kamp led the 1981 political-administrative campaign to keep Sirhan locked up. He ordered his staff to research legal means for prolonging Sirhan's confinement, resulting in a 235-page legal brief arguing against release. At a press conference, DA Van de Kamp brandished 13 media editorials opposing parole – an "outpouring of concern," he called it.

The District Attorney stated: "It is not that we should consider Senator Kennedy's life of more value than any other individual. That is not the point. But who knows what role Kennedy might have played in the history of this country and, for that matter, the world had he gone on to become President."

Van de Kamp won. The Board did not overturn its cancellation of automatic release in 1984 nor did it grant parole. Sirhan's freedom had become an emotionally charged political issue. Dr. M. T. Mehdi, head of the Arab-American Relations Committee, told the press: "I have said that Sirhan Bishara Sirhan is legally guilty and Robert Kennedy is morally guilty. Sirhan is responsible for the death of one person directly. Robert Kennedy is responsible indirectly for the deaths of thousands of Palestinians, Libyans, Syrians. What do you say to that?" Sirhan's memory and motive would not be at issue in the battle over his freedom but would be stipulated by both sides.

The next round was in 1986. Sirhan, then 42 years old, presented himself to the Board as repentant, rehabilitated, and worthy of society's trust. His attorney, Luke McKissak, told reporters that Sirhan was optimistic: "He anticipates he'll be released because he doesn't see any legitimate reason why he shouldn't be. All the psychiatric reports, and every thing else, show he is suitable for parole. Sirhan has been a model prisoner."

Sirhan told the Board, "I'm not interested in being a trouble-maker anymore." With tears in his eyes he repented: "I'm sorry for what happened. I wish it had never happened."

Deputy DA Larry Trapp rebutted, "This was not an average

homicide. It touched the entire nation." It was, said Trapp, "a crime against the American people. . . . Send a message that this is a crime that will never be tolerated or treated with mitigation."

Through an open microphone, one parole board member was overheard saying, "We'll send his ass down there [California Men's Colony, where psychiatric evaluations are performed on prisoners] and keep him there as long as possible." Sirhan's bid was rejected. The Board said he had changed the course of history and "disenfranchised millions of people."

The Board required that he undergo extensive psychiatric tests, pursue vocational training, remain free of disciplinary actions, complete his college degree, and provide documentation of job offers. It also stipulated that he undergo the Alcoholics Anonymous program, although there was never any suggestion that his drinking had extended beyond the several Tom Collinses he consumed the night of the crime.

In 1987, he was again turned down. The disgruntled prisoner charged, "The American system of justice is going to let me go home in a coffin." Attorney McKissak warned that he wouldn't be surprised if the decision triggered "international reprisal" from Sirhan's supporters in the Middle East. Sirhan, the political prisoner. Sirhan, the Arab hero.

The 1968 jury had found Sirhan to be sane and lacking diminished capacity; therefore, he was given the death penalty. His rehabilitation, a prerequisite for parole, cannot be established with a clouded memory or a muddled motive. He must, therefore, convince the authorities that he understands the cause of his violent act.

Prison psychiatrist Dr. Philip S. Hicks said of Sirhan in 1986 that he was "genuinely rehabilitated and demonstrates no evidence of current political fanaticism or proneness toward violence." Further, said Hicks, the assassination had stemmed from "political fanaticism rather than psychotic violence." Sirhan, the rehabilitated political fanatic.

If we trace the evolution of Sirhan's motive and memory we

find something very different from the mythical images that now dominate the political struggle over his freedom. Part of the allure of a political motive is that it appears so neatly grounded in Sirhan's traumatic formative years. He was born in Jerusalem in 1944.[1] The Sirhans' comfortable middle-class home was engulfed by the escalating violence between Jewish militiamen and Palestinian fighters: bombings, sniper attacks, military patrols everywhere. Four-year-old Sirhan reportedly saw the bloodied, tattered bodies of Arab bombing victims. He witnessed the death of his own brother, killed by an enemy truck as it veered to avoid a Palestinian sniper attack.

In 1948, when Israel declared independence, the Sirhans fled their home under cover of darkness and endured a nine-year exile as starving refugees in Israeli-occupied territory. In 1956, when Sirhan was 12, he and his parents came to the United States, with the help of the United Nations Relief Organization. As he grew up in his new country he continued to follow Middle East politics by reading Arab and American newspapers. The developments upset him. He expressed hostility toward the Israelis and their treatment of his people. After graduating from high school he attended a meeting of the Organization of Arab Students. He was particularly bothered by the Israeli victory over Egypt's President Nasser in the Six-Day War (June 1967), in which Israel captured the old city of Jerusalem where Sirhan had lived as a child.

This, says the official version, is the background that pushed Sirhan to political violence against Robert Kennedy, a strong supporter of Israel. Retired FBI Agent Amadee O. Richards, who was the RFK-case supervisor, told me in a 1986 interview that the Bureau's background investigation on Sirhan showed a "clear motive." "Sirhan's motive," said Richards, "was easily understood."

At his trial Sirhan was questioned extensively by his attorney Grant Cooper about his life in Jerusalem. "The Jews kicked us out of our homes," said Sirhan. He described an Israeli attack on an Arab village in which Arab girls whose breasts had been mutilated were paraded in front of villagers. He delivered soliloquies on Zionist power that reminded some observers of classroom lectures.

With a general political motive provided by Sirhan's background, the only question for officials was how his rage came to be specifically targeted on Kennedy (in a manner that Sirhan's own notebook described as an "obsession"). Candidates Hubert Humphrey and Eugene McCarthy were strong supporters of Israel, as was President Lyndon Johnson who demonstrated his support in foreign policy decisions. Richard Nixon was no exception. So why, then, Kennedy? At first Sirhan could not answer. He could not articulate the catalyst that focused his hatred on the Senator. In discussions and hypnotic sessions with defense psychiatrist Dr. Bernard Diamond, the alleged catalyst would be produced: Robert Kennedy's pledge to send 50 Phantom jets to Israel.

In January 1968, Israeli Prime Minister Levi Eshkol visited President Johnson at the White House. Israel had lost a considerable number of aircraft during the Six-Day War and Eshkol wanted to purchase 50 fighter-bombers from the United States. Johnson reportedly promised to sell Israel replacement planes and weapons. The sale came up in the debate between McCarthy and Kennedy the weekend before the June 4 California primary. Kennedy endorsed the sale.

An entry in Sirhan's notebook repetitively scrawls "Robert Kennedy must be assassinated . . . My determination to eliminate RFK is becoming more the more [sic] of an unshakable obsession." It is dated May 18, long before the debate. However, a television documentary aired in Los Angeles in May in which Kennedy is alleged to have been shown pledging to send jets to Israel. Sirhan's attorney, Luke McKissak, told a radio interviewer in 1988 that this was the catalyst to violence:

> He felt after seeing Kennedy make the statement that he was gonna send . . . with the yarmulke on him in the temple . . . he was gonna send 50 Phantom jets to Israel, that was interpreted by Sirhan as basically sending planes to bombard and kill his own people.

The problem is that the documentary aired May 20 – two days after the dated entry in Sirhan's notebook regarding an obsession to kill Kennedy. Recognizing this problem, political scientist James W. Clark developed a more timely route for the jets-to-Israel catalyst. He pointed out that in the January 9, 1968, *New York Times,* which announced Johnson's agreement to sell planes and weapons to Israel, there was also an article about a Kennedy speech that reported: "Mr. Kennedy said he thought the United States should supply Israel whatever weapons it needed to offset whatever the Russians were supplying the Arabs so that Israel can protect itself. He specifically included the 50 supersonic jets the Israelis had been seeking."

The next day, Kennedy met with Prime Minister Eshkol and pledged whatever assistance necessary to maintain Israel's territory. Says Clarke, "It is most unlikely that news of this importance would have been overlooked by the Arab newspapers Sirhan faithfully read."*

Perhaps, but this is a very tenuous and diffuse linkage considering that it supposedly drove Sirhan to commit murder. Whereas the official version has Sirhan reaching a flash point of hatred before

---

* Clarke writes (p. 84) that Sirhan's first written mention of killing RFK was dated January 31, 1968 (which was on the heels of the January 9 newspaper article that discussed Kennedy's support for the sale of bombers). Clarke then describes the rest of this entry in which Sirhan scribbles repeatedly about: "practice," "mind control," "drinking Tom Collinses," "the girl," "coffee," "where is the [gun or girl]," "Kathleen," "RFK must die."

Professor Clarke concludes: "While the identity of 'Kathleen' remains a mystery, the similarity between this entry and the events of June 5 is remarkable. It strongly suggests that the notebook contained not the incoherent writings of a paranoid schizophrenic but the efforts of a determined assassin to prepare himself psychologically for an assassination as well as for his anticipated capture and defense if he survived."

The similarity lacks eeriness once one understands that these pages were not from the original notebook. They were written by Sirhan after the crime, while the hypnotized prisoner performed automatic writing for Dr. Bernard Diamond, the defense psychiatrist. The date on the entry is written twice: once as "Friday 31 January 689"; and a second time, alongside the first, more clearly says, "Friday 31 January 69." One page of ex post facto prose contains the phrase "this is the way you wrote at home."

the documentary was even aired, Clarke has Sirhan on a very slow boil, four months long; either that or Sirhan sustained for four months the homicidal rage that washed over him when reading the news in January. But at that time, Lyndon Johnson was the President, and could make the sale a reality; Kennedy was merely a Senator from New York who would not be a presidential candidate for two months. Whichever of these two scenarios one chooses, the kindling or rekindling of the assailant's rage is left unexplained. No discussion of the bombers was ever attributed to Sirhan in the six months between the January newspaper articles and the June assassination.

Amazingly, in the dozens of interviews conducted with virtually everyone known to have had contact with him during the year prior to the assassination, there emerged not a single instance of Sirhan having commented on Kennedy's support of Israel, on the impact of the Senator's possible presidency on Middle East politics, or on anything at all relating Kennedy to the Jews, Israelis, or the Middle East. No one has come up with a valid means of exposing or re-exposing Sirhan to the issue of jets-to-Israel prior to May 20.

At his trial Sirhan had yet another sequence.[2] He claimed to have seen the television documentary "about three weeks before the assassination," but he attributed his exposure to the bomber issue to radio. Sirhan testified: "It was the hot news on this KFWB station where the announcer said that Robert Kennedy was at some Jewish club in Beverly Hills, or Zionist club, or whatever it was; and he had committed himself to formally giving or sending 50 jet bombers to Israel."

Sirhan went on to describe how this enraged him. However, in questioning it was revealed that the radio program came after the television program – "sometime thereafter," said Sirhan Attorney Grant Cooper. Thus, Sirhan's new scenario had the same problem of timing and sequence regarding his notebook entry as did the other scenarios.

Sirhan's alleged motive did not emerge immediately and clearly. Instead it was an evolutionary product of his sessions with the defense team. During his interrogations by police following the shooting, he never mentioned the jets or his reason for the violent assault, nor was there any defiant proclamation of political purpose.

Sirhan himself brought up seeing the documentary and recalled the pro-Israeli content.[3] He even speculated that he may have seen it on May 18 because of the entry in his notebook. Unfortunately, not only did it air too late to explain the May 18 entry, but its substance presented another failure for the official version of Sirhan's motive: It made no reference to the sale of bombers or to military aid to Israel. The film showed an Israeli flag and the announcer said that Kennedy had decided to play a role in the affairs of men and nations.* There is nothing more specific in the entire film: The documentary fails to provide the linkage between Sirhan, Kennedy, and the bombers.

Considerable reinforcement for this phantom linkage would come in Sirhan's sessions with defense and prosecution psychiatrists. Dr. Bernard Diamond, defense psychiatrist, suggested that Sirhan undergo hypnosis to help him remember. According to defense investigator and author Robert Blair Kaiser, when Dr. Diamond asked the hypnotized Sirhan why he shot Kennedy he had no answer.[4] When Diamond asked again, Sirhan mumbled "the bombers." But he could not say *when* he had decided to shoot Kennedy.

Under hypnosis Diamond instructed Sirhan to visualize "the bombers" dropping their deadly payload on Jerusalem, where Sirhan grew up. He wept, then burst into loud sobs. When Diamond turned to the subject of Kennedy, Sirhan stopped sobbing. Kaiser observed that while the topic of the bombers was traumatic for the tranced prisoner, the topic of Kennedy was not. Kaiser wondered what the connection in Sirhan's mind really was and opined that no one would ever know for sure.

At a later point when Diamond brought Sirhan out of his trance, the doctor asked him to tell about the bombs that had been so

* Notice how tame the actual Israeli imagery is compared to Attorney McKissak's description of the documentary referred to earlier in this chapter. McKissak said Kennedy was in a temple wearing a yarmulka and stated his intention to send the jets to Israel.

traumatizing to visualize. He didn't remember anything about them, even though the sale of bombers would eventually be designated – by almost everyone, including Sirhan – as the political symbol that drove him to violence.

There is a problem regarding the law-enforcement uses of hypnosis. Diamond spent approximately 20 hours with Sirhan, including an unspecified number of hypnotic sessions. Sirhan was walked through the crime and the writing of his notebooks in order to try to restore his failed memory regarding both. Moreover, as is clear from the previous excerpt about the bombers, Diamond discussed motive as well. The potential problem is that while hypnosis is capable of enhancing recall, it is also capable of influencing the subject to believe that hypnotic experiences or images are real when they are not.

A 1984 research brief put out by the U.S. Justic Department states: "In short, hypnosis can allow a person to honestly and compellingly report pseudomemories as fact – indeed, more convincingly than actual recollection."[5]

I consulted Dr. Herbert Spiegel, Jr., of the University of California, Berkeley, one of the country's leading experts on the uses of hypnosis in law enforcement. Spiegel has consulted on numerous cases, using hypnosis to work not only with witnesses but also with accused criminals. Spiegel said there is always a danger of contaminating the subject by artificially reinforcing or creating impressions that will seem real but are not. A vivid hypnotic experience can be mistaken by the subject as true memory. This is why the use of hypnosis to obtain confessions of testimony is a complex, controversial area of law enforcement. As we shall discuss later, Sirhan was exceptionally susceptible to hypnosis – an almost perfect subject. Thus, the danger was that in trying to visualize the jet bombers while under hypnosis, and also being told to visualize Kennedy approaching and to reach for the gun, Sirhan was inadvertently being hypno-programmed to connect RFK, the jets, and the shooting.

While in a trance in his cell, Sirhan was instructed to do

"automatic writing":* repetitive references to killing Kennedy and to other aspects of the case. This was supposed to help him remember how and when he wrote the notebook, but it also could have reinforced in his mind the seeming reality of the thing being written about.

Even apart from hypnosis, Sirhan was receiving heavy doses of suggestion about politics and motive. It seemed that, at times, prosecution psychiatrist Dr. Seymour Pollack was more intent on telling Sirhan what Sirhan thought than eliciting his thoughts from him. Pollack was a distinguished forensic psychiatrist from the University of Southern California who headed an institute on Psychiatry and the Law. He was hired as a consultant to the District Attorney's office because, according to Kaiser, the prosecutors knew that Sirhan's only available pleas were insanity or diminished capacity, both of which would require expertise the DA's office did not have.

Kaiser writes, "As an agent of the District Attorney's Office, Pollack could not talk to the defendant but he could observe him in the courtroom."[6]

He did, in fact, talk to Sirhan, one on one, for several hours. A tape of the 1985 session(s) was among the files released by the DA's office in 1986.[†] Pollack delivers long, often animated soliloquies about Sirhan's motive, state of mind and legal situation. Sirhan mostly listens, saying very little.

Pollack asks, "Now that was in May of '68, '68, that you saw the television program, is that right?"

"Right."

"He was already running in the primaries. Now you mean until that [TV documentary], up until that time, you were for Kennedy?"

"Hell, I was for him, sir."

Pollack says, "Apparently what was eating at you was these elections and how strongly you felt about the American political figures, figures letting the Arab world down. . . . It isn't just letting the Arab world down, it's building up Israel."

---

* Automatic writing is a technique used by some hypnotherapists. The patient is taught to write repetitively and almost subconsciously while in a hypnotic trance, as a way of expressing and reinforcing ideas and feelings.
† From the tape it is not clear whether it is one or several sessions.

Sirhan agrees that this is correct.

Pollack continues, "You saw Kennedy [a crashing sound obscures the rest of his characterization]."

Pollack seeks to broadly define Sirhan's political hatred:

It might not even have been just Kennedy [inaudible] so strong, if [Hubert] Humphrey were there, it might have been anybody else. Somebody who was big, someone who was big, tough, somebody who was – it wasn't necessarily Kennedy – it could have been somebody else but someone who would still represent American policy that was pro-Israel. In fact, it – for example – might have been Humphrey. Because Humphrey was a person you didn't particularly like either.*

Pollack previews the upcoming trial for Sirhan in terms of its political theme.

"The trial is a trial in which you are sort of accusing America of . . . burying a million Arabs."

"In fact!" Sirhan agrees heartily.

"And that's, that's, that's your – in a sense – that's your plea. But that isn't really the issue . . . Although, maybe I'm wrong. Maybe it is the issue."

Sirhan says nothing and continues to listen to Pollack's sudden insight about the trial as a political showcase.

"You see," says Pollack, taking a long pause as if deep in thought, "If I, if I assume that this is so, that you really want the Arab – the world, not the Arab – want the world to see the Arab suffering, the Palestinian Arabs particularly, but all of the displaced Arabs . . . [Pollack is really getting enthusiastic, and it begins to sound like a stump speech by a political candidate] Arabs suffering . . . to see that American policy has helped [cause] that suffering."

Although Sirhan expresses his concern for the plight of the Palestinians and his antipathy to Israel, some of his comments to Pollack seem very strange for a man who is supposed to have murdered for a cause; and who, as Pollack envisions it, is supposed

* Humphrey is not mentioned in Sirhan's notebook. This author knows of no instance where Sirhan expressed personal or political dislike for Humphrey.

to be looking forward to something of a political show trial.

"I would love to die here right now," says Sirhan. "You don't have to take me to court, sir, and bring charges there."

"Hmm," says Pollack, who sounds taken aback.

"My conscience doesn't agree with what I did."

"Your own conscience?" Pollack asks incredulously.

"My own conscience."

"In what way?"

"It's against my upbringing." Sirhan sounds distressed.

"My, my, my childhood, family, church, prayers . . . the Bible and all this, sir. [Sirhan was not a Moslem; he had been raised Christian.] 'Thou shalt not kill.' Life is the thing, you know: Where would you be if you didn't have life? And here I go and splatter this guy's brains. It's just not me."

Sirhan Sirhan had considerable incentive to embrace a political motive. Kaiser observed that the prisoner feared being branded insane more than he feared punishment for the crime.[7] He adamantly refused any suggestion of an insanity plea and insisted his notebook not be brought up at the trial for fear people would think he was crazy. His lack of memory about the crime and the notebook must have made him wonder if he was insane. Kaiser reports in one of his five handwritten notebooks that chronicle the case that Sirhan stated, "I want to plead guilty. I don't want to have those people proving I'm insane."

Eduard Simpson, the San Quentin psychologist who worked extensively with Sirhan in 1969 after his conviction, did not believe the political motive was genuine. In 1974 he told researcher Betsy Langman, during a taped interview, that Sirhan manifested a curiously detached and stereotypic view of his own political motive – a "rather stereotypic version" that seemed devoid of real conviction. Simpson found Sirhan's comments about Arab-Israeli politics relating to the assassination to be "very repetitious," spoken "like an actor playing a role, reading a script." The doctor also noted that Sirhan's descriptions failed to evince the hesitancy or rephrasing that are common in genuine expressions of one's own thoughts and emotions.

If Sirhan seemed somewhat miscast in the role of a classic political fanatic, authorities could still fall back on his notebook as evidence of both political zeal and premeditation. The notebook is a bizarre hodgepodge of repetitive writings and doodles, the most notable of which, in the eyes of the authorities and the media, are references to killing Kennedy.

As with most everything in this case, the substance of the notebook has been generally misunderstood. Professor James W. Clarke says in his book *American Assassins*, "The persistent theme of his writings, however, was a trance-like preoccupation with Senator Kennedy's assassination: 'Kennedy must fall,' 'Robert Kennedy must be sacrificed for the cause of poor exploited people,'[8] 'Kennedy must fall.' "

The fact is, however, that this was not the persistent theme, nor was it as persistent as other themes – if "persistent" at all. This raises questions about the depth of Sirhan's alleged fixation for eliminating Kennedy.

The notebook was sometimes referred to by authorities and the media as a diary, which it is not. Pages of strange, repetitive writing are interspersed with classroom notes that he took at Pasadena City College as well as with blank pages. The entries are not in neat chronological order from front to back but, instead, seem to have been placed on any blank page(s) that turned up when Sirhan opened the book.

My content analysis of the notebook reveals a very different artifact than the prevailing myth that it is the classic diary of a political crackpot. Presuming that the substance of the writing really betrays Sirhan's concerns – this is by no means certain, as we will see – RFK was not his major preoccupation. Excluding blank pages and classroom notes, there are 48 pages of weird entries (released among FBI files). Only two refer to killing Kennedy, or to Kennedy at all. Each of these two pages contains numerous, repetitive references that fill the page. The RFK page closest to the front of the notebook is dated May 18; the other appears 28 pages later and is undated. There is no assurance that the second page was written later or even at a different sitting. For example, four pages after the May 18 entry is a two-page discourse on how "American capitalism will fall" to a "workers' dictatorship," and it is dated almost a year earlier (June 2, 1967). It is therefore possible that Sirhan's May 18 Kennedy entry, which asserts that killing the Senator has become an "unshakable obsession," was the second and last. At most, he wrote of his obsession only once more between May 18 and the June 5 assassination.

The dominant theme of these scribblings is money – twice as many references as to any other subject. Seventeen pages – including the two RFK pages, which say "pay to the order of" – refer to money. For example, he wrote, "I have often wondered what or how it feels to be rich rich rich rich rich." Nine pages link violence and money: "please pay to the order of . . . one hundred thousand dollars ... he should be killed." Five entries refer to killing or violence that have nothing to do with RFK. Five pages talk of killing or removing "the President": "Sirhan must begin to work on uphold [sic] solving the problems and definitions of assassinating the 36th president." "I advocate the overthrow of the current president of the fucken United States of America."

At a 1968 press conference, Los Angeles Mayor Sam Yorty was asked what he could tell the press about Sirhan. "Well," said the staunchly anti-communist Mayor, "he was a member of numerous communist organizations, including the Rosicrucians. It appears that Sirhan was sort of a loner who favored communists of all types." Hoisting Sirhan's notebooks in front of the TV cameras, Yorty asserted, "He does a lot of writing, pro-communist and anti-capitalist, anti-United States."[9]

Sirhan was not a member of any communist organization, nor were the Rosicrucians a communist group. Walter Crowe, a friend of Sirhan's from Pasadena City College, was an avowed communist. He told the FBI that he tried to interest Sirhan in Marxism or communism but couldn't. Crowe told Robert Kaiser that Sirhan was left-leaning but erratic. Sirhan showed no interest in joining

Crowe's local chapter of the radical Students for a Democratic Society, so Crowe didn't bother trying to recruit him to the Communist Party. Crowe also recalled that when he last saw Sirhan on May 2, he seemed to have lost some of his political idealism. Sirhan allegedly told Crowe that his primary interest now was to "make a lot of money."[10]

Yorty was right about one thing: Sirhan's notebook contained heavy doses of pro-communist, revolutionary zeal and anti-Americanism, as if Sirhan *were* a member of the Communist Party or were centrally interested in communist ideology. But he wasn't; next to money, this is the second most common theme. Twelve pages contain leftist-revolutionary and/or anti-American sentiments like the following: "I support the communist cause and its people – whatever Russian Chinese Albanian Hungarians – workers of the world unite you have nothing to lose but your chains." And: "the American, sheep like bourgeois masses by their selfish (capitalistically permissible) sinister and power hungry . . . overlords (who are bribed, paid homage to and toyed with by lobbyists) who are in turn treated the same way by lesser power hungry (political & economic) patriotic (understated) individuals (bastards)."

What is most incredible and casts doubt on his motive for the assassination is that the notebook is devoid of any reference to the alleged spark for Sirhan's violent political mind set – not a single reference to jets or bombers,[11] not a single reference to Zionism, Israel, Palestine, occupation, genocide, homeland or any of the themes or buzzwords for Middle East politics (the terms Sirhan would spout at his trial as propelling him to murder). Only six references cite anything Arab at all. Four sing the praises of Egyptian President Nasser, but these could be considered as much a manifestation of leftism – Nasser's leftist leanings troubled the United States – as Middle East politics. The Nasser references fail to manifest any linkages to Israel or military conflict. Two references are to Sirhan himself as an Arab.

While the dramatic "RFK must die!" pages were seized upon by nearly everyone, the notebook should be considered in toto. If one takes it at face value (as officials did with the RFK pages) it makes a better case that Sirhan was some sort of anti-imperialist hired gun than it does he was an anti-Zionist political fanatic.

There are only two possible exceptions to the notebook's blackout concerning the Middle East. One of the violent references is to killing Arthur Goldberg, a Jewish Supreme Court justice. One of the RFK scrawls says, "Robert F. Kennedy must be assassinated before 5 June 68." June 5 was the starting date for the 1967 Arab-Israeli War. Sirhan was cognizant of this date; at his trial, he said it had significance for him as "the beginning of the Israeli assault, the Israeli aggression against the Arab people." There is, however, no content that would clarify whether the notebook entry is a reference to the symbolic importance of killing Kennedy before the Middle East anniversary or whether it is a reference to the fact that California presidential nomination politics would probably end on that date.

The problem here is that Sirhan recognizes some references in the notebook as things that have significance to him; while others he does not. He has no recollection of doing the writing. Despite extensive interrogation and hypnotic sessions, Sirhan never could remember executing either the diary or the assault. This created monumental frustration for defense and prosecution alike: The failure of recall seemed genuine and, therefore, raised complex and weighty questions about Sirhan's mind, motive and modus operandi.

Dr. Diamond had Sirhan, under hypnosis, read his notebook aloud: "RFK must be assassinated." He then asked the prisoner, three times, *when* he had written this. Finally, Sirhan replied that he didn't know.[12]

When he was not under hypnosis Sirhan seemed about as familiar with his scrawled writings and doodles as he was with ancient Etruscan cave paintings. After Diamond had him read aloud one of his political ramblings, he whistled incredulouly. "This sounds . . . big," he said. He then noted, as if observing the notebook for the first time, that the writing was not his usual style.[13]

In reading another passage Sirhan seemed confused by his own handwriting. ''The man who triggered, triggered . . . What's this?'' he asked.

''Triggered off,'' responded Diamond.

Sirhan asked if the District Attorney's office had placed dates on some of the pages. He was told that *he* had written the dates. Diamond pressed him hard to recall a particular phrase. Sirhan tried, then gave up: ''I can't, Doc. My mind's a blank. I don't remember this.''[14]

Prosecution psychiatrist Dr. Seymour Pollack confronted Sirhan with the memory problem in the following soliloquy on legal strategy:

Cooper and Diamond [defense attorney Grant Cooper, defense psychiatrist Bernard Diamond] believe . . . they believe that the more clear the whole thing is, the better defense you will have . . . In my opinion, Sirhan, and irrespective of my, as . . . I don't think you have any chance, I really don't. I don't . . . as good a lawyer as he is, I just don't think you have much chance. That's my honest opinion and I feel bad about it.

So being that you don't have – as I say – much chance, I think that they believe that . . . I think they want you to testify and I think they've already told you: The clearer you are about all this, the clearer you are, the better chance they think you'll have. Because the jury, listening, will be negative rather than positive if you don't remember.

Now I say this, and I don't want you to fake; I don't want you to make up anything. But I do know there are lots of things about all of this that you, you, you apparently still say either you don't remember or you don't wanna remember.

''You hypnotize me,'' Sirhan responds, ''and whatever I say under hypnosis or under this truth serum or whatever the hell it is, I will face when I'm done . . . But right now, as I speak to you now, sir, I have no recollection."

Pollack talks specifically about the notebook: "Those diaries and those writings, you will admit, don't look good for you, do they? As a psychiatrist, there are peculiar conditions, but I don't know of any peculiar mental conditions that would allow you to write and then appear normal and write and then not know what you've written."

Pollack's frustration is manifest: "If I had made some notes, I would remember, generally, that I had written them. The fact that you maintain that you don't remember, that they look so strange to you, is, doesn't make sense to me from any psychiatric conditions that I know of."

Pollack accuses Sirhan of either feigning memory loss or purposely blocking things out of his mind "because they are so incriminating."

Sirhan seems almost embarrassed by his evident mental fog: ". . . Really, maybe I, ah . . . Maybe I don't know it [that he wrote the notebook]. I know that sounds silly, kind of silly. But really, ah, I can't explain it."

Pollack is persistent. "Don't you remember writing the love letter?" he asks Sirhan. "Why don't you remember this [the notebook]?"

Sirhan sounds distressed: "When I wrote it, I don' remember. I'm not functioning, sir, I don't . . ."

"The thing that bothers me," Pollack interrupts, his voice escalating, "is that you say you don't remember any part of it!" Pollack is now incredulous and seems upset. "Anything that's written there! Not a single damn thing! That bothers me."

Later Pollack remarks ruefully, "Ah, what a crazy, mixed-up case."

In spite of Pollack's exhortations, Sirhan told the jury (when questioned by his lawyer, Grant Cooper) that he could not remember the notebooks.

COOPER: Well now, let me ask you this. You still don't remember writing this?

SIRHAN: I don't remember it. I don't remember writing it.

Cooper became more specific.

COOPER: Do you remember writing this: "Please pay to the order of of of of of . . . this or that"?

SIRHAN: No, sir, I don't remember that.

COOPER: What significance does this have to you?

SIRHAN: Nothing to me. I don't have a bank account. I don't understand it.

COOPER: Well, can you understand why you put the name of a race horse in there, "Port Wine"?

SIRHAN: No, I don't.

COOPER: But you don't deny writing it.

SIRHAN: No, I don't deny it. It is my writing.

On cross-examination, prosecutor Lynn Compton pressed the same point.

COMPTON: What about your notebook? You don't remember when these were written?

SIRHAN: No, sir, I don't.

COMPTON: You had a habit of writing words or even sentences of things that were on your mind?

SIRHAN: I don't know, sir. I didn't sit there and doodle intentionally. . . .

COMPTON: Did you ever look at your notebooks, at the things you wrote?

SIRHAN: I guess sir. I don't remember.

COMPTON: You don't remember looking and thinking, "Gee whiz! Here I wrote that Kennedy must be assassinated!"

SIRHAN: No, sir, I don't.

COMPTON: On this envelope,* see the writing? "RFK must be disposed of like his brother." Did you write that?

SIRHAN: It is my handwriting.

COMPTON: You have no memory of ever writing that?

---

* The envelope was found in a trash can outside the Sirhan house in Pasadena.

SIRHAN: No, sir, I haven't.

The hypno-sleuths had no better luck when trying to get the prisoner to reconstruct the crime. Sirhan remembered having coffee with a pretty girl, then being choked after the shooting, but nothing in between. Sirhan told Diamond he wished he could remember. He told Kaiser that the assassination was "all mixed up like a dream."[15]

NBC-TV newsman Jack Perkins interviewed Sirhan at the conclusion of his trial and asked, "You were planning to kill Senator Kennedy?"

"Only in my mind," said Sirhan. "I did it but I was not aware of it."[16]

Robert Kaiser, defense team investigator and author, told author Jonn Christian that he was convinced Sirhan had some kind of amnesia concerning some of the important critical evidence against him.[17]

In a 1970 magazine interview, Dr. Diamond admitted that "Sirhan executed the crime in a twilight state, knowing next to nothing about what was happening." Diamond reassured his readers that "by having Sirhan under hypnosis we cleared up many doubts about the crime itself as well as about Sirhan's mind."

Dr. Diamond put Sirhan through a series of highly intense, detailed, hypnotic re-enactments of the crime, sternly ordering him to act out the shooting:[18] to see Kennedy approaching, to look at his face, to reach for the gun.

Despite Diamond's claim to have assuaged doubts, the hypnotic sessions hardly produced a clear picture of the shooting, either in Sirhan's mind or for those watching him perform.[19] After recalling absolutely nothing, Sirhan finally remembered, under hypnosis, that Kennedy was in the room at the time of the shooting – hardly a major breakthrough in understanding Sirhan's *modus operandi*. When he woke up he couldn't remember even that. With regard to most other points, it was no better.

Sirhan recalled wanting to shake hands with Kennedy. Diamond asked him why, but Sirhan didn't know. Under hypnosis the doctor asked if Sirhan knew that Kennedy was coming through the pantry. He answered negatively. Was Sirhan waiting for Kennedy? Again he answered no.

Sirhan finally had a vision of Kennedy, but the Senator was running toward him – another unreality. Of Kennedy's presence in the pantry, Sirhan asked aloud in his hypnotic state, "What's he doing here?"

Diamond stated during his 1970 magazine interview that, "We didn't even know, until he grabbed his belt on the left side [under hypnosis] where he carried that .22 revolver." Indeed, when Dr. Diamond asked the hypnotized Sirhan where he carried the gun, he mumbled incoherently. Diamond asked if he kept it in his pants. Again, no comprehensible response. Kaiser reported that when Sirhan came out of his trance he was asked where he had carried the gun. Kaiser observed that Sirhan's response was only a guess.

Diamond then instructed his hynotized subject to reach for the gun. Sirhan moved his right hand over to his left hip bone. Diamond was encouraged, for this is how one witness thought Sirhan had drawn his gun. Remarked Kaiser, "This was the first time Sirhan gave any indication he knew where it was."[20] But did he? At other points during his sessions with Diamond, the spaced-out, slow-drawing Sirhan reached for the weapon in the waistband of the front of his pants, in his lap, or by grabbing his penis. Ten years later Sirhan would allegedly show fellow prisoner Carmine Falzone how he drew the gun with his left hand, despite his being right-handed and numerous witnesses having seen the gun in his right hand.

One apparent breakthrough came when Sirhan spontaneously uttered "son of a bitch!" when visualizing the oncoming Senator, matching what several witnesses overheard him say just before he fired ("Kennedy, you son of a bitch!"). This hardly constituted hypnotically rehabilitated memory. And Sirhan apparently did not remember the phrase, or its significance, once he was out of hypnosis. In Pollack's non-hypnotic, one-on-one session with Sirhan the doctor says, "Did you know when you were hypnotized and you were . . . I was hoping you would remember that, when Diamond had you go through this, you said just before you shot him:

'You son of a bitch.' "

"Yeah, that's right – you son of a bitch again," said Sirhan laughing.

Pollack then suggests that Sirhan doesn't really want him to know what happened.

At another point Pollack announces, "I have a clear picture of what you did. You were waiting for Kennedy. You were actively looking for him . . . There are enough witnesses." The relevant point, of course, is not how clearly Pollack can envision the crime or how many witnesses there were, but what Sirhan can remember.

In another exchange between these two, a frustrated Dr. Pollack candidly reveals that the hypnotic reconstruction process was far from a smashing success. In response to Pollack's exhorting him to remember, Sirhan says, "You've gotta hypnotize me. You better hypnotize me."

"I hypnotized you, and you wouldn't talk to me at all about those things. You just refused to talk to me for three hours."

Sirhan mumbles something and says "Three hours?"

"You refused to tell me about the things in the diary."

"Did I talk at all?"

"You refused to open your mouth."

"Well, why is that?" asks Sirhan. "Why would I talk with Pollack [he means Diamond] and not you?"

In a voice tinged with irritation, Pollack answers, "Whenever we try to get you to talk about these things that are important, you pull away, you fall asleep. We spent a half hour trying to find out where the gun was. How could you carry the gun from your car . . . near Wilshire. How could you carry a gun from there back to the Ambassador Hotel and not know that you had it. How could you? How could you do that? Obviously you don't remember and I'll buy that – I'll buy you don't remember it. But are you trying to tell me you could carry a gun without knowing you have it? . . . What did you think it was in there? Ah, ah, ah, ah, ah applesauce?"

"Ah, I don't know," Sirhan responds, "the, the newspaper [inaudible] newspaper."

"Then you must have carried it in a newspaper. But you mean to tell me that you carried a gun without ever knowing whether it was a gun or a newspaper?" The question seems rhetorical: Pollack doesn't wait for an answer but proceeds to tell Sirhan that the more he remembers the more they can help him.

While Sirhan was languishing on death row in San Quentin, the prison psychologist, Dr. Eduard Simpson, was assigned to work extensively with him. The prison's chief psychiatrist, Dr. David D. Schmidt, wrote to Warden L. S. Nelson: "I asked Dr. Eduard Simpson to see him on a fairly regular basis because it was my opinion that Dr. Simpson would be more effective working with him than any other staff member. . . . "

In a 1974 tape-recorded interview with researcher Betsy Langman, Simpson described his work with Sirhan. A veteran of 20 years of clinical experience, Simpson claims to have developed a good rapport with the prisoner. Estonian by birth, Simpson believes that his understanding of regional political conflict in Europe, coupled with his apolitical stance concerning the Middle East, caused Sirhan to trust him more than he trusted Diamond and Pollack.

During the 20 hours he spent with Sirhan, Dr. Simpson became troubled by the seeming artificiality and superficiality not only of the political motive but also of Sirhan's descriptions of the crime. Simpson observed that these descriptions were "not genuine – [they were] generalities, like reading a newspaper." They lacked specific details. It was as if Sirhan was "acting a part he had memorized."

Very significantly, according to Simpson, Sirhan had finally reached the point where he had "twilight feelings that there was more to it [the assassination], and it's in me; and I have to have some help to uncover it fully. . . . He himself wanted to know. He wanted to find out something that he was sort of vaguely aware [of] or was on the verge of being conscious of."

Also according to Simpson, Sirhan kept saying, in a contemplative way, "The human mind is so complicated." He asked the doctor to use hypnosis to plumb the depths of his foggy psyche in search of answers, in an atmosphere free of the pressures of legal maneuvering that had shaped the pre-trial hypnotic sessions. Simpson believed that conditions were very favorable for achieving a breakthrough. But he would never have the opportunity.

Just before the first hypnotic session, says Simpson, his visits to Sirhan were terminated by his superiors. The reason given was to allow the doctor to spend more time with other prisoners. Simpson finds the timing of the decision somewhat suspicious. He says Sirhan feared the room where they met was bugged and the prisoner speculated that the authorities might not want him to break through the memory barrier.

Six years later Sirhan still had made no progress in ending his mental blackout. A 1975 "psychiatric evaluation" written by the then-chief psychiatrist of San Quentin, Dr. Leo Loughlin, states: "Mr. Sirhan continues to be very close to his family, specifically his mother and brother. They visit regularly. Mr. Sirhan continues to be amnesic to the events surrounding the murder of Robert Kennedy. He states that frequently he has tried to remember what happened, but he has been unable to do so."

In his cell, before the trial, the accused assassin said to Robert Kaiser, "My body outsmarted my brain, I guess." All indications are that it was the other way around.

Chapter 11

THE ROBOT ASSASSIN

*Let me specifically state that it was immediately apparent
that Sirhan had been programmed . . . His response to
hypnosis was very different . . . strange, in many respects.
And he showed this phenomenon of automatic writing, which
is something that can be done only when one is pretty well
trained.*

— Dr. Bernard Diamond, 1974,[1]
chief psychiatrist for Sirhan's defense team

One of the widely stipulated, albeit bizarre, facts of this case is
that Sirhan Sirhan was in an altered mental state during the
assassination of Senator Robert F. Kennedy.* There the agreement
among knowledgeable observers ends. What kind of mental state?
How was it created? What accounted for his lack of memory and his
strange behavior? Three theories have been expounded concerning
what really happened to Sirhan's mind.

One, put forth by defense psychiatrist Bernard Diamond, is that
Sirhan programmed himself. It is known that he did practice mind-
control techniques, as well as self-hypnosis, at home in his
bedroom, mesmerizing himself with lighted candles and his mirror.

* The prosecution rejected this and Los Angeles authorities buried some of the
evidence indicating that Sirhan was in a trance or stupor, for fear it would hinder
the attainment of a first-degree murder conviction.

He had also joined the Rosicrucians, whose heavy doses of mysticism reinforced his interest in mental manipulations. "AMORC" (the Ancient Mystical Order of the Rosicrucians) was written several times in Sirhan's notebook.

Dr. Diamond claimed to have investigated "who or what" had influenced Sirhan.[2] He described his findings:

> No one was more surprised than I to find out how the programming had been accomplished . . . that he programmed himself . . . [He took a] correspondence course in self-hypnosis. . . . This seems the most logical explanation of all the things that happened. . . . As far as I can form a judgement, he was programmed by himself. But there is no way of being, ah, you know, of certifying the validity of that.

Diamond said in a 1970 interview that Sirhan "programmed himself exactly as a computer is programmed by its magnetic tape."

Indeed, there is no way to verify Diamond's theory, especially when Sirhan cannot remember his automatic writing or trying to program himself. To Diamond, however, Sirhan was a muddled lunatic who employed mind control to gear himself up for murdering a man who would allow the Jews to rain death on his homeland.

Robert Blair Kaiser had a different theory. In a 1970 interview with the *Chicago Tribune* he flatly stated what his book *"RFK Must Die!"* had only hinted at: "Sirhan was programmed to kill Bob Kennedy and was programmed to forget the fact of his programming." Although Kaiser allowed that this was only his "personal opinion," he went even further and claimed, "I think I know who the programmer is." He refused to name the individual. If one reads Kaiser's book, it seems likely that he might have suspected someone with the Rosicrucians or perhaps a friend of Sirhan's who was interested in mind control.

The third option is the Manchurian Candidate theory, put forth by Jonn Christian and William Turner in their 1978 book *The Assassination of Robert F. Kennedy*.[3] In this scenario Sirhan was programmed not by a friend or associate dabbling in mentalism but by a professional expert or experts working for, or in the shadow of, U.S. intelligence. Such an expert(s) programmed Sirhan to attempt the assassination on cue, without remembering the shooting or his programming.

The scenario of programmed assassination was first put forth by Richard Condon in his 1959 best-selling novel *The Manchurian Candidate*, later made into a movie starring Laurence Harvey and Frank Sinatra. The plot involved an American prisoner of war who was brainwashed into becoming a remote-control assassin and sent to kill the president of the United States. The assassination attempt was cued by turning up a specific playing card that had been burned into the hit man's psyche by North Korean brainwashers.

The sensational nature of the Manchurian Candidate theory has caused it to be misunderstood and largely rejected by scholars and journalists – many of whom are unfamiliar with the available technology for programming assassins, the history of efforts to do so, or both. In 1968, the scenario of a hypno-programmed killer was generally considered to be a Hollywood sendup, and most experts derided it as an impossibility ("A crackpot theory," said Dr. Diamond). Twenty years later the possibility is still rejected by most mainstream experts.

Authors Alan W. Scheflin and Edward M. Opton, Jr., assert that it is impossible: "Psycho-surgery and electric shock therapy, behavior modification and electric stimulation of the brain are not sufficiently sophisticated to wipe away the will yet leave the functioning person. Of the techniques which remain – brainwashing, drugs and hypnosis – each has such serious limitations as to make the Manchurian Candidate scenario virtually impossible."[4]

In 1987 I talked with three prominent hypnotherapists in the Los Angeles area whose skills enable their clients to bolster their professional poise (as lawyers, salespeople or actors), reduce weight, quit smoking, cure sexual dysfunctions, concentrate on hitting baseballs for the Dodgers, improve their memories, etc. All three, two of whom requested anonymity, were sure that the robot assassin was, for a variety of reasons, technologically beyond the capacity of their profession. The third, Dr. Robert Fields, maintained, ''You simply cannot go beyond what the subject is willing to do . . . you cannot control people for long periods of time and require them to forget, while still having them function. It's an impossible feat.'' One of the other therapists, told me that the key to his influence over the subject was not the power of hypnosis but the subject's eagerness to believe, created by shelling out a hundred dollars per session to get help with a problem. He argued that without this will to believe – almost like a placebo effect – hypnosis would have very little power over the person's mind and behavior. ''You could conceivably help homicidal types to become more confident and focused murderers, but you cannot create assassins and program them to kill and to forget.''

Patients are told that hypnosis is not something that controls them so the doctor can help them, it is, instead, a technique by which they can help themselves, with the doctor acting more as a kind of broker than a Svengali. This is the professional shibboleth – that practitioners are healers, not controllers who have power over peoples' minds and bodies. Many upstanding practitioners believe this.

In contrast, a great deal of solid evidence and expert opinion exists that creating a hypno-programmed assassin is not only possible but *was* possible in 1968, conventional wisdom notwithstanding. No one who has seen the awesome power of the skilled stage hypnotist – ''programming'' people to run from the auditiorium believing their pants are on fire, one half hour after they were instructed under hypnosis to do so when the word ''blueberry'' is mentioned – can deny the manipulative potential.

One expert, demanding anonymity, cynically referred to the irresponsible and unscrupulous uses of hypnosis by some of his professional peers. He also spoke of a military experiment in which Navy personnel were plunged naked into water so frigid that it is normally fatal within seconds. They survived because they had been instructed under hypnosis not to succumb to the cold.

This same hypnotherapist demonstrated audio equipment that subliminally bombards patients with voices while they are waiting for, or chatting with, the doctor. The voices instruct the listener to be "more receptive to hypnosis." With the sound muted, receptivity to hypnosis can be increased; the patient can unwittingly be set up for hypnosis while reading a magazine in the waiting room or giving the doctor a history of the problem. This practitioner asserted that he would never use the device subliminally because it would be unethical.

He enthusiastically recounted one of his most unique uses of hypnosis – to "prepare" patients for surgery that they fear. Under hypnosis he creates a "warm, positive" feeling about the impending operation. The patient is instructed that this feeling will kick in when the operating physician says, "Hi, I'm Dr. Jones." On cue, some patients are able to lapse into a hypnotic stupor of positive emotions, to the extent they forego anesthesia during the surgery.

This hypnotherapist also conducts workshops for attorneys, training them in the fine art of selecting jurors who will be receptive to carefully staged verbal suggestion. Then he teaches the lawyers how to implant in jurors' minds powerful messages they will remember and act on in their deliberations. The technique involves using speech patterns, tonality, phrasing and voice modulation to give selected phrases ("messages") particualr punch – to set them up so they will stand out and "stick" in jurors' minds (like a catchy tune they can't stop remembering). This he described as "talking to the jury and knowing how to get them receptive to the message and remember it." He concluded, "Remember, a lawyer's job is to protect his client at any cost."

What about professionals whose tasks include assassination? One expert who believes that it is possible to create robot assassins is Dr. Milton Kline, a New York psychologist who once served as president of the American Society for Clinical and Experimental Hypnosis. He was also one of the numerous outside experts consulted (on an unpaid basis) by CIA researchers. Kline told author John Marks that while he had refused to cross the ethical line in mind-control research, he was sure intelligence agencies had done so. Regarding the creation of a Manchurian Candidate, Kline observed, "It cannot be done by everyone. It cannot be done consistently, but it can be done.'" He estimated it would take him six months to create one.

Beginning in the early 1950s and possibly continuing to the present day, Soviet and American intelligence agencies raced each other to the frontiers of mind-control research. Needless to say, this endeavor was – and still is – one of the most secretive and manipulative enterprises the CIA has engaged in. One expert who was both a stage hypnotist and a clinical practitioner alleged, to journalist Martin A. Lee, that the secrecy was definitely enforced:[6]

> These people [hypnotists who worked for the CIA] are very closed-mouthed. They've been indirectly threatened by the government. Retaliation could occur; or, rather, retaliation is possible. I think you are going to get a pretty mute ear [sic] even if you were to hit one of these people directly. I'm referring to conversations I've had with hypnotists who could possibly be involved in the situation and I [they] scattered his brains all over the countryside before we started. He's the only one I've heard admit directly that he was involved in it.

After World War II, the American military discovered through captured files that the Nazis had been conducting mind-control experiments with drugs and hypnosis. Indications were, however, that they never succeeded in gaining control of their "subjects' " minds. When the German experimental data was sent back to the U.S, the question quickly arose as to whether the Soviets could, or had, succeeded where the Nazis had failed: Could the Russians produce a "sleeper killer" as a weapon against the West? U.S. intelligence soon began to suspect the Soviets of using drugs and hypnosis to gain control of refugees before they came to America from Eastern Europe, or to control captured spies and political prisoners who might later be exchanged or released to the West, where they would do Moscow's bidding. Hypnosis became yet another of the Cold War's weapons-development races.

In 1951, CIA behavioral research coordinator Morse Allen became enamored of hypnosis and began voraciously reading the literature on it. He then took a four-day crash course from one of New York City's leading stage hypnotists. Among other impressive uses of hypnosis, the mentor regaled Allen with stories of using it to seduce women. In one case the practitioner convinced a woman, under hypnosis, that he was her husband and that she desperately desired to make love to him. Allen wrote back to the CIA touting the espionage uses of hypnosis. He also duly noted that his New York teacher "spent approximately five nights a week engaging in sexual intercourse with his various female subjects."

In addition to tales of sexual exploitation, Allen learned enough from the brief workshop to be able to put on a little demonstration back at CIA headquarters. He experimented on his office secretaries, hypno-programming them to "steal" secret files and pass them to total strangers. Allen induced one of his secretaries to report to the bedroom of a complete stranger, where she fell into a pre-programmed trance. "This activity clearly indicates," he wrote, "that individuals under hypnosis might be compromised or black-mailed."[8]

If spying was that amenable to the uses of hypnosis, then what about killing? By 1954, the CIA's pursuit of the robot assassin was proceeding in earnest. An Agency memo dated January of that year discusses a "hypothetical problem": "Can an individual of [de-leted] descent be made to perform an act of attempted assassination involuntarily . . . ?" It describes using a particular person, name deleted, to turn him into a "trigger mechanism" whereby he can be "induced to perform the act of attempted assassination at a later date. All of the above to be accomplished at one involuntary uncontrolled social meeting. After the act of attempted assassination was performed it is assumed that the subject would be taken into custody by the [deleted] government and disposed of."

The target of the attempted assassination was to be "a prominent politician [of the foreign country] or *if necessary an American official* [emphasis added].''

The memo (see photo/documents section) warns that this hypothetical operation would probably not be successful because access to the subject would be too limited and the man would be acting involuntarily. Despite such problems, and despite the fact that this operation is described as ''insignificant'' in the overall mind-control project, the memo concludes that ''under crash conditions'' and appropriate authority from HQ, the ARTICHOKE [code name for the mind-control project] team would undertake the problem in spite of its operational limitations.''

Limitations notwithstanding, Morse Allen ready to put on a stage show of his own, performed at CIA headquarters only two months after the memo was written. Having put one of his secretaries into a deep trance, he instructed her to stay that way. He then hypnotized one of her colleagues and told the second woman that if she could not awaken the first woman she would be so enraged that she would ''kill'' her while she slept.

Allen's hit woman, who had previously expressed a fear of firearms, dutifully picked up a hand gun left by her boss and ''shot'' her dozing colleague. When Allen brought the assailant out of her trance, she not only had no memory of the ''shooting'' but she denied that it ever occurred.[9]

By 1957, the CIA's projected experiments with hypnosis were at a point where, as CIA researcher Alden Sears wrote, ''they could not be handled in a university situation.'' Concluded author John Marks (in *The Search for the ''Manchurian Candidate''*): ''Nothing Sears or the others found disabused them of the idea that the Manchurian Candidate is possible.''[10] One expert, who did not participate in the CIA effort but knew some of those who did, told writer Martin A. Lee that there were numerous researchers involved: ''There had to be because there was a huge department [program] . . . the volume of work could not have involved simply one man or two men.''

The CIA has steadfastly maintained that the Manchurian

Candidate program was never operationalized. Even if it is true that the Agency never did so, this does not mean that no one else did. The technology was not under strict CIA control as was the deadly shellfish toxin that the Agency developed for assassinations. Mind-control research was conducted at an unknown number of hospitals, private clinics and institutes, and by a diverse group of CIA-recruited experts that included renowned academicians, stage hypnotists and clinical practitioners. One source familiar with some CIA researchers opined that the Agency "approached a lot of the wrong people" in its program. As we shall see in the next chapter, this is an understatement. If some of the CIA researchers were out of control, so too was the technology they developed.

Moreover, at least one clandestine use of hypnosis appears to have been implemented by the CIA. One area of the Agency's research was to discover whether hypnosis could be used to create a totally new and separate personality for a subject. If so, this second one could work for the Agency as a courier or operative, using the "original" personality as a cover – a perfect secrecy shield. Such experiments were carried on with CIA money.[11]

A 1976 book entitled *The Control of Candy Jones* by Donald Bain told the bizarre story of an attractive Chicago model and cover girl who claimed to have been used by the CIA as a courier, after a doctor installed a second personality under hypnosis.[12] Jones asserted that she was approached by the medical doctor to work as a CIA courier for a lot of of money. Instead, she was unwittingly installed with a second personality that would perform the chores for free. She alleged that the doctor surreptitiously hypnotized her, programmed her and carried on a love affair with her. As her alter ego Arlene Grant, Miss Jones carried messages and data to foreign countries, sometimes being tortured by foreign intelligence agencies.

Jones later married New York radio personality "Long John" Nebel, who dabbled in hypnosis and used it to help her relax. On one such occasion, he accidentally discovered Arlene Grant and, with the help of an expert hypnotherapist, began to reconstruct what had happened. Jones's story sounded so wild that many people dismissed it as a fabrication. Most experts believed it could not possibly be true.

In the year the book appeared, the CIA's mind-control experiments had not yet come to public attention and the documents describing the research were still secret. Subsequent to the release of these documents, several knowledgeable researchers have marveled at how closely her alleged experiences parallel the CIA file's goals and techniques. John Marks, who first obtained the CIA's file on mind-control research, has concluded that the similarities are rich enough to convince him that she could not have invented the story and it is probably authentic. [13]

One aspect of CIA research was the so-called "terminal experiments" to see if hypnotized and/or drugged subjects could withstand various types of torture without breaking down and revealing information. Jones claims she was taken by her doctor-programmer to CIA headquarters in Washington where she was part of a "demonstration" in which several hypnotic subjects were put through their paces by their controllers – a deep-sleep dog-and-pony show far exceeding the little ones Morse Allen had conducted. Jones says that after being tranced and instructed not to feel pain, a lighted cigarette was inserted into her vagina. To the delight of the CIA audience, she reportedly didn't feel a thing.

In 1986, I contacted a leading New York psychiatrist and expert on hypnosis, Dr. Herbert Spiegal, who was familiar with the literature on CIA research and the Sirhan case. He indicated that success in programming an assassin would depend upon the susceptibility of the subject, the skill and ruthlessness of the programmer, the amount of access to the subject, and the circumstances of access. "It is by no means simple," said Spiegal, "but under the right circumstances it is definitely attainable."

There appears to be one point of considerable agreement among experts, and it is damning to Dr. Diamond's theory that Sirhan programmed himself. Dr. John Walters, a leading hypnotherapist, opined in a 1974 interview with researcher Betsy Langman:

You can get into a self-hypnotic state . . . but when you start giving yourself a suggestion, it's back at a conscious level again, so you're no longer in a hypnotic state where I interject thoughts and pictures and you don't have to think, only absorb.* That's quite a difference . . . [when being hypnotized by someone else] you have no way of analyzing 'cause you're only absorbing . . . [to perform] an act contrary to your normal behavior you have to be hypnotized by someone else.

One non-CIA expert talked to journalist Martin Lee about the CIA-military applications of hypnosis. From some of his peers who worked on mind control and hypnotic research, he had learned that a subject could be put through a "conditioning process" that would hide information: "They [the programmers] could condition in such a manner that the very information they [the interrogators] were seeking would only become blurred under pressure."

If Sirhan could not program himself to kill and forget it all – to do automatic writing to gear himself up for the kill and to forget he ever wrote it – then someone else did. Could this be a mysterious friend or acquaintance, as in Sirhan defense investigator and author Robert Kaiser's theory? Would such a person have the expertise to create a programmed killer, when the professionals and experts on the frontiers of hypnosis regard the task as exceedingly tricky and demanding? It is possible, but it does not seem likely.

The risk for such a person would lie in being identified as the programmer. Once the authorities discovered that Sirhan was programmed, as they indeed did, there would be a good chance that he might recall being hypnotized or influenced by this person, whose identity he could reveal to authorities. It would be very difficult for someone who was not a high-powered, expert practitioner to work extensively with Sirhan and leave no clues.

* Walters described how a skilled hypnotist who understands his subject can "reach the subconscious directly." "Once you bypass the conscious mind you are all set." At that point, said Walters, "You can create reality for the subject by implanting thoughts and images: dreams become reality . . . your body cannot distinguish between dream and reality. It secretes adrenaline in fear whether [the fear is] real or not."

Is it possible for a highly skilled hypnotist to write himself out of the subject's mind, as if he never conducted the programming and never existed? The three mainstream practitioners I consulted greeted this possibility with extreme skepticism or, in one case, derision.

In 1987, I interviewed a renowned hypnotherapist whose clients included federal agencies. He boasted that he knew how to write himself out of the patient's consciousness, as if he were never there "because," he said proudly, "I have a double-blind maneuver." The subject ends up believing he has done nothing more than have a conversation with "a close friend, a lover or a family member," and will "never remember" the hypnotist.

According to both Diamond and Kaiser, Sirhan seemed to possess at least one of the necessary conditions required for someone to create a robot assassin: He was an excellent hypnotic subject. Dr. Diamond found that Sirhan could be hypnotized extremely quickly, simply by having him look at a coin. No protracted suggestions of sleepiness or prolonged, mesmerizing motions were required. Sirhan's trances were sometimes so deep that he appeared to be asleep, and he was difficult or impossible to question. Indeed, he had to be prevented from going too far under.

Diamond also graphically illustrated Sirhan's excellent capacity to internalize and act out hypnotic suggestion. Under hypnosis, the doctor told the prisoner that when he awoke he could climb the bars of his cell like a monkey. He actually did just that. While he was hanging on the bars Diamond asked him why he was there. Sirhan replied that he was exercising. He remembered nothing about the hypnotic suggestion.[14]

Dr. Herbert Spiegal told this author that in 1976, at the request of Jonn Christian and William Turner, he had studied Dr. Diamond's testimony regarding Sirhan's behavior as a hypnotic subject. Spiegal also read Kaiser's accounts of the hypnotic sessions. Even without examining Sirhan directly, Dr. Spiegal confidently concluded that the prisoner was a "grade five" on a scale of one to five. A grade five is the best hypnotic subject. "Less than ten percent of the population rates a grade five," claimed the doctor.

Spiegal also noted that Sirhan's status as a Palestinian refugee with a childhood plagued by political violence provided a ready-made entry for the programmer's manipulations, a strong hook for the programming. Intense emotions and past traumas could be conjured up and directed toward the desired goals of the programming.

Sirhan was not just a susceptible subject but one who, in the year and a half preceding the assassination, developed an intense interest in mysticism, self-hypnosis and mental self-improvement. His keen interest in mental manipulations made him a more willing subject who would be less likely to resist hypnosis than would someone who feared or distrusted it or believed he or she could not be hypnotized.

John Strathman had been friends with Sirhan since they attended junior high school together. Sirhan visited John and his wife Patricia several times in 1964 and 1965; the couple saw him "now and then" in 1966-67.[15]

Patricia recalled that when Sirhan visited in May of 1967 he talked about mysticism, in which they shared an interest. One night that year in a restaurant he told her he had an ability to "see mystical bodies" out of the corner of his eye. He also claimed he could conjure up a vision of his "guardian angel" for the couple to see. When the Strathmans confessed that they couldn't see it, Sirhan confided that his powers were not yet fully developed.[16]

Patricia told the FBI that after Sirhan fell from a horse in 1966 he "changed." He was "brooding more," she testified at the trial. He no longer talked of becoming a jockey and making lots of money. These previously overriding interests were now replaced by mysticism.

He had nurtured his dream of becoming a successful jockey by working around horses since 1965. The 5-feet 4-inch, 120-pound Sirhan was an exercise boy at Granja Vista del Rio Ranch in Corona in the summer of 1966. On September 26, 1967, there was to be a race, staged by various horse owners with exercise boys doing the riding. The morning fog was so thick that some owners withdrew.

Three horses were allowed to race, including one ridden by Sirhan. As they thundered around the track at full speed, the fog suddenly closed in, causing the horses to bump into one another. Sirhan fell and hit his head. As he lay crumpled up, his head cut and bleeding, he screamed. [17]

His injuries were not severe, and he was discharged from a nearby hospital after a brief stay. But he was plagued by blurred vision and pain. He successfully settled a workman's compensation claim for $2,000, but his career plans ended abruptly.

Those around him noticed the marked change described by Patricia Strathman. He became more withdrawn and irritable. Terry Welch was a co-worker of Sirhan's at the Corona horse ranch when Sirhan had the accident. Welch told the FBI that before the fall Sirhan was "extremely intelligent, neat, clean, gentlemanly and ambitious." He was "an avid reader especially interested in the law." After the mishap Sirhan underwent a "complete personality change," said Welch. He was "quiet and aloof, unpredictable and a loner. He started showing resentment toward people with wealth."

Tom Rathke, a friend and co-worker of Sirhan's, told LAPD that "something happened to him after he got hurt. He just wasn't the same kid. . . . You really couldn't even talk to him. I mean, he had his mind made up and that was the end of it. He was just a different person altogether. Before, he was a likable boy and you'd talk and laugh and have fun . . . and there was no more laughing. It was just rigid . . . like somebody that's a . . . like a paranoid. Just rigid."

Sirhan's older brother Sharif lamented about the change to police. "He was so nice [before the fall]; everybody liked him." But he changed suddenly – "snap" – and became reclusive, disappearing for four or five hours at a time. "The way he acted was abnormal," observed Sharif.

Perhaps to fill the void created by his shattered dream and to overcome the physical pain, he embraced the realm of the mind: self-hypnosis, mind control, mysticism. Thus, Sirhan was more than someone who was amenable to hypnosis – he was a veritable mind-game junkie. He joined the Ancient Mystical Order of the Rosicrucians (AMORC), practiced mental projection of images and ideas, and frequented a bookstore in Pasadena that specialized in the occult.

During this period he also saw numerous medical doctors in search of diagnosis and treatment for the elusive maladies caused by the accident. Thus we have Sirhan Sirhan, an excellent hypnotic subject, bouncing from doctor to doctor while developing a voracious appetite for mental gymnastics. This surely increased his chances of falling into the clutches of a CIA-sponsored headhunter, a mind-control researcher capable of programming him.

Sirhan's behavior before, during and after the shooting is replete with bizarre manifestations as well as striking contradictions. While everyone agrees he was in some sort of twilight zone, the questions are: What sort? How did he get there?

At 10:00 p.m. the night of the assassination, Carrilo Cetina, a waiter at the Ambassador, encountered Sirhan outside the men's room near the Palm Court Bar.[18] Cetina stood waiting for a fellow worker when Sirhan approached him and commented, ''It sure is crowded here.'' Sirhan asked the waiter if he would hold his drink. After Cetina obliged, Sirhan asked, ''Can I use one of the chairs?'' pointing to a stack of chairs in the hallway. Cetina said yes; he handed the drink back and departed with his colleague when he came out of the rest room.

Cetina is positive it was Sirhan. He saw him again in the kitchen just before the shooting, but did not talk with him. The waiter reported nothing odd about Sirhan's behavior or demeanor during their brief, close encounter outside the rest room (an encounter that would have been forgettable had the man not turned out to be an alleged assassin).

Approximately a half hour after that encounter, Sirhan was behaving very differently. Something had changed. Robert Kaiser, defense-team investigator and author, came across a brief LAPD summary of an interview with Mary Grohs, a teletype operator who was stationed at a machine in the Colonial Room near the pantry.

The report intrigued Kaiser because she described Sirhan as "staring fixedly" at the teletype at about 10:30 p.m. Kaiser tracked her down but found her very reluctant to talk.[19]

She described the encounter: "Well, he came over to my machine and started staring at it. Just staring. I'll never forget his eyes. I asked him what he wanted. He didn't answer. He just kept staring. I asked him again. No answer. I said that if he wanted to check the latest figures on Senator Kennedy, he'd have to check the other machine. He still didn't answer. He just kept staring."

Grohs asked for Kaiser's name and informed him that she was going to tell the police about his visit; they had instructed her not to talk to anyone about the incident, she said. Grohs also made a point of telling Kaiser that she didn't smell any alcohol on Sirhan. As we shall see shortly, LAPD may have been fearful that the assailant's spacy behavior was due to alcohol consumption and that this might provide the basis for a legal defense of diminished capacity. Evidently LAPD had discussed the alcohol problem with Grohs.

LAPD's chronology of Sirhan's movements the night of the shooting lists his "Activity/Location" as "unknown" between 11:00 and 11:30. At 11:45 to 12:00 he was seen inside the pantry by busboy Jesus Perez. During or shortly after his unaccounted-for half hour, he would follow the mystery girl toward the pantry. His last memory until after the shooting would be of drinking coffee with her.

If, in fact, the infamous polka-dot-dress girl was with Sirhan at this time, an hour or so before the shooting, she could have triggered or cued or reinforced his programming for both the assault and the loss of memory. A preprogrammed phrase or reference would do the trick, perhaps augmented by something slipped into his coffee – something that would enhance hypnotic control and/or help him to conjure up the tremendous energy he would manifest during the struggle for the gun, after initially feeling so tired that he had to rest on a table in the pantry area before going through with the attack.[20]

Two of the experts I consulted stated that a subject could be programmed to lapse into a trance not only by the use of a cue or phrase but also simply upon meeting a certain person. Whatever the cause of the changes, Sirhan degenerated from normal conversation, at 10:00 p.m., to unresponsiveness as demonstrated by the conversation with the teletype woman, to feeling extremely fatigued, to summoning fanatical strength.

Karl Uecker grabbed the assailant's gun hand and was joined in the struggle by ex-football player Roosevelt Grier, Olympic champion Rafer Johnson and several others. Sirhan's hand gripped the gun with such intensity that he managed to fire six shots after his arm was grabbed. It took thirty to forty seconds to get the gun away.[21] Radio reporter Andrew West described the struggle: "His hand is frozen." "Break it if you have to." Writer George Plimpton observed, "He [Sirhan] was very strong for a small man." Did one cup of coffee turn this sleepy wanderer into an unstoppable shooting machine? Was it adrenaline, fanaticism, drugs – or hypnosis?

Then there was Sirhan's eerie smile. Vincent Di Pierro, a college student working as a waiter, told LAPD that he saw Sirhan moments before the shooting, standing in the pantry next to the attractive girl in the polka-dot dress. When asked what most stood out in his mind about Sirhan, Di Pierro said, "That stupid smile. A very sick-looking smile."

Both Sirhan and the girl were smiling. "He had that same stupid smile." Sirhan turned as if to say something to her. She did not speak, "just smiled." Said Di Pierro, "When she first did it [smiled] she looked like she was sick also."

Hotel waiter Martin Patruski saw Sirhan approach his target. "The guy looked like he was smiling," Patruski recalled.[22] Busboy Juan Romero, in a handwritten statement to the FBI on June 6, described Sirhan as "smiling" when he approached Kennedy. Patrolman Arthur Placencia rode with Sirhan from the hotel to the police station. The prisoner had a smile on his face, Placencia recalled, a kind of "smirk."[23]

Buried among the tape-recorded interviews conducted with

dozens of witnesses in the hours immediately following the shooting is a brief account provided by a hotel cook, Yosio Niwa. Most of his story was duplicated by dozens of other witnesses (he heard shots, then saw the struggle for the gun). Nevertheless, he did have a singular encounter with Sirhan after the shooting.

Niwa thought of joining the fight for the gun but saw that there were already too many bodies involved. He stood and watched. When Sirhan had been subdued, Niwa got very close to him.

"I'll never forget that guy's face," said the incredulous cook. "I'll never forget. I was so upset. I told him, 'You got mother or father?' . . . He was smiling too."*

"Say anything to you?" asked the policeman.

"No. He was looking at me. I was so excited, upset. He was smiling."

"That's hard to understand, isn't it?" the officer commiserated with Niwa.

"I don't know why," said the puzzled witness.

Despite his strength and zeal – yelling "Kennedy, you son of a bitch!" – Sirhan seemed eerily serene. Joseph Lahive, president of a local Democratic club, noted that during the struggle Sirhan looked "very tranquil."[24] George Plimpton was taken aback by Sirhan's "dark brown and enormously peaceful" eyes just after the shooting.[25] Was this the inner calm of a well-motivated political fanatic, fulfilling his plan of violence; or was it a further manifestation of programmed disassociation, of a compartmentalized psyche?

It is clear that LAPD's most famous prisoner exhibited some very abnormal traits when first arrested. Since he had imbibed three or four Tom Collinses, the question of sobriety arose. Police wanted to squelch any notion of intoxication for fear it could cost the DA's office a first-degree conviction by providing the basis for a plea of diminished capacity. By insisting the prisoner was normal, LAPD inadvertently covered up something far more powerful than alcohol, something that could make Sirhan smile, shoot, struggle, be

---

* Niwa's interview is not summarized in written form nor is it listed in the *Summary Report*, which purports to be a complete list of all witnesses. I found it after analyzing the recently released LAPD files.

peaceful and never have any memory of it.

If Sirhan was drunk enough to be resting on a table and to have his memory go totally blank, it's a wonder he could pull off the assassination in the manner credited by the official version. His "intoxication" was of a different kind, mentally induced rather than physically.

Officers Travis White and Arthur Placencia rode with Sirhan after he was shoved into a police cruiser, barely escaping a crowd determined to tear him apart. The prisoner was taken to Rampart station, where Placencia conducted a standard examination of Sirhan's eyes with a flashlight to determine if the suspect's pupils were dilated, signaling the possible presence of drugs or alcohol. At the trial, Placencia was evasive about both performing the test and its results.

Under questioning by Sirhan's attorney, Grant Cooper, he responded, "Well, actually what I did, I shone a light in his face and I really didn't examine them [Sirhan's eyes]." When asked how Sirhan's pupils reacted, the officer said he couldn't recall. Asked if he shined the light in order to see if Sirhan was intoxicated, Placencia answered, "No, sir."

Cooper pressed him hard, and the policeman finally admitted, "The reason I checked them [the eyes] was because when I have been out in the field the more experienced officers check suspects' eyes to see if they were under the influence of drugs."

"Or alcohol?" asked Cooper.

"Yes, sir."

In a pre-trial interview with Ron Allen, one of the defense team's investigators, Placencia had stated that Sirhan's pupils were dilated. In court, when Cooper asked the results of the test – specifically, concerning Sirhan's pupils – Assistant District Attorney John Howard strenuously objected to the question and asked to approach the bench. Howard told the judge that Placencia had not been qualified to administer the test since he was only a rookie policeman. Howard further asserted that the flashlight test was performed later by a more experienced officer who compared the suspect's eyes to someone else's (as a control for the test), which Placencia had not done. Sirhan was normal, the prosecutor told the judge. Later, Officer White testified and confirmed that he properly administered the test a few minutes after arriving at the station. He found nothing abnormal.

If LAPD was truly interested in finding out whether Sirhan was drugged or drunk, they seemed to blow their best chances to do so, for the Rampart station where Sirhan was first taken had a special "Breathalyzer room" equipped with a machine to test alcohol levels. Sirhan was actually put in this room before being taken to an interrogation room,[26] but supposedly he was not tested.

Dr. Martin Schorr, a psychiatrist consulted by Sirhan's defense team, expressed a very skeptical view of the police's handling of the sobriety issue.[27] Schorr claimed to have heard a police tape on which one of the officers booking Sirhan said, "Here's another drunk."* The doctor asserted that Sirhan was very disoriented when brought into custody: "He didn't know who he was or why he was there. He was too drunk even to know where he was."

Dr. Schorr also harbored deep suspicion about the blood test administered to Sirhan by police. According to Schorr, the only result reported by the lab was that the suspect had tested negative for syphilis. Some error was allegedly made in testing or reporting whereby there was no data regarding drugs or alcohol. Schorr skeptically asserted to researcher Betsy Langman that he had never heard of such a gross error even in the most routine case.

In pursuing the possibility that Sirhan was intoxicated, defense investigator Ron Allen interviewed Sergeant William Jordan, one of Sirhan's primary interrogators who spent considerable time with him in the first few hours after his arrest. An audio tape of the interview, released among DA files in 1985, reveals that Allen was very jittery when he popped the big question. He coughed nervously

---

* There is no such reference on the released tapes but the earliest recording of Sirhan's handling at Rampart station starts in the middle of a conversation between him and a policeman. There is no way of telling how much conversation preceded this, or if the tape Dr. Schorr claims to have heard was destroyed by LAPD along with the other missing tapes and photos.

and rephrased the question: Had Sergeant Jordan been informed by Officers White or Placencia about the results of the flashlight test?

Just as he would do in court, Deputy DA John Howard intervened, telling Allen the question violated the ground rules for the interview. Since Jordan didn't perform the test himself, Howard asserted, he had no direct knowledge of it; he, therefore, should only be asked about those things of which he had direct knowledge.

After a conspicuously long silence Allen again rephrased his question: "Did you examine Sirhan's eyes?"

"Not specifically," Jordan answered, "no."

Jordan sat across the table from the suspect during the interrogation sessions and had plenty of chance to observe him close up. The officer told Allen that he did observe that Sirhan "wasn't using any drugs or alcohol or anything like that."

"Did you look at his eyes?" asked Allen. "Did you notice his pupils?"

"Not specifically," replied Jordan.

The defense team obviously had not heard the audio tapes of Sirhan's interrogations, occurring between his arrival at Rampart at around 12:45 a.m. and his 7:00 a.m. arraignment. Allen asked Jordan where the tapes were. The officer replied that they were "somewhere in Parker Center [police headquarters]," but he didn't know precisely where.

One of those tapes contains a comment made by Jordan that the defense surely would have been interested in questioning him about. In one of the later interviews, Sirhan complained that he was not dressed properly for his arraignment; the clothes given him didn't fit well. Sergeant Jordan observed, "You look very presentable compared to when I first saw you. You're clean; you're neat; *your eyes are clear* [emphasis added]."

The subject of his eyes was brought up by Sirhan himself in a pre-trial taped session with Dr. Seymour Pollack, the DA's psychiatric expert.

"The policeman, when he flashed the thing in my eyes, he said there was no tears."

"Say that again," says Pollack.

"You know, when I was riding in the car . . . flashlight in my eyes, and there were no tears."

"No tears!"

"No tears," repeats Sirhan.

"No tears." Pollack sounds puzzled.

"Yeah, you know that's a sign of alcohol in the system."

"I'll have to check," says Pollack. "I don't, I don't, I don't really know what the significance is . . . *No tears* . . . " he repeats, bewildered. "No tears. No tears."

Getting back to defense-investigator Ron Allen's attempts to find out from Sergeant Jordan if Sirhan appeared abnormal during his interrogation, Allen asked if Sirhan "spoke irrationally" or "mumbled." Jordan replied, "No, definitely not."

Allen inquired whether Sirhan's behavior changed during the course of the three interviews conducted in the early morning hours.

"Yes," said Jordan, "I would say there was a slight change."

"In what way?"

"During the initial interview he was more quiet. He didn't wanna talk. He was very restrictive with his words, very careful about saying anything. My third interview with him he would almost volunteer to talk about various things."

Jordan's statement is accurate and born out by the tapes, but it fails to describe how precipitous and multidimensional the change is – not just in the amount of conversation, but in Sirhan's general behavior.

In the very first available recording of Sirhan's interaction with police (at about 12:45 a.m., prior to the first interview) he is indeed reticent. More importantly, he is mumbling and talking very rapidly in a voice that is both hoarse and weak. The listener is struck most by the way he draws deep, erratic breaths while talking, gasping for air almost as if hyperventilating.

· Sirhan, who is nearly inaudible, asks for a sip of hot chocolate from a police officer's cup. When the policeman refuses, the prisoner kicks the cup out of his hands, spilling it on the floor.

During the first interview, conducted shortly after the kicking incident, Sirhan displays these same traits. The volume of his voice fluctuates between very low and considerably louder, but both levels are nearly incomprehensible to the listener because of the rapidity and mumbling nature of his speech. He breathes heavily between answers, as he refuses to reveal his name or make any statement. It would seem that the defense lawyers never had access to these tapes, because they would probably have introduced them as evidence that raised questions about Sirhan's state of mind.*

By the second interview, conducted at 3:15 a.m., Sirhan had undergone a remarkable transformation. As LAPD's *Summary Report* described, "He was relaxed, polite, composed" and "alertly responded" to questions.[28] "Officer Jordan was impressed with Sirhan's composure and relaxation. He appeared less upset to Jordan than individuals arrested for a traffic violation."[29]

What the *Report* inexplicably glosses over is that this was only true of the second and third interviews, not the first. In contrast to the first interview and to the interaction that preceded it, Sirhan talked more slowly, his voice stronger and louder. His words, no longer mumbled, were well articulated, and breathing was normal. The prisoner seemed quite cheery and deferential, even initiating philosophical discussions about law enforcement, with a sense of humor.

What caused the change? Since the first two tapes of Sirhan mumbling and gasping were made some time apart from one another and in different rooms with different law officers present, it does not seem likely that the prisoner's condition stemmed from a whack in the solar plexus by an overzealous policeman. He was apparently treated very well by police and never charged that he was physically mistreated. If you recall how he was described right after the assassination – as he stood smiling – just after the prolonged struggle with the men in the pantry, he seemed calmer and more placid than he did a half-hour to an hour later at the police station, where he was kicking drinks out of officers' hands. One explanation is that Sirhan was coming out of a deep hypnotic trance, an experience that caused

---

* The tapes of the first interview and the conversation that preceded it.

him to behave similarly when the defense psychiatrist, Dr. Diamond, was working with him prior to the trial.

Was Sirhan merely a drunk sobering up, as Schorr suspected? On the early tapes Sirhan sounds like a man overwhelmed with anxiety rather than one who is in a drunken stupor or haze. The police certainly did not ply him with caffeine between his first and second interviews, in order to rejuvenate him. At the start of the second interview, Sirhan got his first cup of coffee, which he sipped during the questioning. Jordan told Sirhan that it was only fair that he get a cup since the officers had already had two or three and he had had none.

Before the trial, when Dr. Diamond first hypnotized Sirhan in his cell, the session was traumatic for the prisoner. Author Kaiser described Sirhan's voice as high-pitched and punctuated by deep breaths. When Dr. Diamond slapped Sirhan's face and brought him out of the trance, he made "wheezing sounds."[30] Shortly thereafter, he started to shiver, complaining of the cold and hugging himself to keep warm.[31] The cell was reportedly quite warm (it was summer in California), except for Sirhan.

Another example of Sirhan's unexplained shivering occurred in the hours immediately following the shooting, when LAPD brought in the jail's medical examiner, Dr. Marcus Crahan, to check the prisoner. During the examination Sirhan began to shiver violently, embracing himself to keep warm.

"It's chilly," Sirhan mumbled.

"You're *cold*?" asked the doctor in surprise, because the room was comfortably warm.

"Not cold," said Sirhan.

"*Not* cold. What do you mean?"

"No comment," the prisoner responded. Sirhan may have reacted this way because he was coming out of a trance on both occasions.[32]

He could not program himself to forget or to block out of his mind certain responses or events, nor could he program himself to give false answers or a cover story.

Kaiser observed that during Dr. Diamond's hypnotic sessions, Sirhan seemed to have a mental block on key questions.[33] When Diamond asked him if he thought up the assassination entirely by himself, there was a five-second delay before he answered affirmatively. When asked if he was the only one involved, there was a three-second pause before he answered. Such delays in responding can be caused by the time it takes for the programming to be recalled and to take over the response – to kick in, as it were.

A sophisticated programmer could also build in disinformation or a cover story to conceal the origins of the programming. This was previously illustrated by one expert's claim that he could write himself out of the patient's mind and replace his presence with that of the subject's friend or relative. The authorities could have been predicted to discover that Sirhan was in a trance during the shooting and that he had had past experience with hypnosis. In order to conceal the fact that Sirhan had been hypno-programmed by an expert, his manipulator could have programmed him to practice self-hypnosis and to join the Rosicrucians, and to believe that these were the exclusive sources of his experience with hypnosis. Both Doctors Diamond and Simpson quickly discerned that Sirhan had been subjected to extensive hypnosis. Sirhan told Simpson, "The Rosicrucians taught me everything." Under hypnosis Sirhan told Diamond that the Rosicrucians and his mirror were the source of his previous experience. Were the Rosicrucians really responsible for Sirhan's status as a well-practiced hypnotic subject? A close examination reveals the answer is clearly no.

Before Diamond hypnotized Sirhan he asked him if he knew what hypnosis was. Sirhan replied that he'd never really studied much about it, but the Rosicrucians had mentioned a fellow named Mesmer.[34] In fact, neither the Rosicrucian literature nor the organization itself taught hypnosis or self-hypnosis or automatic writing – only mentalism, mysticism and positive thinking.[35] When Sirhan was asked under hypnosis who taught him automatic writing, he indicated the Rosicrucians by penning "AMORC [Ancient Mystical Order of the Rosicrucians]."[36]

Diamond first asked Sirhan about automatic writing when he was not under hypnosis. He didn't even understand the concept.[37] He said he had heard of it but mistakenly defined it as transferring words to a blank sheet of paper using mental telepathy. He was very interested in mental projection and transference but seemed not to comprehend the notion of using repetitive, subconscious writing to create or reinforce ideas.

If someone programmed in the Rosicrucian angle as a cover for robotizing Sirhan, it worked. The authorities eagerly accepted the cover as real, even though it made little sense.

Kaiser believed that Sirhan's automatic writing was spawned, at least in part, by an article in *Rosicrucian Digest* entitled "Write It Down." Kaiser's belief that there may also have been an additional source probably stemmed from his hypothesis that there was a shadowy programmer behind Sirhan. The prosecution, which rejected the latter idea (partly because it would make the crime a conspiracy that was not yet solved), seized upon the article as the source, partly because it could be used to imply premeditation regarding Sirhan's writing about RFK's death (even though he did not remember the assassination or substance of the writing).

At the trial, prosecutor Lynn Compton asked Sirhan if he had believed that if you write something down "enough times" and think about it hard enough, the goal will be accomplished (of course, given the paucity of RFK references in the notebook, Compton's assumption would lead us to believe that Sirhan was trying 20 times as hard to acquire money as he was to kill Senator Kennedy, because of the plethora of references to money).

Sirhan replied, "I don't know. You read that article, sir, in the *Rosicrucian Digest*, sir. That's the best explanation to it."

This "best explanation" still leaves Sirhan's mind a complete blank as to when, where and how he applied the article.

The article itself was hardly very instructive regarding what seemed to be going on when Sirhan's notebook was written, except that *both* involved writing. The *Digest* piece stressed the power of positive thinking reinforced by seeing the written word. Here are some excerpts from the text, which was read into the trial record:

> Plan to do something different, something exciting. But here's a word of advice: put it in writing. Put your plan, your goal, your idea in writing and see how it suddenly catches fire. See how it gains momentum by the simple process of writing it down.
>
> Writing it down brings it into focus, clarifies it, makes you pin down exactly what you wish to achieve.
>
> Try it: Pick a goal. Set a target date. Now start working to make it come true.
>
> Read that goal every morning when you get up and every night before you go to sleep.

Sirhan certainly failed to heed this advice. The article describes a very conscious process, not an unconscious one. Sirhan could not recall doing the writing, much less ever reading what he wrote. No doubt we are to believe that he decided to embellish the Rosicrucians' prescription by adding self-hypnosis and automatic writing, neither of which he was ever familiar with.

Sirhan had precious little contact with his alleged mystical mentors of self-induced mind control. Other than mailings, his interaction consisted of attending a single Rosicrucian meeting on May 28, 1968. He had paid 20 dollars to join in March (after allegedly seeing an ad in the newspaper) but was never curious about checking out the organization until two months later.

According to FBI interviews with people who had been at the meeting he attended, he volunteered from the audience to participate in one of the "experiments" in sensory perception. The "tactile experience experiment" involved the "Lodge Master," a Mr. Livingston, who blindfolded Sirhan and touched various parts of his body with different objects to see if he could identify the object doing the touching.

Prior to the meeting, Sirhan introduced himself to Livingston and told him he wanted to chat with him afterward. When the event broke up at about 9:00 p.m., the Lodge Master saw Sirhan standing alone browsing through some literature. When Livingston finished talking with someone else and looked for Sirhan, he was gone – never to be seen again until his picture appeared in the news.

Despite this meager contact, Sirhan seemed to have developed some sort of bond with this organization, whose methods about "writing it down" he did not follow and with whose members he could not take time to talk. Sirhan asked Kaiser if the defense investigator had found anything in police reports concerning the Rosicrucians. Kaiser replied that there was a small amount about him attending one meeting. Sirhan became markedly upset and insisted that this not be brought up at the trial.[38]

Kaiser told him that his lawyers had not decided on the meeting's significance yet.

Kaiser observed that nothing sinister seemed to have gone on at the Rosicrucians' meeting, as if wondering what Sirhan was so worried about. Kaiser later suggested to Sirhan that because his notebook was partly inspired by the Rosicrucian article, the organization was distantly involved in the assassination.[39]

Sirhan nearly came unglued: "Yeah, but I don't want – oh, shit – I don't want to put any blame on them in that way, oh, hell, no. No, shit, no. Hell, no."

It was almost as if Sirhan was trying to protect friends, which the Rosicrucians were not, or accomplices, although he had no notion of his own role much less someone else's. Yet he would also claim that the Rosicrucians taught him everything he knew about trancing and writing. One explanation for these almost schizophrenic responses – not wanting them involved but involving them by virtue of his own statements, while at the same time not being able to provide any specifics of their linkage – is that Sirhan was responding to two post-hypnotic suggestions: that AMORC (Ancient Mystical Order of the Rosicrucians) taught him and that the organization must be protected.

The authorities chose to believe that Sirhan was being evasive or deceptive about precisely how the Rosicrucians influenced him to scribble and "space out." In reality, he simply didn't know. And why should he, since AMORC did not teach what he had done? Furthermore, he didn't remember how, when or why he had done it. There is a more logical explanation of how AMORC and Sirhan ended up linked to hypnosis and automatic writing (when neither practiced it previously or knew about it): Someone familiar with these techniques – and with ancient mystical orders (such as the Rosicrucians) and Sirhan – linked them all together in Sirhan's mind, as a cover for creating a robot assassin with no recollection of who gave the orders.

Sophisticated robot-like programming could also have effectively used Sirhan as the best propagandist for the lone-gun theory. "You can program basic messages," said Dr. Eduard Simpson, "and they will affect the rest of your thoughts because they are basic guidelines for thinking."

Dr. Martin Schorr agreed that if Sirhan underwent skilled programming he would become highly defensive concerning any questions or evidence that challenged whatever the programmers wanted people to believe. In Sirhan's case, it would appear that he took great pains to back up his lone-assassin status, even when evidence to the contrary might have helped him in court.[40] Sirhan steadfastly insisted that no one manipulated him; he refused to plead insanity; and he accepted a convenient political motive. He ended up being slated for the gas chamber rather than exploring the possibility that someone may have tampered with his mind.

It is also unbelievable that Sirhan could not remember anything about planning to kill Kennedy, preparing for it, or executing the attempt. Yet the spaced-out assailant seems to have undertaken a series of minor preparations, as if he (or someone else) wanted to assure that there would be a good case against him or, at least, assure that the motive for his attack was clearly understood by the authorities (even if he himself could not comprehend it). The perpetrator who cannot recall how he concealed the gun or that he was about to shoot Kennedy had taken the trouble to carry no wallet or identification. To some this suggested that he knew he would be captured at the crime scene and wanted to temporarily confound the authorities, which he did for several key hours (right after the assassination, when the trail of co-conspirators would have been hot) by refusing to reveal his identity.

When captured, he had on his person a series of little artifacts that, taken together, presented a better picture of the ostensible motive and planning than Sirhan's whitewashed psyche could provide. He carried a large amount of cash: four $100 bills, one five, four ones. Was this getaway money, just in case he somehow managed to escape? This is precisely how some of the official investigators interpreted the presence of the cash, and to them it was further evidence of premeditation.

In his pocket was a column, clipped from a May 26 Pasadena newspaper, entitled "Paradoxical Bob." The piece served as an advertisement for what would be Sirhan's alleged motive: It chided Kennedy for opposing the Vietnam War while supporting Israel (although it did not mention the jet bombers for Israel). Sirhan also carried a Kennedy campaign song sheet and a five-by-five-inch clipping of a newspaper ad inviting the friends of Robert Kennedy to attend a rally at the Ambassador on June 2. Sirhan had gone there. This was perceived by many as evidence of premeditated stalking of Kennedy.

In addition, Sirhan had a ballistics exhibit: two unspent .22s and the copper-jacketed casing from a spent slug. Was he planning to reload (this would not explain the purpose of his carrying the spent shell), or was this a convenient sample from the same batch of ammunition as the bullets fired by Sirhan at the crime scene, programmed in by someone other than Sirhan, in order to provide a clearer trail of ballistics evidence once he was caught?

Other odd artifacts include two envelopes found by Pasadena police during a search of the Sirhan family home. Although no search warrant had been obtained, the envelopes were admitted as evidence at the trial. One had the return address of "U.S Treasury Department" and was supposedly found in a dressing- table drawer in Sirhan's room. On it, apparently in Sirhan's handwriting, was the inscription "RFK must be disposed of like his brother." A second envelope (with the return address of the Argonaut Insurance Company) was found in a trash can outside the house. It had a reference to killing RFK that was akin to the repetitive ramblings of the notebook: "RFK must be disposed of DDD disposed of disposed disposed of properly Robert Fitzgerald [*sic*; really Francis] Kennedy must soon die die die die die die die die die die."

The incongruity here is that the other two references to killing Kennedy contained in the notebook were in the repetitive scrawling of automatic writing, and they filled two pages. They were written while he was in a trance. The first envelope is not similarly scrawled and there is only one sentence. Was this written while Sirhan was not hypnotized? Did he want to leave a political message? Whatever the origin of the envelopes, Sirhan claimed to be as unfamiliar with them as with the notebook. The reader will recall that, at his trial, he said he could not recall writing the envelope he was shown, although he agreed that it was in his handwriting.

This little group of exhibits – a supply of cash, no identification, extra bullets, political and scheduling information about Kennedy – seemed to be the product of premeditation and forethought, if in fact this was assembled by Sirhan. Was all this really part of Sirhan's plan – one that did not manifest itself in the actual carrying out of the assault, one that Sirhan does not remember? Were these artifacts a reflection of his latent desire to be an Arab hero, or to get caught; or were they someone else's sophisticated plan and idea of how to create a patsy?

In his book *The Search for the "Manchurian Candidate,"* John Marks quotes an unidentified, veteran CIA researcher as saying that it would be much easier to create a "patsy" than a programmed robot assassin. The patsy could be programmed to perform a series of tasks or engage in a series of incidents that, as Marks described it, "will make the authorities think the patsy committed a particular crime." Hypnosis expert Milton Kline, who served as an unpaid consultant to CIA researchers, estimated that he could create a patsy in three months.[41] Sirhan Sirhan may have been a robot gunman and a patsy all in one.

Doctors Diamond and Pollack could not restore Sirhan's memory. Even so, Sirhan still could be deprogrammed. The psychic barriers and disinformation could be penetrated, and his memory could be restored.

In 1987, I re-contacted Dr. Herbert Spiegal, with whom I had discussed programming a year earlier, and queried him about deprogramming. He asserted that deprogramming was definitely possible, partly because Sirhan is such an excellent subject. If an expert could establish a good rapport with him, Spiegal believes that deprogramming "might be done in a few days."

Spiegal said that in 1980 he was actually approached by Sirhan's lawyers about the possibility of using hypnosis to restore the prisoner's memory. According to Spiegal, the discussion terminated when he could not guarantee what might tumble out if Sirhan's mind were unlocked. The lawyers were put off by the prospect that something inimical to their client's prospects for parole might turn up. Spiegal remains ready to work with Sirhan, but has not been asked.

Dr. Spiegal may be somewhat overly optimistic about the ease with which he could penetrate the psychological fortress erected by a master programmer. On the other hand, the experts I talked with agree that no programming is so perfect as to be beyond penetration by a skilled prober. It would be a complicated battle for the truth and for Sirhan's mind. If successful, it could provide solid clues to unraveling the conspiracy behind the assassination of Robert F. Kennedy.

Chapter 12

HOLLYWOOD
HYP

BETSY LANGMAN (researcher): *"Do you think Sirhan used self-hypnosis?"*

DR. WILLIAM JOSEPH BRYAN, JR. (CIA-linked hypnosis expert): *"I'm not going to comment on that case, because I didn't hypnotize him."*

– From a 1974 interview

The 1966 accident that ended Sirhan's career plans (his fall from a horse) also sent him searching for medical and mental help. But where, and from whom? His mentalist meanderings were broad enough to have put him in the clutches of a skilled programmer. In fact, his medical and mentalist contacts were not thoroughly traced by the investigative agencies.

One heavily deleted FBI report, unusual in that it deletes the name of the interviewee, states, "[deleted] advised that Sirhan had indicated that he was studying mysticism with an individual named Paul, who was unknown to [deleted]." The report goes on to indicate that "subsequent investigation determined that [name deleted] was an associate of Sirhan and this associate was interviewed 7/10/68. He should be reinterviewed to determine if he studied mysticism with Sirhan.''

A follow-up memo tells us that Sirhan's acquaintance Paul Khoury ''denied studying mentalism with him.'' The suggested ''leads'' for further investigation are to ''contact cooperative family members for possible identification [of Paul]'' and to ''review AMORC [the Ancient Mystical Order of the Rosicrucians] for any Pauls.'' There no indication in available documents that Paul was ever identified.

In the months after his accident, Sirhan consulted numerous medical doctors, mostly opthalmologists and neurologists. He complained of pain and muscular difficulty in his left eye. Seeing at least nine (known to us) physicians, his medical odyssey could have inadvertently landed him in the web of mind-control research, just as could his mystical odyssey.

I attempted to contact these doctors to find out if any of them referred Sirhan to a psychiatrist or hypnotherapist or if they knew of his receiving any such treatment. Seven physicians either could not be located or refused to respond, citing patient confidentiality. The others said no to both questions.

After his fall from the horse, Sirhan's behavior changed noticeably. The young man who had generally seemed polite and talkative was neither. Dr. Milton A. Miller told the FBI that he treated Sirhan on four occasions two months after the accident. He described the patient as ''angry and nervous.'' He concluded that Sirhan was a ''malingerer'' and refused to certify his alleged injuries as worthy of compensation by the insurance company. Miller then referred him to another doctor in Pasadena. Miller claims that the irate patient telephoned him and threatened to ''get him,'' in some unspecified manner, if he did not certify the injuries. The doctor refused.

Sirhan's brother Sharif told LAPD that Sirhan changed gradually but markedly after the accident.[1] He became withdrawn and irritable; he no longer listened when family members tried to engage him in conversation. Sharif discussed the problem with his mother, who also agreed something was wrong. When Sharif suggested

Sirhan should see a doctor, Mary Sirhan reportedly responded that he was already seeing one.

It was also during this period of medical-mystical wandering that Sirhan did something that should have given investigators considerable pause: He dropped out of sight just six months before the assassination. Beginning in January of 1968, he left the family home in Pasadena for nearly three months. An FBI report states that a neighbor described Mary Sirhan as having been "extremely worried" because she "did not know his whereabouts for quite some time." LAPD's detailed reconstruction of Sirhan's life, from birth to the assassination, was diagrammed in an eleven-page, month-by-month flow chart. It reveals only that Sirhan worked at a Pasadena health-food store during this time, but gives no specific listings of other contacts or involvements as it does at the end of this three-month period. Christian and Turner in *The Assassination of Robert F. Kennedy* claim to have written confirmation, provided in 1975 by an LAPD officer who insisted on anonymity, that there was indeed a "three-month gap" in LAPD's tracing of Sirhan's activities.[2]

Whatever Sirhan was up to; whomever he was consulting or getting advice from; whoever may have been working with – or on – his mind, his interest in mentalism had grown. He began collecting relevant books and soon joined the Rosicrucians.

In 1978, Christian and Turner implied that Sirhan's programmer might have been the late Dr. William Joseph Bryan, Jr., a bizarre figure in government-sponsored mind-control research. By all indications, Bryan is indeed a likely choice to have created a Manchurian Candidate. (Drawing upon my own investigation and upon files provided by two journalists who have developed additional information on the search for the programmed robot assassin and its links to the RFK case, this chapter will present new data on Dr. Bryan and will probe beyond Christian and Turner's original suspicions, into the strange and secretive world of the intelligence community's hypno-headhunters.)

Bill Bryan, Jr., was a hypnosis-superstar. His friends and associates included some of the nation's most prominent lawyers, among them F. Lee Bailey of Boston, who consulted Bryan on the Boston Strangler case and Los Angeles attorney Henry Rothblatt, who defended the Cubans charged in the Watergate break-in. Bryan's applications of hypnosis to criminology were overtly solicited by a variety of agencies, including LAPD. His professional stature was exceeded only by his ego – and his weight. Tipping the scales at close to four hundred pounds, the obese and bearded specialist in "sex therapy," criminology and mind control, unhesitatingly billed himself as "probably the leading expert in the world." He once announced on a Los Angeles radio show that he was the "chief of all medical survival training for the United States Air Force, which meant the brainwashing section."[3]

Christian and Turner's suspicion that Bryan programmed Sirhan stemmed from some intriguing tidbits of circumstantial data-data, which has since been expanded by the work of other investigators. Two prostitutes who claimed to have serviced Bryan regularly told Christian that Bryan indulged his enormous ego by bragging about his most famous cases, including those of Albert Di Salvo (the Boston Strangler) and Sirhan Sirhan. The women thought nothing about the mention of Sirhan because they understood that Bryan had been called in by law-enforcement authorities to hypnotize some infamous criminals.[4]

Christian and Turner also asserted that within hours of the shooting, before Sirhan's identity was known, Bryan made an interesting comment while being interviewed on KABC radio in Los Angeles by host Ray Briem. The show was not about the assault on Senator Kennedy, but when the subject briefly came up Bryan offhandedly opined that the assailant may have been acting under "post-hypnotic suggestion."[5]

In 1974, researcher Betsy Langman interviewed Bryan in his Sunset Strip office. She found his boundless ego still intact. Reaffirming his status as the world's leading expert on hypnosis, he boasted – or warned – "I can hypnotize everybody in this office in five minutes." He recounted his work with the Boston Strangler and the Hollywood Strangler.

When Langman casually asked him if he thought Sirhan had used self-hypnosis, his mood changed abruptly. "I'm not going to comment on that case," said Bryan, "because I didn't hypnotize him." Langman explained that she was only soliciting his opinion. He immediately terminated the interview and stormed out of his office.

The truth about his possible involvement with the Kennedy case cannot come from Bryan himself. He was found dead in 1976 in his room at the Riviera Hotel in Las Vegas, apparently from natural causes. Hollywood reporter Greg Roberts queried Bryan about the Sirhan matter just before his death. Bryan forcefully denied involvement. Roberts claimed to know from Congressional sources that Bryan's name had been given to the House Select Committee on Assassinations, as a key witness in the RFK case.[6]

Like the New York stage hypnotist who first taught CIA official Morse Allen the wonders of hypnosis, Bryan made liberal use of his craft for sexual exploitation. He once told a *Playboy* interviewer that he liked getting to know people at a "deep emotional level. One way of getting to know people is through intercourse." Unfortunately, for some of Bryan's female patients, the hypnosis prevented them from knowing what was happening while Bryan was getting to know them, under the guise of curing their "sexual disorders." In 1969, the California Board of Medical Examiners found him guilty of sexually molesting women patients whom he had hypnotized. He was put on probation for five years.

One hypnosis expert who knew Bryan well, and despised him, told journalist Martin A. Lee that Bryan's workshops on sex and hypnosis, which he gave around the country, went beyond the professional norm: "It's better to call them something else. I give a lecture on sex and hypnosis in my classes, but the lecture I give on 'sex and hypnosis' is on the sexual aspects of hypnosis. His would have been better named, as blunt as it sounds, fornication and hypnosis. His article [interview] appeared in *Playboy*; I figured out once that he would have to have had sex 12 times a day if it [his frequency of intercourse] were true, and we do have other things to do." Of Bryan's expertise, he said, "I'll give the enemy his just credit. I was dealing with a misguided genius and I knew it. He's a very intriguing person. If there's anything ordinary about him I don't know what it is."

"In what sense 'misguided'?" asked Lee.

"So damn sexually motivated that nothing else seemed to be in the offing when he was talking."

Regarding Bryan's secretaries, the same source cynically observed, "They were receptionists, and bed partners, or they didn't stay. Bryan was quite a hunk of man physically. He was 386 pounds. There were some girls who just didn't dig fat; they didn't last long."

Another Los Angeles practitioner who knew Bryan, whom we shall give the pseudonym Dr. Ellard, said that he was interested in more than sex.

"He's connected to everything . . . William Bryan is connected to anything you can name – legally, illegally. He specializes in anything that makes money." Ellard then referred to Bryan's seducing his patients. "He's not afraid of anything."

Still, Bryan had impressed some of the country's top lawyers. L.A. Attorney Henry Rothblatt sang Bryan's professional praises in a 1974 interview with researcher Betsy Langman. He described him as "the most brilliant man in the field of hypnotism," as well as the "most knowledgeable and imaginative." Rothblatt said Bryan "lives, thinks, breathes and dreams this [hypnosis]. There is nothing he hasn't experimented with." The attorney had used Bryan as an expert consultant on one case and indicated to Langman that if Sirhan's subsequent lawyers wanted to probe Sirhan's mind, Bill Bryan would be the man for the job. Unknown to Rothblatt, Bryan might then have been in the position of checking his own work, if not reinforcing it.

Boston superlawyer F. Lee Bailey, in his book *The Defense Never Rests*,[7] described how he first met Bryan in 1961 at a hypnosis seminar for trial lawyers put on by Bryan and San Francisco attorney Melvin Belli. Bryan wowed the audience by hypnotizing three lawyers, including Bailey. He instructed the trio to hold their right arms outstretched as he droned on about the arms feeling rigid, stiff, "very numb." The subjects felt their arms being lightly rubbed but were getting impatient waiting for something interesting to happen. They were not aware that they were in a deep trance. When Bryan brought them out they were horrified to find hypodermic needles dangling from their outstretched hands, stuck into their flesh.

Bryan announced to the assembly of attorneys that they had just witnessed a demonstration of hypnosis as anesthesia. He pointed out that there was no blood emanating from the punctures. Hypnosis could reduce bleeding during surgery. He then instructed his subjects, "As I speak you will observe a slight drop of blood commence in response to my suggestion." The three attorneys bled on cue.

Bryan's work for Bailey included using hypnosis to bring out the beast in two accused murderers. He studied the background of Harvey Bush, the so-called Hollywood Strangler who had killed three elderly women.[8] Bryan decided that Bush's hatred for his mother had motivated the killings. Bush was hypnotized in his cell, and Bryan cast Bush's attorney in the role of the prisoner's mother. The hypnotic psychodrama succeeded in getting the tranced prisoner to let out a scream and violently attack his attorney. According to F. Lee Bailey, "If Bryan hadn't been there to grab Bush and bring him out of his trance, Matthews [the attorney] might have been victim number four."

Similarly, Bryan hypnotized Albert DiSalvo, the Boston Strangler. The doctor repeated over and over to him the hypothesis that he had been symbolically murdering his daughter who had diverted his wife's affection from him. Bryan activated DiSalvo's murderous impulse: The prisoner's hands lurched up from his lap and grabbed for Bryan's throat. The hefty therapist deflected the thrust and slammed DiSalvo into the wall. Simultaneously, he put his hands on the attacker's shoulders and forcefully yelled, "Sleep!" The prisoner relaxed.

In 1966, Bryan got Bailey involved in another celebrated case.

According to Bailey, Bryan telephoned him and asked him to take the case of Dr. Carl Coppolino, who was about to be charged with the two separate murders of his first wife and his mistress's husband. Bryan told Bailey, "I haven't known Carl for a long time, but I know him well enough to be convinced he's no killer."[9] Coppolino, a 34-year-old anesthesiologist forced into early retirement by a heart attack, was, as Bailey described it, "an expert hypnotist." His former mistress, Marjorie Farber, claimed that Coppolino had used his powers of mesmerization to become intimate with her and then to manipulate her into helping him to kill her husband.

According to Bailey, Bryan pitched in by assisting in the selection of jurors for the New Jersey trial, by "interpreting unarticulated response[s], or what it has become voguish to call body language." Mrs. Farber's contention that she was tranced into sex and mayhem was refuted by the testimony of Drs. Leo Wollman and James A. Brussel. Wollman stated that it was impossible to get a hypnotic subject to perform an act "which they felt they are morally unable to do." Brussel opined that no amount of hypnosis could cause a person to commit a criminal act "if he or she did not want to commit it without hypnosis . . ." If Bryan was watching, it must have been very difficult for him to keep a straight face or to refrain from jumping up and performing a little experiment to show how powerful his manipulative skills were.

Did Bryan participate in the search for the Manchurian candidate? One colleague who knew him well, whom we shall call Gilbert Marston, said that Bryan flatly announced to him that he worked for the CIA. Marston also recalled another startling manifestation of Bryan's compulsion to talk about his involvements: He asserted that the authorities summoned him to hypnotize Sirhan. "It was actually, I believe, conducted in a prison cell," said Marston. "That's what I got [from Bryan]." There is absolutely no evidence in official records to suggest that Bryan worked on Sirhan *after* the assassination.

Marston also recalled hearing through the professional grapevine that Bryan was the technical consultant for the film *The Manchurian Candidate*. It seems very likely that Bryan lent his expertise to more than the fictional version. It is difficult to imagine that the MK ULTRA* crowd, .. assembling its cadre of stage hypnotists, clinicians and ivory-tower experts, could have failed to recruit a man who could make subjects bleed, attempt to kill and submit to sex. This was precisely the kind of manipulation that so titillated the Agency spooks. With Bryan's insatiable appetite for power, intrigue and action, it seems unlikely, given his compulsive self-promotion, that he would have sat out the CIA's mind wars.

Christian and Turner reported that they asked Sirhan about the DiSalvo reference in his notebook: "God help me, please help me. Salvo Di De Salvo Die S Salvo." He replied that it was entirely foreign to him.[10] The authors were unaware that his dissociation from the name was also captured on an audio tape of a conversation in Sirhan's cell. Within hours after the shooting, the prisoner was engaging in idle chatter with his jailer, a Mr. Foster. Sirhan's notebook, of which he had no recollection, had not yet been discovered by authorities, much less analyzed.

Foster told Sirhan of a book he was reading: "It's about the Boston Strangler."

"Oh, oh," Sirhan said evenly.

As Foster described the grisly murders and the *modus operandi,* Sirhan expressed interest: "Oh, a pattern?"

He wondered aloud why someone would sexually molest and kill elderly ladies. Foster explained that it had something to do with the killer's mother.

Then Sirhan thought he recalled the "story": The police did not believe the killer's confession and the real killer remained free.

"No," said Foster. "The guy's last name is DiSalvo."

"Yeah," said Sirhan in a flat tone.

"See, this is a true story," Foster corrected.

Sirhan now thought he remembered this real-life case: "This was just recently wasn't it? They tracked him in the snow."

* The CIA's code name for its mind-control research project.

Foster replied that he didn't know anything about tracking in the snow, but this case "was back in '63, '62 or '63."

"Oh, no, no, no," said Sirhan. "This was, like, last . . . nearly a year."

If Bryan's enormous ego compelled him to talk about having hypnotized Sirhan – an inherently risky boast – it is not unthinkable that the evil genius compulsively left his calling card in Sirhan's mind, like a crime-scene trademark left behind by some cat burglars or serial murderers.

The reader will recall the earlier-described case of Candy Jones, the attractive model who told of being a hypno-programmed courier for the CIA. The best evidence is that her recruiter and primary programmer, who also programmed himself into the role of her lover, was not Bryan but one of his late associates. This author has learned, from a knowledgeable and reliable confidential source, that during her deprogramming Miss Jones recalled under hypnosis that her programmer talked about a racetrack in California and "bragged" about hypnotizing Sirhan. It is possible that her main programmer was sharing her case, or even her sexual exploitation, with Bryan.

Among the elite group of hypnosis experts whose knowledge would have been invaluable to the CIA's research was a doctor I'll refer to as Jonathan Reisner.* In a 1987 interview I conducted with him, Reisner said he had known Bryan "very well." "He was brilliant," said Reisner, "but a discredit to the profession – too flamboyant, a genius but a grandstander." Reisner denied working with Bryan.

Two sources who knew both men claim that they jointly conducted workshops on sex and hypnosis. Both men had an interest in the links between mystical orders and hypnosis, as well as in the uses of auto-hypnosis. Bryan wrote about ancient Egyptian "sleep temples." The group that Sirhan joined, the Ancient Mystical Order of the Rosicrucians, traced its origins to "mystery schools or secret schools" of learning established in Egypt in 1500 B.C. The group's San Jose, California, headquarters includes an ancient Egyptian museum.[11]

* A pseudonym provided by the author.

Bryan authored a book entitled *Religious Aspects of Hypnosis,* an excerpt of which reads: "The prophets produced their visions by a form of auto-hypnosis and, in the Middle Ages, most of the prophets who heard the voice of God actually disassociated their own voices and heard themselves. . . . Many elements of hypnosis remain in religion today . . . The chanting testimonials, the flickering candles, and the cross as a fixation point for our vision."

Returning to Sirhan's notebook, it may well be true that it does provide clues about this crime, but in a very different manner than the authorities imagined. One page contains numerous references to "God" and a cross was drawn. In one passage Sirhan seems to be describing mass mentalism practiced by religious cults or political movements: "The importance of will power of the many [illegible] may be sent so that it can be taken up by thousands. A proof of this is the various suicide and murder epidemics."

The mixing of drugs and hypnosis was one avenue of CIA research. The most strangely written, wildly scribbled page in the notebook contains very few words. It is the least substantive page, filled with extensive doodling instead of words. But the word "drugs" is written four times.

Electric shock was another favored stimulus of CIA headhunters. One entry – written upside down, as if the notebook were turned around exclusively to write this – says, "elec. equip. this seems to be the right amount of preponderance."

The notebook also contains some rather odd third-person references. Bryan had written about getting the subject to "depersonalize" in order to advance "therapy":

"Sirhan Sirhan has been determined" . . . "You will not be required to do anything that may require any great or ungreat stipulation against the Arab People" . . . "is paid to say, is paid to say, say" . . . "Arab you, Arab you" . . . "Sirhan heard the order of" . . . "Documentations prepared by Sirhan Sirhan."

Sirhan also wrote the phrase "heat is seldom," which could relate to the chills he experienced when coming out of a deep hypnotic trance – within hours after the assassination and later when Dr. Diamond hypnotized him.

Harold Tabor* lived at Dr. Reisner's Hollywood home for an extended period during the early 1960s. In 1987, Tabor told me that Reisner had hung in his office at that time a federal license to dispense LSD. In fact, LSD was outlawed during this period and only federally licensed practitioners could dispense it. The Food and Drug Administration wanted to restrict use but not inhibit "legitimate research." Permission was supposedly granted only to those researchers exhibiting "scientific integrity and moral and ethical responsibility."[12] Such regulation aside, the record clearly reveals that the CIA was unwittingly dispensing acid trips under conditions that lacked both scientific and ethical integrity.

Both Bryan and Reisner believed that the mesmerization of an audience by a political speaker was a form of hypnosis. Reisner explained this to me during lunch in a fashionable Hollywood restaurant. After touting Hitler as the greatest mass hypnotist in history, he proceeded – much to my embarrassment – to deliver three "*Sieg Heil*s!", complete with arm salute, uttered at a level considerably above normal conversation but short of a yell. Facing the bar, I did not look back to see how many patrons were annoyed or appalled by the outburst.

One L.A. hypno-clinician who knew Bryan told Martin A. Lee of an incident that occurred when the two hypnotists made a joint television appearance to discuss the Sharon Tate murder case: "There was one point there where he's talking about Hitler, and he says '*Sieg Heil!*' about seven times."

Then there is the process of automatic writing under hypnosis. Reisner explained to me that the patient becomes disassociated from his writing hand, which may produce different substantive responses than the patient would give verbally. Reisner insisted that the patient would easily recognize what he had written. But he neglected to add the caveat that this is only true if you are not programmed to forget. Reisner boasted he could write himself out of the patient's memory by adopting the role of a lover, relative or close friend, through execution of a maneuver (which he did

* A pseudonym provided by the author.

210

not explain) that would render the patient "amnesic" regarding the hypnotist.

One hypno-expert who knew both Bryan and Reisner was shown examples of the released CIA documents on hypnosis from the MK ULTRA file. His first comment after perusing the exhibits was that it read like a textbook written by Jonathan Reisner. But Reisner flatly denied to me any connection with CIA research.

This same source said that while Bryan was definitely CIA, Reisner "could very well have been." The source referred to a gap in Reisner's career, which he speculated might have been spent in intensive federal service.

Harold Tabor described Reisner's home as "possessing a commune-like atmosphere centering around drugs and hypnosis. Reisner was always into digging up exotic people," said Tabor. "It was a pretty wide-open place . . . A lot of people would come and go," including foreign students from nearby universities.

My own 1987 encounter with Reisner found him to be a rather strange character whose vast expertise was exceeded only by his enormous ego. He agreed to talk with me if I would meet him in the waiting room of a medical doctor with whom he supposedly had an important appointment half an hour later. When I approached him in the waiting room and introduced myself, he said, "Let's go," and walked out of the office without talking to the receptionist.

He had me drive him to an elegant restaurant in Hollywood. On the way he droned on about hypnosis like an audio-taped textbook. Hypnosis had gotten a bad rap from the press and public, he contended: It is not a manipulative, Svengali-like craft.

As I drove and he filibustered, he fixed his large, piercing, blue eyes on me. He touched my temple as if feeling for a pulse. "Touching helps relax," he said. In retrospect, this apparently general discussion was much more: Reisner was sizing me up as a subject.

He kept reiterating that the power of hypnosis was derived from the subject's willingness to participate, not the hypnotist's power to control. I found this more than a bit disingenuous coming from the man who could fix it so patients didn't even know he had worked on them.

During the luncheon discussion, Reisner was extremely guarded. In response to my question about the possibility of programmed robot assassins, he pompously asserted that the notion was "preposterous." "It can't be done." He then elaborated the standard arguments ("You can't force people to do things against their will," etc.).

Bill Bryan, Jr., had claimed publicly that he was the technical advisor for the film *The Manchurian Candidate*.[13] One of his professional peers who knew him well was told this by Bryan himself. Now Reisner made the claim about an advisory role, while disclaiming any association with Bryan and after having stated 20 minutes earlier that the idea of a programmed assassin was preposterous.

I looked across the table at him. "Oh, really?"

"Well," said the doctor, realizing his inconsistency, "I advised . . . it was impossible."

Changing the subject, I aked, "Did LAPD ask you to consult on the Sirhan case? There were hypnosis experts on both sides [defense and prosecution] and some fascinating dimensions."

"No," he replied flatly, showing no reaction.

"Did Bryan work on Sirhan?"

"I don't know."

Reisner disclaimed any knowledge of the hypnosis angle of the Sirhan case. After I described Diamond's and Pollack's efforts to probe Sirhan's failed memory by using hypnosis, Reisner stated evenly and declaratively, "They didn't get anything." It was Reisner himself who, with no prompting, brought up a subject I was anxious to ask him about.

"Ever read *The Control of Candy Jones*?" he asked.

"Yes."

He then delivered a five-minute mini-lecture on why the story was fictitious: It is impossible to program people in the manner claimed by Miss Jones.

We finished lunch and Reisner suggested we talk more at his office. We drove to his spacious and richly furnished headquarters. After making a phone call, he suggested we go outside and look for his secretary who was taking a walk. Once outside, he suggested we sit in the back seat of his new BMW, parked on the street, because there was an article he wanted to show me. Making no attempt to look for his secretary, the doctor led me into the back seat. It was a hot June afternoon with the temperature near 90°. The bright California sun had heated the inside of the vehicle to the level of a sauna. We cracked open the windows and doors and began to talk.

Reisner started lecturing again, as if a cassette inside his head had been tweaked on by an unseen hand. The clinical wonders of hypnosis washed over me, as did the drenching perspiration.

Finally his secretary showed up. An attractive woman some 20 years his junior, she introduced herself as she stood outside the car. She suggested that Reisner and I retire to his air-conditioned office to finish our talk.

"It's quiet in the car," Reisner replied tersely. "We like it here."

When she departed, Reisner made his move. He asked me for piece of paper so he could diagram the "hypno-feedback loop of the brain." Holding the paper two feet in front of my face, he drew a series of connecting circles and squares that was supposed to represent a "brain synapse."

As he drew, his voice became repetitive and droning: "The input goes around and around." He punctuated the mesmerizing doodling with very pronounced eye contact, locking his eyes to mine. "Do you understand the diagram . . . Look at the diagram."

By now the "diagram" was starting to look like a steam-bath version of Sirhan's weird doodling. This reminded me of the danger of the situation and my defense mechanisms kicked in. I couldn't believe he was actually trying to hypnotize me!

"Hear the sound of the traffic," he intoned like the voice of God. "It's not disturbing; it's quiet. It helps us concentrate."

I thought of how disruptive the traffic was. I refused eye contact with Dr. Strangetrance. I looked away from the diagram and began to concentrate very heavily on which restaurant I'd choose for dinner. I made it away from him.

Of course, given what has already been said about Reisner's ability to cloak his role as hypnotist, and his probable ability to program people to forget, the reader will have to take my word that I escaped. Hopefully, this book serves as testimony to that fact. Otherwise, I probably would have immediately changed projects and written *The Wonders of Hypnotherapy: The Incredible Story of the Genius of Dr. Jonathan Reisner.*

We were both tired from the heat and the mental jujitsu. Hoping his guard might be lowered I again brought up the subject of Candy Jones, in a general non-threatening manner. Reisner's response was indeed interesting.

"There was a real problem with that book," he said, staring through the windshield, his eyes half closed. "I haven't told too many people about it. There was supposed to be a doctor described in that book and, except that he was supposed to be in northern California, people could have thought it was me. I told the publishers that; I threatened to sue. You see, the problem was that I dated Candy a couple of times way back . . . when she was a model."

If you will now recall Miss Jones's remembrance that her programmer, now deceased, mentioned a racetrack and bragged about hypnotizing Sirhan. Reisner has denied association with either Bryan or Jones's programmer. This would render his association with Miss Jones a coincidence of major proportion.

The real proof that Reisner had not captured my mind was that he became rather insistent about a follow-up chat. He wanted it to take place at his estate in the San Gabriel Mountains. There, said Reisner, I could have access to his vast files on hypnosis. I politely declined, not wanting to press my luck at being tranced or tripped-out on some hallucinogen.

The smoking gun of Sirhan's hypno-programming does not lie in strictly kept medical files because the secretive files on CIA mind-control subjects are either destroyed, doctored or withheld in perpetuity. It is not likely that anyone involved would ever admit it, because of the legal-professional consequences and, perhaps, the reprisals for violating the oath of secrecy. If the egomaniacal loose-lipped Bryan left behind papers or a diary, they have never surfaced nor are they likely to. The Kennedy case aside, there may be untold thousands of U.S. citizens who were unwitting targets of the Agency's mad researchers and who suffered horribly from the consequences. Such data, and all access to it, would create a deluge of legal, financial and political trouble for the Agency, and particularly for the researchers whose participation is secret or underreported.

The smoking gun for the hypno-programmed assassination of Senator Robert F. Kennedy lies in the mind of Sirhan Sirhan. Indeed, there are some good clues to go on in trying to find it – clues that could help clarify any new data culled from the shadows of Sirhan's memory by a highly skilled deprogrammer.

Chapter 13

THE FEMALE ACCOMPLICE

Sirhan Sirhan was hypnotized in his cell. Prosecution psychiatrist Dr. Seymour Pollack then asked him to write the answers to the questions asked:[1]

POLLACK: *Did anyone help you shoot Kennedy?*
SIRHAN (wrote): *No No No . . .*
POLLACK: *Was anyone with you when you shot Kennedy?*
SIRHAN: *No No N . . .*
POLLACK: *Who was with you when you shot Kennedy?*
SIRHAN: *Girl the girl the girl . . .*

— From a 1968 interview

LAPD's conclusion that there was no sinister female presence in this case is refuted by numerous witnesses, all of whom the official investigators would reject or discredit. The All Points Bulletin for the polka-dot suspect was canceled. As will be discussed in detail in the next chapter, Kennedy volunteer Sandra Serrano heard a fleeing girl in a polka-dot dress say, "We shot him!" When Serrano asked who, the girl replied, "Senator Kennedy." Information provided by an older couple who overheard this exchange with Serrano was inexplicably lost by police.

While all of the above data would be somehow lost or rejected by LAPD, other important witnesses also claimed to see a suspicious female not only at the crime scene but also in troubling incidents several weeks before the shooting. These too were dismissed. Each witness, each incident, was compartmentalized by police investigators and dealt with as if it existed in a vacuum. The entire body of data, strongly suggesting a female accomplice, was never assembled or interrelated. Having decided early on that the sinister woman did not exist, LAPD was not about to let a critical mass of speckled evidence form. Instead, it sought to extinguish each sighting as if dealing with a series of troublesome brush fires that, left unchecked, could meld and burn down the lone-assassin façade.

Sirhan is acknowledged to have been at the Ambassador Hotel on the night of June 2, when Kennedy was also there. He was not seen with a woman. All other alleged sightings of Sirhan at Kennedy-related places were rejected by the authorities. The primary reason for this was that he was seen with an attractive young woman.

On June 7, 35-year-old Albert LeBeau contacted the FBI to relate an incident that occurred at Robbie's Restaurant in Pamona on May 20. When LeBeau saw Sirhan's picture on TV he recognized him as the young man who had acted so strangely at the luncheon for Senator Kennedy. He picked Sirhan's photo from a batch as "closely resembling" the man he saw. LeBeau's five-page, signed statement to the Bureau described the incident as follows.

He worked as the night manager at Robbie's but was serving as ticket taker at a luncheon for 400 guests. As he collected tickets he heard a commotion on the stairway just behind him. He saw a young woman who "had to climb over the rail from a booth and over a brick flower casing in order to get behind me. I saw a man coming over the rail and dropping onto the stairs behind the girl."

LeBeau grabbed her to stop her from crashing the luncheon.

"Do you have tickets?" he asked the couple.

"We are with the Senator's party," the woman replied.

LeBeau again asked for tickets. The woman claimed, "We are part of the Senator's party. He just waved us to come upstairs."

Her companion said nothing, but constantly held his hands against the woman's back, as if pushing. LeBeau also noticed that he had a coat draped over his right hand and forearm.

The couple returned to the bottom of the stairs and LeBeau proceeded to admit those with tickets. The would-be crashers did not attempt to go through the line and he lost sight of them.

The woman was Caucasian, 25 to 30 years old, with "medium blond," shoulder-length hair. She appeared to be about 5-foot-6, somewhat taller than the man (Sirhan was 5-foot-4). She also had a "nice shape, built proportionately."

After taking the tickets, LeBeau journeyed upstairs to find "a runner" for one of the many newsmen present. He again saw the couple, standing against the back wall of the dining room. Robert Kennedy was giving a speech. There were 100 standees admitted, but these people also needed tickets.

As LeBeau moved through the crowd searching for a runner, he bumped against the man he later thought was Sirhan.

"Pardon me," said LeBeau.

"Why should I," the man replied, his coat still draped over his right arm on this warm May afternoon.*

This was the last LeBeau saw of the couple. No one else at Robbie's would positively identify Sirhan as having been there, but there was corroboration for the basic events of the incident. William Schneid, a Pamona policeman assigned inside the restaurant, told the FBI that he too saw the couple on the stairs. Independently corroborating LeBeau's account, Schneid said it appeared that the woman had crossed over the "brick façade adjacent to the stairs and over the stair railing behind persons apparently checking for tickets at the foot of the stairs." He saw the couple being briefly detained.

Schneid said the man bore some resemblance to Sirhan. He

---

* The reader will recall that Sirhan's notebook had an entry dated May 18 that said that his "determination to eliminate RFK" had become "more the more [sic] of an unshakable obsession."

described him as Caucasian, Latin or Mexican, slender, with dark curly hair, 5-foot-6 to 5-foot-7. Schneid's FBI summary states, "He did not feel the man observed by him would have been Sirhan Sirhan."

However, the policeman was obviously focusing his attention much more on the young woman. He saw her three separate times, and his FBI interview mentions the man only at the very end, when it briefly refers to "the man observed by him in the company of the woman." Apparently Schneid only saw the man when the couple was detained by LeBeau. The officer did say that he might recognize both of them if he could see them in person. Not only did LAPD not offer Schneid a lineup of Sirhan but police did not bother to interview him. His LAPD interview sheet consists of two handwritten notations: "See FBI report attached," "Sirhan in Pamona at RFK [illegible]."

Schneid described the woman as Caucasian, in her mid-20s, 5-foot-4 to 5-foot-7, medium- to light-brown hair, 110 to 125 pounds. She was also "proportionate," "attractive" and "officious."

The officer first encountered her just prior to Kennedy's arrival. She was standing by the door of the restaurant's kitchen apparently trying to get in. He approached her and told her that she could not go inside. She asked which way Kennedy was entering the luncheon. Schneid told her the Senator "would probably go up the stairs to the second floor."

The policeman next saw her as Kennedy entered and ascended the stairs. She "bolted toward the area at the foot of the stairs," as if trying to "get to someone she might have recognized."

Officer Carl Jackson told FBI agents that he had observed his colleague Schneid talking with a young woman at the kitchen door. A few minutes later he saw her at the foot of the stairs "apparently having been detained by one of the persons taking up tickets." Jackson had no recollection of the man and described the girl as Caucasian, 25 to 30 years old, 5 foot 5 inches tall, 135 pounds, brunette or black hair.

Felicia Maas, the owner of the restaurant, saw the couple being stopped by LeBeau but paid little attention and had no descriptions.

Albert LeBeau is obviously the witness who had the most contact with the suspicious young man. On June 12 he picked Sirhan's mug shot for FBI agents as "closely resembling" the individual, and indicated that if he saw the couple in person he might recognize them. Incredibly, LAPD never afforded him the chance to see Sirhan.

LeBeau was interviewed by LAPD on June 26. The summary states that he was also "interviewed" previously by "Officer Thompson." There is no record of this interview.

LeBeau picked Sirhan's mug shot from a batch of 25 photos of male, Latin types 20 to 25 years old. LAPD summary states that he failed to pick out a "racetrack" ID photo of Sirhan taken by the Racing Commission in 1965.

When it was singled out and shown to him he allegedly said it resembled Sirhan but the skin was too smooth. LAPD seemed to imply that the failure to recognize an outdated license picture was a severe blow to the witness's credibility. The interview summary bears the approval signature of Lt. Manuel Pena, but the box entitled "Investigators Making Interview" is completely blank. This is most unusual in other LAPD files.

The last sentence of the summary states, "Just before the conclusion of the interview LeBeau was asked, 'Could you under oath swear that Sirhan is the man involved in the incident on May the 20th?' LeBeau hung his head, stared at the floor for several long moments and replied, 'No.' " Such histrionics are exceedingly rare in other LAPD summaries. So too are the frequent quotations from LeBeau and from the unknown interviewer(s) that pepper the unusual three-page, single-spaced document. The unidentified officer(s) must have taken unusually meticulous notes: No audio tape of this interview appeared in released files.

LAPD's 1,500-page *Summary Report* says of LeBeau that he "initially stated the man was Sirhan, but later admitted he lied." There is no record of any such admission. If the synopsis in the *Summary Report* chose to portray uncertainty under oath as confession of falsehood, the question arises as to how accurately LeBeau is quoted and reported on in the three-page interview summary.

Another stalking story emanated from the Kennedy campaign headquarters in Azusa, California. Laverne Botting, a 41-year-old volunteer, told the FBI of an incident occurring on May 30. Two men and a woman entered the office. A man whom she would later recognize as "Sirhan or a person who very closely resembles Sirhan" approached her desk and inquired whether Senator Kennedy would be visiting the area. She replied negatively. Botting recalled that the man said he was from RFK headquarters in Pasadena (Sirhan lived in Pasadena). The other man and the woman stayed in the background throughout the brief conversation. Botting had no description of the man. The woman was a 22-year-old Caucasian, 5-feet 7-inches tall, slim, with an "excellent figure" and "dishwater blond" hair.

Mrs. Botting told the Bureau that while "there is a reasonable doubt" about whether it was Sirhan, she could make a definite judgment if she saw him in person. LAPD never gave her the opportunity. Police interviewed her three weeks after the FBI did. Although she picked out Sirhan's mug shot, the report states that she described the man she saw as having a broad nose and shoulders, which Sirhan does not have. Yet she also said the man was 5-foot-4, 20 to 25 years old, with dark eyes and black kinky hair (characteristics closely resembling Sirhan). This same interviewing officer, patrolman C. B. Thompson, would reject the identification of Sirhan by Botting's co-worker, 45-year-old Ethel Creehan, because she placed Sirhan's height at 5-foot-8 when it was 5-foot-4. Botting received no credit for getting the height correct (or the age, hair color and eyes) but was ignored for allegedly describing two of Sirhan's features as "broad."*

Officer Thompson reports that Botting said she received a threatening, anonymous phone call: "I hear you think you saw Sirhan. You had better be sure of what you are saying." If true, one wonders who beyond LAPD would have an interest in trying to exert pressure on her degree of certainty? Who besides LAPD even

---

* No audio tapes or transcripts for the interview of Botting and her co-worker were among released files.

knew of her sighting?

Thompson's logical frame of reference escapes the reader of his police report. He concludes, "Witness has obviously made an honest mistake." Earlier in the report he said he asked her if she would take a polygraph and she agreed. The final sentence says, "The officer has requested Lt. Hernandez to administer the polygraph examination for Mrs. Botting." But LAPD's polygraph log lists no test for her.

Ethel Creehan told the FBI that she overheard the brief exchange between Botting and the man she too thought was Sirhan. She also thought the man might have said he was with the Pasadena headquarters – as reported by Botting – but she was not certain.

Creehan told FBI agents she was "fairly certain" it was Sirhan, but she would not want to "testify to the fact without first seeing Sirhan in person." Like Botting and LeBeau, she was not offered a lineup.

Khaiber Khan,* another witness who claimed that Sirhan and the polka-dot girl were at a different Kennedy headquarters, allegedly refused an opportunity to view Sirhan in a lineup. Police took note of this in their interview report, implying that he was uncooperative. Perhaps the lineup was only afforded to witnesses who seemed disinclined to participate.

Ethel Creehan was first interviewed by LAPD on June 7, the day she phoned police to alert them to her story. She positively identified Sirhan as the person asking about Kennedy. The woman with him was thin, perhaps 19, but with makeup that made her appear 23 to 25. She had brown or blond hair.

Creehan was re-interviewed a month later by Officer Thompson. She repeated her story and picked Sirhan's picture as looking like the man she saw at campaign headquarters. Like Botting, she too reportedly agreed to take a polygraph test. None was given, according to LAPD records. Creehan augmented her previous description of the woman who was with Sirhan: Her hair was shoulder length and her nose was "prominent." While there are many varieties of prominence, witness Sandra Serrano said the

---

* Khan is also a mystery figure in his own right and will be discussed in the chapter "Iranian Enigma."

polka-dot-dress girl fleeing the Ambassador had a "funny nose." Vincent Di Pierro, a young waiter who claimed to see the polka-dot girl standing next to Sirhan in the kitchen, told the FBI that she had a "pudgy" nose.

Officer Thompson's bottom line on Creehan was, "The person described by Mrs. Creehan as possibly being Sirhan is 4 inches taller than Sirhan. It is doubtful if the person she observed was Sirhan." Recall that Thompson did not give Laverne Botting any credit for saying Sirhan was 5-foot-4. Moreover, if accuracy of estimated height were to be the litmus test for good witnesses, the prosecution's ability to prove Sirhan was in places where they wanted him would be greatly impaired. As FBI and LAPD files richly illustrate, estimated height varies considerably among witnesses observing the same person, depending on how close they get to the subject, whether the witness is sitting or standing, whether they have a good frame of reference, etc.

In another strange twist of investigative logic, Thompson writes that he talked with a woman from the Kennedy headquarters in Pasadena who said there was no reason why they would send anyone to Azusa to obtain information on the Senator's schedule. This is stated as if it reflects negatively on Creehan and Botting's story when, in fact, it would render the trio of visitors all the more suspicious if one of them claimed to be from the Pasadena office.

The Azusa headquarters incident parallels another that occurred on June 2 at the Wilshire Boulevard Headquarters. No attractive young woman was involved, but two campaign workers identified Sirhan as the man who came inside and said he was "with" Khaiber Khan, an Iranian who recruited Arab volunteers for the Kennedy campaign.*

After "Sirhan" was standing near a desk at the headquarters, a copy of the Senator's itinerary was missing and never found, according to Laverne Botting, despite a concerted effort (the itinerary was not considered a public document and copies were selectively distributed). This adds a measure of corroboration to the

---

*This incident will be discussed in detail in the "Iranian Enigma" chapter.

implicit notion in Botting and Creehan's story – that Sirhan was stalking Kennedy.

At the Ambassador Hotel the night of the assassination, several witnesses would claim to have encountered the polka-dot girl or to have seen a woman with Sirhan. The accounts vary in their richness and conspiratorial implication, but LAPD would reject or ignore all of them, no matter how consistent the witness or how cross-corroborative the data.

Lonny L. Worthy had a brief sighting of Sirhan standing next to a woman shortly after 10:00 p.m. While getting a soft drink for his wife, Worthy bumped into a man he would later identify as Sirhan, standing at the end of the bar. Worthy excused himself for the bump. Sirhan said nothing. A few minutes later Worthy noticed him standing next to a woman, and thought they were together. According to the summary of his FBI interview, he did not see them talk and provided no description of her. Worthy's LAPD interview summary says he saw Sirhan earlier in the evening, but inexplicably there is no mention of a woman.

Kennedy volunteer Susan Locke told the FBI on June 7 about the suspicious polka-dot-dress woman she saw in the Embassy Room just prior to Kennedy's speech. Locke said the woman seemed "somewhat out of place" and stood "expressionless" in the midst of the joyous victory celebration. Locke also noted that the woman had no yellow badge (necessary for admission to the ballroom). She pointed the woman out to Carol Breshears, in charge of a campaign support organization called the "Kennedy Girls," who in turn pointed her out to a nearby guard. The FBI report has no further information on what, if anything, the guard did.

Locke described the woman as Caucasian, in her early 20s, with long brown hair pulled back. She was "well proportioned" and wore a white dress with blue polka dots. Unexplainably, none of this would appear in Locke's LAPD interview, even though the polka-dot story comprised about a third of the information she gave to the Bureau.

Thirty-three-year-old George Green was a real estate salesman who headed New Images, a community action organization. Green told the FBI[2] that at about 11:15 to 11:30 he was in the corridor leading to the pantry area, watching Kennedy's press secretary Frank Mankiewicz talk with reporters. At the edge of the crowd Green noticed a man he would later positively identify as Sirhan, standing near a tall, thin man and a blond female Caucasian. The woman appeared to be in her early 20s. She wore a white dress with black polka dots and had a "good figure." Green accurately described Sirhan's attire and told police that Sirhan was conspicuous because he was wearing neither a suit nor a kitchen uniform.

Green went into the pantry just as the shooting was unfolding. From outside in the corridor he heard popping noises that sounded like firecrackers. When he entered the room he realized the sounds had been shots. Before he joined the struggle to overpower the assailant, he noticed a man and a woman running out of the pantry. They were conspicuous because everyone else in Green's area seemed to be trying to get in. The woman was in her early twenties, had long blond hair and wore a polka-dot dress. He did not see her face.

Green told both agencies that, in between his two sightings of Sirhan, he went down to one of the bars in the lower ballroom and had "several drinks." Neither of the two FBI interviews mentions "wandering." But the term appears three times in Green's LAPD interview report: Green "continued to wander around the hotel"; he "wandered from the Ambassador Room to the lower floor." LAPD's *Summary Report* falsely states that in two prior interviews with the FBI, Green indicated he "wandered between the first and second floors." The implication is that Green is a spaced-out partygoer, though he claims to have seen Sirhan standing near a polka-dot-dress woman before he went to the bar for drinks. As with Susan Locke's detailed account and Lonny Worthy's fleeting sighting of a female near Sirhan, Green's story of seeing Sirhan standing near a polka-dot woman would disappear between his FBI interview and his later LAPD interview. There is only a mention of him seeing Sirhan, but, as was the usual pattern, nothing at all about another man and the polka-dot woman.

The *Summary Report* attacks Green's credibility by alleging two major discrepancies in the story he told LAPD compared to what he told the FBI. First, he "described Sirhan's height as 5-foot-8 in one interview, 5-foot-0 in another." Second, he "described the dress, as white with black polka dots, in one interview and as a dark dress, which may have had some type of white dots, in this latest interview."

If real, these discrepancies would certainly be significant. However, LAPD's polka-dot file is replete with misrepresentations of witnesses (Booker Griffin and Sandra Serrano are two glaring examples that will be discussed shortly). No tape recording exists of Green's interview. LAPD has already misrepresented his "wandering" and excluded entirely the story about his earlier sighting of the polka-dot woman near Sirhan. Since Green's earlier FBI interviews were available to LAPD, they should certainly have questioned him about it and placed a report of the results in their case record, if they were really interested in determining the truth about the third major American political assassination in five years.

Green was by no means the only witness to see a polka-dot woman running from the pantry. Jack J. Merritt, a uniformed security guard working for Ace Guard Service, reported his sighting to both agencies. Just after the shooting, amidst the confusion of the struggle to disarm Sirhan, he noticed "two men and a woman leaving the kitchen through the back exit." He did not get a good look at the woman's face, but she was approximately 5-feet 5-inches tall, had "light colored" hair and wore a polka-dot dress. The two men wore suits. As sketchy as Merritt's information was, he provided one eerie detail to LAPD: "They seemed to be smiling."

Merritt was not discredited nor was his polka-dot sighting left out of the *Summary Report*. However, it was stated briefly, without comment, and ignored, as if it had been a report that there were sandwiches in the pantry. This witness, one of eight guards responsible for the Senator's security, was, strangely, not among the 3,470 people interviewed by LAPD.

Shortly after hearing shots while standing outside the pantry, 21-year-old Richard Houston asserts that he saw a woman run out of the room. She wore a black-and-white polka-dot dress with "ruffles around the neck and front." As she fled, she said, "We killed him"; she then "ran out onto a terrace area outside."

The official disinterest in exploring this account, which relates to those of Sandra Serrano, the Bernsteins and other witnesses, is conspicuous, to say the least. LAPD did not mention Houston in its polka-dot-dress investigative file. He was apparently never re-interviewed or polygraphed. His name is totally excluded from the *Summary Report,* which purports to synopsize all LAPD interviews. The summary of his LAPD interview states that he "has not been interviewed by the FBI." His account was simply buried in the files, as has become the norm with all witnesses who had seen the polka-dot-dress girl.

Evan Freed was a freelance photographer who had stepped inside the pantry to fix his damaged camera. When shots rang out he was pressed up against the wall by the crush of bodies. He fell backwards. On regaining his balance he witnessed the struggle to disarm the assailant. He also saw three persons, two men and a woman, running to the exit at the east end of the pantry. One man wore a light blue sport coat, and it seemed to Freed that this man was being chased by the third man. Freed told LAPD that he had no description of the woman except that she was Caucasian and "possibly wearing a polka-dot dress."

Freed was subsequently interviewed by both LAPD and FBI on the same day (September 11). As we have come to expect, the summaries reflect no mention of a fleeing woman – only two men.

It should be recalled that Vincent Di Pierro told both agencies that he saw Sirhan in the east end of the pantry standing next to an attractive girl in a polka-dot dress just before the shooting.* Darnell

* There were two doorways to the pantry – east and west. Five witnesses reported a woman exiting just after the shooting. Interview summaries of both agencies are often frustratingly vague, or silent, on key points such as her direction. The summaries of Johnson and Green fail to pinpoint exactly which exit they are

own mind a connection between [sic] the three women.'' The audio tape also reveals that he admitted he could not be absolutely sure it was the same woman in all three instances, but he did not infer that there were possibly three different women of whom he may have mentally projected a composite. This is yet yet another gross distortion and convenient misinterpretation of an eyewitness report of the polka-dot-dress woman whom law-enforcement investigators steadfastly refused to consider as a suspect in the case.

Griffin was warned by one of the three interviewing LAPD sergeants that he must stick to the "facts" about which he was definite – no "impressions." In a highly unusual version of the *100-percent-certain* test, applied only to witnesses whose accounts implied a conspiracy or contradicted the official findings, Griffin was asked the following tortured question: "If your life depended on it, that we're gonna send this man to the electric chair in another set of circumstances, could you say without any reservations, definitely, positively that this was the same man [Sirhan, on all three occasions] . . . no mistake about it?"

"No, I wouldn't."

"You wouldn't?"

"No."

"How about the girl?"

"No."

"So if we're dealing with facts now, you couldn't definitely say that she [the woman fleeing the pantry] was the same woman you saw earlier?"

"No."

In putting additional heat on Griffin, his police questioners also derided his claim of having made "negative eye contact" with Sirhan. The officer asked, rhetorically, if there were a thousand people at a function, would they all have to look happy? LAPD suggested that the woman fleeing the pantry "possibly could have been running out because of the shooting situation." Griffin did not deny the logical possibility but said he saw no one else trying to escape the room at that time. The sergeants told Griffin that

Kennedy staffer Judy Royer was probably the woman he saw with Sirhan, because she was in and around the pantry, had seen Sirhan before the shooting, and had told him to leave. But Royer was wearing a white suit, not a dress made of "flowing material" with contrasting colors, as Griffin described.

It was in the context of being asked to describe the woman that the police brought up the subject of mental projection. LAPD claimed that Griffin admitted he was probably projecting descriptive traits from the first sighting, when he had a better view of the woman, to the woman fleeing the pantry.

The policeman sums up: "So the description you gave me earlier then was not really a description of what you saw then [the girl fleeing the pantry] but rather a projection from the girl that you had seen earlier."

According to the police, Griffin agreed.

LAPD's *Summary Report* discredited Griffin with an allegation that is completely baseless in any of the tapes, transcripts or summaries of his law-enforcement interviews: "Later he stated that the story of the male and female escaping was a total fabrication on his part."

This conclusion on the part of the police is simply unwarranted and so transparent in its goals of discrediting a witness that it serves as further evidence of the existence of another agenda on the part of those neatly choreographing the final *Summary Report* on the assassination.

In June 1987, I interviewed Griffin in the offices of the talent agency he runs on Sunset Boulevard in Hollywood. He reiterated his account of seeing Sirhan and the girl. It was consistent with what he had told LAPD, the FBI and CBS-TV, in 1968. I showed him the recently released *Summary Report* alleging he admitted he lied.

Griffin reacted with disbelief, then anger.

"This is *not* true," he said forcefully. "This is totally untrue." He glared at the document, transfixed. "Law must not perjure itself. How can the police department say that I say that I fabricated?" he asked incredulously. He wanted to telephone his attorney.

Griffin indignantly but calmly defended his credibility: "I am a trained newsperson and I had been taught to watch details. . . . I was not there with the lay eye. I had covered, you know, shooting stories and others, and I was raised in a neighborhood situation where seeing people shot and being around bullets was something I was used to, and I was always taught to keep a kind of cool head. I'm not blind. I'm not a dishonest person. I know what I saw."

I asked him if the police had requested that he take a polygraph. Griffin asserted that he brought up the subject. "I mentioned it to them and they said it's unreliable." This is extremely hypocritical on LAPD's part, since, unknown to Griffin, two key polka-dot-dress witnesses (Serrano and Di Pierro) were rejected for failing the polygraph.

Concerning his treatment by LAPD, Griffin recalls: "They really tried very hard to break me down and lead me, as opposed to listen to me."

At the conclusion of our interview he said affirmatively, "I have not recanted a statement. I will not recant a statement."

Marcus McBroom, Ph.D., headed a local speakers bureau formed to support the Kennedy campaign. He had accompanied the Senator on his visit to the riot-torn Watts ghetto of Los Angeles. McBroom told the FBI that he saw a man whom he would later recognize as Sirhan in the kitchen at about 10:30. Sirhan was sitting on a table and looked out of place. He was not a kitchen employee; and his clothes were "dirty."

After the speech, McBroom entered the kitchen with the senator's party. At first he thought the series of popping sounds was exploding balloons, but he saw Kennedy's hands go up as if to protect himself. In the aftermath of the shooting he ran from the pantry into the Embassy Room in search of a doctor. It was then that he saw a Caucasian woman heading toward the exit. She was dark-haired, about 25 years old, 5-feet 4-inches tall, 126 pounds, and wore a white dress with black polka dots. He did not hear her speak. She attracted his attention because she was "calmer than everyone else" and "appeared to be trying to leave the room as soon as possible."

Two months after he talked to the FBI, McBroom was interviewed, and discredited, by LAPD: "Investigators feel this witness would be unreliable as he has given statements that he alleged were fact and could easily be disproved." The interview summary alleges that he mistakenly positioned Roosevelt Grier and shooting victims Evans and Weisel. It also claims that his own position was misstated; he was shown a photo of himself outside the kitchen when he was supposed to be inside. McBroom asked police when it was taken. He was told, "five seconds after the first shot was fired." Given the record LAPD treatment of polka-dot-dress witnesses, a prudent person would require independent verification to establish that McBroom was really in the wrong place at the wrong time.

The LAPD interview summary tells us that McBroom was "informed that the statements were not consistent and when used in court would certainly embarrass him . . ." What court? Was LAPD thinking of using him as a trial witness? Or did they conjure up the vision of a court proceeding in order to intimidate him? Without an audio tape we will never know for sure.

Conspicuously, but consistent with the pattern that I have uncovered, his polka-dot-dress story is never mentioned in his LAPD interview report or in the *Summary Report*. The clearly most controversial aspect of his account was simply ignored, following the established pattern of the authors of the *Summary Report*.

The *Summary Report* conveniently claims, "All additional statments made by McBroom were later retracted and are not reported here." The alleged retraction must indeed have been forceful since it prevented the polka-dot story from even being mentioned in the report. It was simply buried, as so many other accounts had been. Other polka-dot-dress witnesses who allegedly retracted their controversial assertions at least had their stories reported.

What about Sirhan himself? Does he remember a mystery woman? Recall that his last recollection before the shooting was of having coffee with a girl; the next thing he remembered was being pummeled by the men who disarmed him.[5]

He remembered bright lights and mirrors; he followed a girl through a door to a dark place. Sirhan was tired. She was tired. She wanted coffee. There was a shiny coffee urn and cups near the pantry. He poured for her.

"And I made some for me and we sat there. Then she moved and I followed her. She appeared to be Armenian or perhaps Spanish."

A year after the assassination Sirhan told NBC newsman Jack Perkins, "There was a girl there."

"A pretty girl?" asked Perkins.

"I thought she was."

"Did you think about trying to pick her up?"

Sirhan laughed.

"Did you try?" asked Perkins.

"I don't know [inaudible] what I was thinking about."

"After you poured coffee for the girl, then what happened?"

"I don't remember much what happened after that."

"You don't remember much?"

"I don't remember."

"Do you remember anything that happened after that?"

"I remember choking and the commotion."

"You remember nothing in between [coffee and choking]?"

"If I do, sir, I don't know it."

Here was the would-be assassin, a .22 pistol concealed on his person, about to kill a presidential candidate very soon and in this particular locale. He did not remember thinking of shooting Kennedy, but he recalled seeing a policeman. He told Dr. Bernard Diamond that he could not remember where on his person he was carrying the gun, or whether the girl saw it on him. Nor did he remember having any reaction when seeing the "policeman."* He recalled only the girl and the coffee.

Who was the girl with Sirhan just before he pulled the trigger, the girl whose presence coincides with his loss of memory? LAPD

---

* It must have been a uniformed fire marshal or security guard (there were no policemen), but it doesn't matter since Sirhan thought it was a policeman and still remembers no reaction.

does not know. Was she not the polka-dot-dress girl? No one came forward claiming to have innocently and coincidentally shared coffee, conversation and a walk to the murder scene with Sirhan.

Descriptions of the mystery woman vary significantly, especially regarding hair color, for example. Still, witness descriptions of Sirhan, in places where he was known to be – the rifle range, the crime scene – also vary substantially. The woman is described fairly consistently as being in her early to mid-20s, with long hair, and attractive or having a good figure, wearing a long, flowing dress (not a suit or a miniskirt) with polka dots that are characterized rather similarly in terms of color and size.

There is also a rough but significant symmetry to the sightings by witnesses at the Ambassador: earlier in the evening in the Embassy Room, then near the pantry, then in the pantry, running out of it, moving across the Embassy Room, then outside the hotel. It is not as if the majority of sightings can be written off as occurring at the same time in different places, as is the case with Darnell Johnson's report of the girl being in the ballroom when other witnesses placed her outside.

The police never officially collated the information on the polka-dot-dress girl or looked for cross-corroboration. Their effort was primarily directed toward finding inconsistencies – real and in many cases invented by investigators – with which to browbeat and discredit witnesses. LAPD's investigation was more concerned with systematically disposing of troublesome data rather than with effectively searching for the polka-dot-dress girl, ''the girl'' who had coffee with Sirhan, or the woman who may have done both.

Chapter 14

LAPD'S HANDLING OF SANDRA SERRANO

Manny Pena knew that as long as Miss Serrano stuck to her story, no amount of independent evidence would, in itself, serve to dispel the "polka-dot-dress girl" fever, which had by now, in the press and public mind, reached a high point on the thermometer of intrigue. She alone could put the spotted ghost to rest.

> – Chief Robert Houghton,
> in his book *Special Unit Senator*[1]

How Sandra Serrano's story was put to rest is not so much an intriguing sidebar to LAPD's handling of the case as it is a microcosm of it. Her account, as told to the FBI on June 8, was as follows. Having worked as co-chair of the Youth for Kennedy Committee in the Pasadena-Altadena area, the 20-year-old key-punch operator went to the Ambassador with several friends. While waiting for the final election results, she sought escape from the hot, crowded ballroom and went outside. She sat on a stairway, on the fifth or sixth step. It was about 11:30 when three people (two men and a woman) climbed up the stairs. The woman said, "Excuse us," and Miss Serrano moved aside so they could get past her.

She sat there for about a half hour, she estimated, and saw no one else. Then, she heard what she thought were six car "backfires," four or five of which seemed close together. Moments later a man and a woman (two of the trio she had seen previously) came running down the stairs toward her. The woman said, "We shot him! We shot him!" Serrano asked: "Who did you shoot?" The woman replied, "Senator Kennedy."

Serrano went inside where she encountered a uniformed security guard. She asked, "Is it true they shot him?" "Shot who?" he inquired. When she replied "Senator Kennedy," the guard told her she had had too much to drink. Word of the tragedy gradually spread from the pantry to the edges of the gathering and had apparently not yet reached people near this exit. She encountered several other disbelievers as she moved around inside the hotel asking people if they had any confirmation that the Senator had been shot.

Serrano described the woman as Caucasian, 23 to 27 years old, 5-foot-6, with dark brown hair, wearing a white dress with black, quarter-inch polka dots (one and a half to two inches apart). She later recognized Shirhan as the man who had earlier been with the couple she subsequently saw fleeing (the trio had walked up the steps when she was sitting there).

Sandra Serrano was the subject of more attention and investigation than perhaps any other witness. Eventually she was discredited by LAPD via a long, punishing process that seemed at times more like an inquisition than an investigation.

In April 1988, when LAPD files were released, a hungry press seized upon the story of the young woman who claimed she saw the polka-dot girl but admitted she concocted the story after failing a polygraph. But the press failed to report the campaign to discredit her, conducted by investigating authorities, or the corroborating accounts presented by other witnesses who also saw a polka-dot-dress woman fleeing the hotel. Just as Don Schulman was *the* second-gun witness, Serrano was designated by LAPD as *the* polka-dot-dress witness.

While the other polka-dot-dress witnesses described in the previous chapter were also interviewed by LAPD and the FBI, Serrano was unique in that her story was vivid, involved Sirhan and had been broadcast on national television shortly after the shooting. She was interviewed by NBC-TV reporter Sander Vanocur. Her story about the fleeing duo and "We shot him!" was captured on video even before she was interviewed by the authorities. The stunned and blurry-eyed national audience had heard an account fraught with conspiratorial implication from a young woman who was visibly shaken but seemed both sincere and coherent, and who had no motive to lie.

At 2:35 on the morning of the shooting, Miss Serrano was interviewed by LAPD. Her story was essentially the same as what she said on TV. She was re-interviewed at 4:00 a.m. The LAPD *Summary Report* says that "Serrano's statements during the later session were essentially the same as in her previous interview." Considering the hour, the ordeal and her emotional state, such consistency should have been viewed by police as adding to her credibility.

She was perhaps the most extensively debriefed witnesses. On June 7 she was interviewed by two LAPD detectives. She also re-enacted her story at the Ambassador for a gaggle of investigators from LAPD, the FBI and even the Secret Service. On June 8 she was interviewed by the FBI and she was also taken to police headquarters to view Cathy Sue Fulmer, a possible candidate for the elusive polka-dot-dress girl. Serrano rejected her. That same day she was taken to NBC studios in Burbank to view TV footage of the crowd at the Ambassador. She saw none of the three persons she had seen on the stairs.

On June 10 there was another interview, with representatives of several law-enforcement agencies present, as well as a video-taped reconstruction of her story (done at the hotel). Then there was a quasi-fashion show in which she looked at eight polka-dot dresses assembled by the authorities. She was extensively questioned about the detailed characteristics of the mystery woman's garment.

On June 20 she was interviewed for approximately an hour and a quarter by LAPD Lt. Enrique Hernandez. She allegedly failed a lie detector test. Then, after a break to find a tape recorder, she was re-interviewed for 20 minutes, during which time she finally agreed to what Hernandez had been insisting: that her story was false. Even in this session she put up considerable argument, sometimes agreeing in half-hearted, perfunctory fashion ("I guess") with his descriptions of what the police say supposedly happened.

But the true story behind this pivotal investigation would not be revealed until LAPD files were released 20 years later. The striking fact is that it was less an investigation of her story (of how it related to other witness data or to potentially corroborating evidence) and more an investigation of Serrano herself, during which she would be isolated not only personally but in terms of other available, known evidence.

The challenges to her credibility were instant and constant, excluding her two interviews the morning of June 5. As described earlier, seven interviews with no substantive summaries of the interviews, only a couple of hand-written notations, are dated June 6 and 7. This was before the polka-dot investigation had really begun. They are signed by Lt. Manuel Pena. The scrawled notations seem to be in his handwriting: "Polka-dot story of Serrano phony," "Polka dot story Serrano N.G." Each of the seven documents has a notation indicating that the matter was settled, primarily due to the witness's unreliability.

Potentially corroborative evidence for Serrano's story became one of the investigation's several endangered species, disappearing at a rapid rate. If you will remember back to the sequence of events I described earlier, Sergeant Paul Schraga's APB for the polka-dot-dress girl was canceled.[2] The Bernsteins' names and address disappeared (the couple had allegedly also witnessed what seems clearly to have been Serrano's "We shot him!" encounter). Reports of Schraga's APB vanished. Other witnesses with polka-dot stories were being trashed by law-enforcement authorities as fabricators, hallucinators, publicity seekers or excessive revelers.

A June 12 FBI document written by Special Agent Richard Burris reports on his questioning of Serrano at the June 10 interview and reconstruction. It is a unique report not only in the FBI's 32,000 pages on this case but also in comparison to FBI files on the assassinations of President Kennedy and Dr. Martin Luther King, Jr.[3]

Unlike LAPD interview summaries, those of the FBI do not characterize witness credibility or discuss inconsistencies or challenges to the story reported. They simply provide a straight summary of what the witness said, with no evaluation or comment. But this Serrano report conspicuously departs from the norm:

> Serrano was asked by SA [special agent] Richard Burris why, in her interview on television following the shooting, she had not said anything about seeing the woman and the two men go up the stairs but only told about the woman and the man coming back down. It was pointed out to her the fact she claimed one of the men going up the stairs was Sirhan Sirhan was the most significant part of the incident described by her. Serrano stated she could not explain why and accused those present of trying to trick her.

Either Burris and his colleagues woefully misunderstood the sequence of events or they actually *were* trying to trick her. Miss Serrano had not witnessed Sirhan's arrest and his picture had not yet been flashed on TV when she went briefly on camera with NBC. At that point, in the shock of the moment, the big story was the "We shot him!" dialogue she had heard and witnessed. In her original police interview with LAPD, at 2:35 a.m under more detailed questioning, she told of seeing the fleeing couple earlier, with a third man whom she could recognize if she saw him again.

It appears that Serrano was already feeling the pressure on June 10 and did not trust the official investigation. Agent Burris' report tells us that she "insisted" on "having someone present not connected with the investigation" before she would do the videotaped reconstruction of her story. Several Ambassador Hotel kitchen employees were brought in, but she rejected all but two of them and "gave no reason for her rejection."

The audio tape of the reconstruction reveals a young woman who sounds beleaguered, occasionally speaking sharply to the investigators; other times, her voice cracks as if overcome with emotion. She was alone in the midst of authorities from LAPD, the FBI and the District Attorney's office. Agent Burris' report states that Serrano told investigators she was very upset and could not continue. She asked to be driven home.

Perhaps she had hoped to bring in an outsider with slightly more protective clout than an Ambassador Hotel busboy. In any event, on June 12 she called the FBI's Los Angeles office and reported that she had engaged two attorneys. She provided their names and phone numbers and, according to the FBI report of her call, told both the Bureau and the police that the lawyers were to be contacted before she would talk any further with investigators.

One identifiable "trick" that the official investigation would employ against Miss Serrano was to use the syntax in her original interview to discredit her. During her 2:35 a.m. interview at the Ambassador she was asked whether she heard gunfire.

SERRANO: Yes.
LAPD: When did you hear the sound approximately?
SERRANO: Well, I didn't know it was a gun, I thought it was the backfire of a car.

She was further questioned about "the gunfire or the backfire or *whatever you thought it might be* [emphasis added]." During her second interview that morning she was asked how many backfires or shots she heard. Henceforth, in summaries of her FBI interviews of June 8 and 10 and another LAPD interview on June 7, she is reported as having said she heard "backfires." There is no report that she claimed to hear "gunfire" or "shots." Yet the police would continue to attribute this claim to her and to use it against her.

She was asked if she heard people screaming from the pantry. She responded negatively; at first, no one in her area was aware of what had happened.

She was sitting outside overlooking a hotel parking lot where cars and delivery trucks came and went. Inside was a victory celebration at which popping balloons were so prevalent that numerous people inside the pantry did not immediately recognize the gunfire. Radio reporter Andrew West narrated the immediate aftermath of the shooting and the struggle to subdue Sirhan. He told his audience, "You heard a balloon go off and a shot. You didn't realize that the shot was a shot."

Rather than entertaining the possibility that the "whatever" she heard could have been firecrackers, backfires, balloons or something else, the authorities seemed intent on misstating her opinion in order to discredit her.

A June 8 FBI memo states that LAPD Detective C. J. Hughes, who participated in Serrano's June 7 re-enactment, informed the Bureau "she claimed to have heard some backfires or shots." He then opines that it would be impossible for her to hear shots from where she was located. He offered no opinion about backfires or balloons.

Evidently, she was challenged by officials about this claim which they attributed to her – challenged sometime between June 7 and June 10. During her June 10 video-taped reconstruction she was asked when she heard the sounds "that you told us sounded like backfires."

Indignantly, her voice choked with emotion, she responded: "It sounded like the backfire of a car. And I've *never heard a gun*. I don't know what a gun sounds like."

Her questioner said: "All right, all right, you heard these sounds that were kind of like backfires."

But LAPD seemed not to care what Serrano was actually claiming. The mere mention of the possibility of gunfire in her first interview (as fatigued and traumatized as she was at the time) was a designated line of attack on her credibility.

At times it seemed that LAPD was more zealous in investigating conspiracy witnesses than evidence that could lead to the conclusion of a conspiracy. On June 20 they fired a .22 revolver in the pantry, being careful to use the same brand and lot of ammunition found in Sirhan's gun. Ironically, the gun was fired "with the muzzle pointed towards the west door of the pantry," where police almost certainly removed the extra bullets on June 5. Sound-level tests allegedly showed that, from Serrano's position, only half a decibel could be registered from the gunfire in the pantry. Two decibels were asserted to be necessary for someone "with normal hearing" to pick up the sound. The experiment was ordered by Lt. Manuel Pena and was conducted by DeWayne Wolfer, LAPD's chief criminologist.

Serrano's fate as a witness was to be entwined, by LAPD, with that of another witness: Vincent Di Pierro, a college student working at the hotel as a waiter, the son of the Ambassador maître d'. As Kennedy entered the pantry, Di Pierro shook hands with him, then moved toward the ice machine. In interviews with LAPD and FBI, and in his June 7 testimony before the grand jury that indicted Sirhan, he put forth a polka-dot-dress story.

He claimed to have observed Sirhan just prior to the shooting, standing near a stack of serving trays in the pantry. He noticed Sirhan only because he appeared to be with a girl who was "very good looking." It seemed to Di Pierro that they were talking, even flirting, because both of them were smiling. Moments later when Sirhan began shooting, he still wore a smile – "a very sick looking smile."

The girl had brown hair and wore a white dress with black or dark purple polka dots. And, said Di Pierro, she had a peculiar nose ("pudgy," he told the FBI). During her first June 5 LAPD interview Serrano described the polka-dot-dress girl as having dark brown hair, a "good figure" and "a funny nose." Similarly, in her NBC-TV interview she said the woman had "dark hair" and a "funny nose."

At the end of his June 5, early-morning interview, one investigator told Di Pierro he was a "very very good witness." On July 1, he was re-interviewed and allegedly failed a polygraph. One investigator referred to the need to "eliminate" what Di Pierro "thought" he saw. Unlike Serrano, Di Pierro was very cooperative and not subjected to pressure tactics – at least, not on tape. LAPD's *Summary Report* concludes: "He admitted that he discussed the polka-dot dress with Serrano prior to his original interview." In his confusion the night of the assassination he may have seen "a girl somewhere" but not with Sirhan. Di Pierro's vivid, consistent account, given to police and FBI, had been expunged. He was told of Serrano's recantation, but he was not told about the numerous witnesses who also claimed to have seen the mystery woman.

When Serrano was flunked as a witness she admitted talking with the young waiter about the polka-dot-dress girl (of course, she had told her story on TV before she ever encounterd Di Pierro). She was never queried as to whether they talked about the girl being in her 20s, about the odd nose, the good figure or the color of the dots. LAPD's *Summary Report* states that during their conversation in the witness room before being interviewed, "The polka-dot-dress was mentioned but was not described."[4] Were the rest of the matching traits merely a coincidence?

A June 13 FBI memo on Di Pierro states that he recalled talking to Sandra Serrano about a woman wearing a white dress with black polka dots while they were sitting together waiting to be interviewed by police after the shooting. They did not describe the dress to each other, except to mention the fact that it was a white dress with black polka dots. Di Pierro said no details about the person wearing the dress were discussed since a police officer saw them talking and warned them not to discuss the case.

Even if we act as the LAPD did and disregard Sergeant Schraga's APB and all the other witnesses, there is a problem in dismissing Serrano's story as the product of collusion with Di Pierro. After the shooting, but before she confronted any of the other witnesses, Serrano encountered Los Angeles Deputy District Attorney John Ambrose.[5] During her first LAPD interview she described how she was looking for someone in authority to tell her story to. She approached Ambrose because he was wearing a suit. As Ambrose described the encounter to the FBI on June 10, she came up to him and asked his help in contacting the "proper authorities." He identified himself, "quieted her down" and listened to her story about the girl in the polka-dot dress saying, "We shot him!" He then took her to the investigating officers. The FBI report says: "Serrano impressed Ambrose as a very sincere person and although she was alarmed and excited over what was told her by the couple, she remained insistent on the wording of the girl's statement ['We shot him!']. In Ambrose's LAPD interview of June 10 he concludes: "Serrano impressed me as a very sincere girl who was a dedicated Kennedy fan, not interested in publicity."

Further corroboration for Ambrose and Serrano's accounts was provided by 21-year-old Irene Chavez, a friend of Sandra's who went to the Ambassador with her. Chavez told the FBI on June 7 that she saw Serrano after the shooting. Sandra was crying and "near hysteria." Chavez' FBI summary describes what Serrano told her: "A man and a woman ran down the stairway where she had been sitting and the woman said something about they had shot Senator Kennedy. Chavez said she understood from Serrano that she thought these people had shot Senator Kennedy and not just the fact that Senator Kennedy had been shot."

Moreover, Chavez' FBI summary states: "Miss Chavez said that after trying to calm Serrano down, they met a man who claimed to be a district attorney and took Serrano to the police for an interview."

Ambrose's LAPD interview asserts "before Serrano appeared on television, another man who identified himself as a witness to the shooting, *was overhearing Sandra relate what she had seen* [emphasis added] and volunteered he had seen a girl of the same description with the same dress, and implied, to the best of my memory, that he had seen her at the time of the shooting." Ambrose said he could recognize this witness (clearly Di Pierro), because he talked with him again later at the Rampart police station.

Ambrose's account allows for Di Pierro's contamination as a witness by overhearing Serrano, but Ambrose's previous encounter with her, during which she told him her story, is damning to the

Terrorism Against
The United States

Top: President John F. Kennedy (right) and then-Attorney General Robert F. Kennedy (*Assassination Archives and Research Center, Washington, D.C.*). Bottom: RFK campaigning the day of the 1968 California primary, June 4 (*Southeastern Mass. Univ. RFK Assassination Archives*).

Top: Senator Kennedy autographs a poster on his way through the Ambassador Hotel pantry, L.A., to make his victory speech. On his return through the pantry, he will be assassinated. Bottom: Senator Kennedy gives his victory speech after winning the California primary (*both AARC, Washington*).

Top: The struggle to disarm Sirhan Sirhan (barely visible in the center of the melee). His gun hand is being slammed against the steam table. Bottom left: The bow tie of uniformed security guard Thane Eugene Cesar lies just beyond Kennedy's hand moments after the shooting. Busboy Juan Romero kneels beside the Senator (*both AARC, Washington*). Bottom right: As Kennedy lies on the pantry floor, Dr. Stanley Abo tries to provide assistance (*SMURFK Archives*).

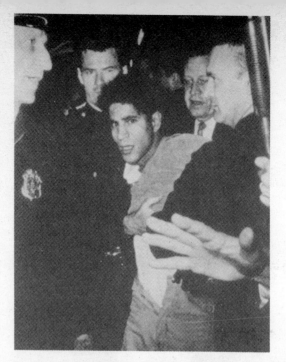

Top: Sirhan Sirhan is taken into custody immediately after the shooting (*AARC, Washington*). Bottom: The author on the Ambassador Hotel stairway, in 1987 – where witness Sandra Serrano encountered the fleeing polka-dot-dress girl and an unidentified man just after the shooting. The girl exclaimed, ''We shot him! We shot him!'' Serrano had seen these two earlier in the company of Sirhan (*Floyd Nelson*).

Top: An FBI photo of the pantry after the shooting. The "X" marks the spot where Kennedy's body allegedly fell (*SMURFK Archives*). Bottom: An FBI crime-scene photo showing numerous ceiling tiles removed by the police (*Castellano-Nelson Collection, SMURFK Archives*).

Top: An LAPD photo of police criminologist DeWayne Wolfer pointing to an apparent ricochet mark in the pantry doorway. Wolfer asserted that no bullets were recovered from the crime scene and that Sirhan's eight shots accounted for all the bullet damage. Bottom: L.A. coroner Thomas Noguchi points to two holes in the doorframe of the pantry doorway. These holes were identified by the FBI, opposite in the photo marked "E2," as "bullet holes." If these are bullet holes, they constitute proof of a second gun (*both SMURFK Archives*).

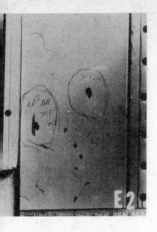

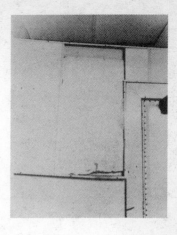

LA 56-156
ACO/S/BIS
4

D-5   Interior view of kitchen serving area looking
      south showing ice machines. The x marks on
      floor reportedly show locations in which the
      injured came to rest. The x shown on floor to
      far left reportedly is the location that
      Senator KENNEDY had fallen after being shot.

E-1   View taken inside kitchen serving showing
      doorway area leading into kitchen from the
      stage area. In lower right corner the photo
      shows two bullet holes which are circled. The
      portion of the panel missing also reportedly
      contained a bullet.

E-2   A close up view of the two bullet holes of
      area described above.

E-3   Close up view of two bullet holes which is
      located in center door frame inside kitchen
      serving area and looking towards direction
      of back of stage area.

E-4   Close up view of upper hinge on door leading
      into kitchen area from back of stage area.
      View shows reported location of another bullet
      mark which struck hinge.

F-1   Interior view behind stage and speakers platform
      area looking in westerly direction and showing
      entrance to stairway which leads down to the
      Casino level and the Ambassador Ballroom.

F-2   View taken from Casino Level or Ambassador Ball-
      room floor level showing base of stairway
      which leads up to Embassy Ballroom.

F-3   View taken from Ambassador Ballroom floor level
      in a northwesterly direction which shows fire
      doors leading to fire stairs shown in photos
      A-1 and A-2.

G-1   View taken from Ambassador Ballroom floor level
      showing foyer area south of entrance to the
      Ambassador Ballroom which leads to fire doors
      shown in photographs A-5 and A-7.

G-2   Close up view of photographed area described in
      G-1 above.

-48-

Top left: FBI photograph "E2" – a close-up of the pantry doorway doorframe, showing two "bullet holes." The number "723" in the "E2" close-up was most likely inscribed by the late Walter Tew, a Los Angeles Sheriff's Deputy whose badge number was 723. Top right: A more distant view of the FBI's "E2" photograph. Right: Page from FBI photo-caption list; items E-1 through E-4 should especially be noted (*all three, SMURFK Archives*).

Left: An LAPD detective wears Kennedy's coat, with a metal rod through the bullet holes to illustrate the shots' flight paths. L.A. coroner Thomas Noguchi stands behind him. Note the sharply upward angles on the shots, which struck the Senator's back rather than his front. LAPD insists that a bullet passing through the coat hit victim Paul Schrade in the forehead. Schrade was several feet behind Kennedy, who was not facing Schrade (*Castellano-Nelson Collection, SMURFK Archives*). Bottom left: LAPD officer Charles Wright and his partner, Sergeant Robert Rozzi, examine what appears to be a bullet in the pantry doorframe. It was labeled as a bullet by the Associated Press in its photo of the two officers at the doorway (*SMURFK Archives*). Bottom right: Close-up of what officers Wright and Rozzi were examining (*Castellano-Nelson Collection, SMURFK Archives*).

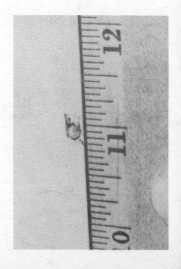

Form 15 7 (Rev. April 1962)

EMPLOYEE'S REPORT

DR

SUBJECT

Kennedy - 187 P.C.

DATE & TIME OCCURRED	LOCATION OF OCCURRENCE	DIVISION OF OCCURRENCE
6-5-68	Ambassador Hotel	Rampart Division

To: (Rank, Name, Assignment, Division)

DATE & TIME REPORTED

7-8-68

Lt. D.W. Mann, O-I-C, Criminalistics Section, S.I.D.

DETAILS:

The weapon used in this case was an Iver Johnson, Cadet Model,
.22 caliber, 8 shot revolver (2½" barrel). This weapon had eight
expended shell casings in the cylinder at the time of recovery from
the suspect. A trajectory study was made of the physical evidence
which indicated that eight shots were fired as follows:

#1 - Bullet entered Senator Kennedy's head behind the right ear
     and was later recovered from the victim's head and booked as
     evidence.

#2 - Bullet passed through the right shoulder pad of Senator Kennedy's
     suit coat (never entered his body) and traveled upward striking
     victim Schrade in the center of his forehead. The bullet was
     recovered from his head and booked as evidence.

#3 - Bullet entered Senator Kennedy's right rear shoulder approximately
     seven inches below the top of the shoulder. This bullet was
     recovered by the Coroner from the 6th cervical vertebrae and
     booked as evidence.

#4 - Bullet entered Senator Kennedy's right rear back approximately
     one inch to the right of bullet #3. This bullet traveled upward
     and forward and exited the victim's body in the right front chest.
     The bullet passed through the ceiling tile, striking the second
     plastered ceiling and was lost somewhere in the ceiling interspace.

#5 - Bullet struck victim Goldstein in the left rear buttock. This
     bullet was recovered from the victim and booked as evidence.

#6 - Bullet passed through victim Goldstein's left pants leg (never
     entering his body) and struck the cement floor and entered
     victim Stroll's left leg. The bullet was later recovered and
     booked as evidence.

#7 - Bullet struck victim Weisel in the left abdomen and was
     recovered and booked.

#8 - Bullet struck the plaster ceiling and then struck victim Evans
     in the head. This bullet was recovered from the victim's head
     and booked as evidence.

A Walker's H-acid test was conducted on Senator Kennedy's suit coat
in the area of the entrance wounds. This test indicated that the
muzzle of the weapon was held at a distance of between one to six
inches from the coat at the time of all firings.

DATE & TIME TYPED	CIVN. RPTG.	CLERK	EMPLOYEE(S) REPORTING	SER. NO.	DIVN.
7-8-68 10 a.m.	S.I.D.	mms			
SUPERVISOR APPROVING		SERIAL NO.			
Lt. D.W. Mann		#2M5	Officer DeWayne A Wolfer #6727	S.I.D.	

The above LAPD document, dated July 8, 1968, describes the department's official accounting of the eight bullets from Sirhan's gun. Supposedly, not one bullet was recovered from the crime scene (*SMURFK Archives*).

ALL 1
b7C

Date 6/8/68

_____ Detective Division,
Los Angeles Police Department, advised that the ballistics
examination regarding the slugs recovered at the shooting
at the Ambassador Hotel on the morning of June 5, 1968,
has not been completed. Examination to date indicates
that the murder weapon was approximately six inches
from Senator ROBERT F. KENNEDY when discharged.

Regarding the two spent bullets found in the
vehicle registered to SIRHAN SIRHAN, one is not capable
of being examined as it is flattened out, appearing to
have hit a piece of metal or rock. The other one has
not been subjected to ballistics examination but from visual
observation indicates that it had been removed from its
casing without being fired.

Examination has indicated that one bullet
located in Senator ROBERT F. KENNEDY was definitely
fired by the murder weapon.

The bullet taken from EDWIN STOLL was a half
slug which cannot be positively identified as coming
from the murder weapon although examination is continuing.
At the present time a ballistics expert will testify to
the fact that it is his professional opinion that this
bullet is a .22 caliber. No further determination could
be made.

The bullet causing the wound to Mrs. ELIZABETH EVANS
cannot be entered into evidence as continuity of the bullet
has been lost.

_____ tated that the ballistics examination
has not yet been completed, however, it is anticipated the
examination will be finished by June 9 or 10, at which time
it will be furnished to the Los Angeles Division.

1082 *

On __6/8/68__ at __Los Angeles, California__ File # __Los Angeles 56-156__

by __SA_____   Date dictated __6/8/68__

An FBI memo discovered by the author, in later-released files, refers to
"slugs recovered *at* [emphasis added] the shooting at the Ambassador
Hotel." If a single bullet was removed from the crime scene, it would be
too many bullets for Sirhan's gun (*SMURFK Archives*).

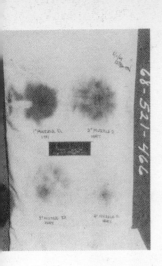
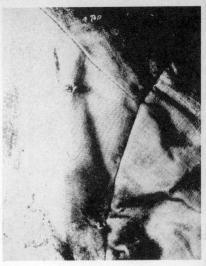
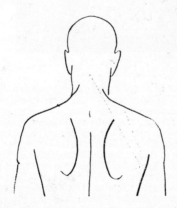

Top left: LAPD powder-burn tests (dating from June 11, 1968) produce a dark, concentrated burn – like those found on Kennedy's suit jacket – only when the gun is fired from as close as 1 to 3 inches away (*Gregory Stone*). Top right: Close-up of Senator Kennedy's suit jacket showing the two bullet holes through the shoulder pad (*Castellano-Nelson Collection, SMURFK Archives*). Bottom: A schematic drawing by Gregory Stone showing the pathways of each bullet that entered Senator Kennedy's body (*SMURFK Archives*).

Top left and right: Never-before-published still photos taken from the 1977 video re-enactment done for Los Angeles authorities by key witness Lisa Urso. The authorities mistakenly believed that Urso would position the gun within inches of Kennedy's head. Instead, she placed it approximately five feet away – and the video tape was suppressed until 1986. In the left-hand photo, Urso, at far right, assumes her crime-scene position while a female law officer plays Sirhan (the gun is obscured by "Sirhan's" head). Note the distance from the gun to the "Senator's" head, as he shakes hands. In the right-hand picture, taken from behind Urso, the gun is visible next to the right side of "Sirhan's" head – a distance several feet from the white-shirted "Senator" (*Judith Melanson*).

Above: Never-before-published still photo taken of a 1971 filmed re-enactment by Los Angeles authorities, suppressed until 1986. The re-enactment is supposed to show "Sirhan" (in the middle of the picture) firing nearly point-blank behind "Kennedy's" right ear and his shoulder area. ("Kennedy" is the figure on the right.) Instead, because actual witness Karl Uecker, blocked from view by "Kennedy," has re-enacted his role by walling off "Sirhan" to "Kennedy's" front-left, the "gun" (a bare hand mimicking a gun) is being fired into "Kennedy's" forehead. This re-enactment disregards Uecker's testimony that Sirhan never got past him to close in on Kennedy (*Judith Melanson*).

Great S.P.I Books
Fact and Fiction

□   **The Super Swindlers: The Incredible Record of America's Greatest Financial Scams** *by Jonathan Kwitney.* They say that crime doesn't pay, but it has paid quite handsomely, thank you, for some of America's greatest swindlers and con-men. Acclaimed investigative journalist Jonathan Kwitney (*The Wall Street Journal, The Kwitney Report*—PBS TV) tracks down these notorious paper pirates who have taken individuals, corporations and governments to the cleaners. In *The Super Swindlers* we find out how these con-men have been operating and how so many of them have avoided prosecution. (ISBN 1-56171-248-5) $5.99 U.S.

□   **First Hand Knowledge: How I Participated In The CIA-Mafia Murder of President Kennedy** *by Robert D. Morrow.* We still have far more questions than facts about that dark November day in Dallas. But now, out of the shadows, comes the only inner-circle operative not to have been mysteriously assassinated. The author's information was the basis of the House Select Committee on Assassinations 1976 investigation. Morrow finally feels the danger to himself and his family has passed and he is ready to talk. (ISBN 1-56171-274-4) $5.99 U.S.

□   **Love Before The Storm: A True Romance Saga in the Shadow Of The Third Reich** *by Roslyn Tanzman.* They were two young Jewish medical students, in love, and studying medicine in Europe's greatest medical schools. The future looked rosy, until the German economy tottered and the right-wing forces marched into power. In this moving, true retelling of her parents' actual love story, Roslyn Tanzman recreates their love at first sight, the class-war between their families and the shadow cast upon the lovers by Hitler's Germany and the impending World War. (ISBN 1-56171-240-X) $5.50 U.S.

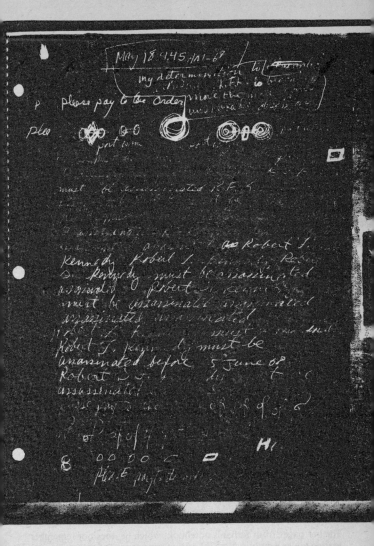

Above: A page from Sirhan Sirhan's notebook, scrawled in "automatic writing," refers to killing Robert F. Kennedy (*SMURFK Archives*).

Further pages from Sirhan's notebook, which he does not remember writing under hypnosis. Note the references to drugs and to communism in which Sirhan's friends and associates say he had no interest. But he did express an interest in money, a predominant theme of his notebook.

A R T I C H O K E

B/3

1. The ARTICHOKE Team visited ~~~~~~~~~~ during period 8 January to 15 January 1954. The purpose of the visit was to give an evaluation of a hypothetical problem, namely: Can an individual of ****** descent be made to perform an act of attempted assassination involuntarily under the influence of ARTICHOKE?

2. PROBLEM:

a. The essential elements of the problem are as follows:

(1) As a "trigger mechanism" for a bigger project, it was proposed that an individual of ****** descent, approximately 35 years old, well educated, proficient in English and well established socially and politically in the ****** Government be induced under ARTICHOKE to perform an act, involuntarily, of attempted assassination against a prominent ****** politician or if necessary, against an American official. The SUBJECT was formerly in ~~~~~~~~~~ but has since terminated and is now employed with the *** Government. According to all available information, the SUBJECT would offer no further cooperation with ~~~~~~~~~~ Access to the SUBJECT would be extremely limited, probably limited to a single social meeting. Because the SUBJECT is a heavy drinker, it was proposed that the individual could be surreptitiously drugged through the medium of an alcoholic cocktail at a social party, ARTICHOKE applied and the SUBJECT induced to perform the act of attempted assassination at some later date. All the above was to be accomplished at one involuntary uncontrolled social meeting. After the act of attempted assassination was performed, it was assumed that the SUBJECT would be taken into custody by the *** Government and thereby "disposed of." Other than personal reassurances by ~~~~~~~~~~ means of security involving the   B/3

B/3

A CIA memorandum, from 1954, proposes using a hypno-programmed assassin, created by the "ARTICHOKE" research project, to attempt the assassination of a "prominent [deleted] politician or, if necessary, against an American official" (*SMURFK Archives*).

PSYCHIATRIC EVALUATION FOR ADULT AUTHORITY
MAY 1975 CALENDAR
SAN QUENTIN PRISON

Mr. Sirhan is a thirty year old Caucasian male who has been in the California Department of Corrections six years for Murder 1st. He was originally sentenced to Death and spent his first years on Death Row. In 1972 his sentence was commuted to Life in Prison.

During his entire stay in the Department of Corrections he has been housed in security housing, mostly for protective custody. Mr. Sirhan has not made any personal enemies. However, it is felt that since he is a somewhat notorious inmate that his safety in the general prison population could not be guaranteed.

My impression of Mr. Sirhan is based on several lengthy interviews and other briefer contacts in the past nine months. I feel Mr. Sirhan has used good judgment in his relationships with other convicts that he has been housed with so that he has not antagonized anyone. This has been difficult as any of the inmates he has been housed with are violent types who easily take offense over small things. Mr. Sirhan has maintained a relationship basically by not relating to them except on a very superficial level. In this way he does not become involved in their many disputes. However, as a result, he feels rather isolated. He does not take part in their every day discussions of criminal activities; rather, prefers to keep to himself, read books that he has and perhaps talk to staff when possible. Mr. Sirhan has always related very well with staff and has never been a management problem. On a couple of occasions over the years Mr. Sirhan has become very frustrated and/or depressed and had an emotional outburst or two. This has never been serious or out of the ordinary realm of expectations for the average person.

At the present time he is still housed in the Adjustment Center but he spends several hours each day working in the office with the counsellors and correctional officers there. He has been very helpful to the staff and this job has also helped Mr. Sirhan to recover from feelings of depression. In recent months he had become increasingly depressed and despondent with feelings of hopelessness of ever being released from lockup. This depression reached the extent as to require hospitalization. In the medical ward where he was able to converse with staff readily, and where he was treated with antidepressant medication. He improved significantly and has maintained his improved spirits now that he has the opportunity to work and talk with more people during the day. I feel this depression was a psychoneurotic reaction to isolation and stress of living with dangerous and violent inmates. He has never shown any signs of psychosis. He has not been delusional. He has never hallucinated. Also he shows no signs of organic brain dysfunction. Both recent and remote memory are intact.

Mr. Sirhan continues to be very close to his family, specifically his mother and brother. They visit regularly. Mr. Sirhan continues to be amnesic to the events surrounding the murder of Robert Kennedy. He states that frequently he has tried to remember what had happened but he has been unable to do this. He expressed remorse over the death of Robert Kennedy and the plight of his widow and twelve children. Over

The first page of a 1975 prison psychiatric evaluation of Sirhan states (last paragraph) that he "continues to be amnesiac to the events surrounding the murder of Robert Kennedy. He states that frequently he has tried to remember what happened but he has been unable to do this" (*SMURFK Archives*).

MEMORANDUM

file

TO: JOHN K. VAN DE KAMP
                District Attorney

FROM: DINKO J. BOZANICH
                Deputy District Attorney

SUBJECT: HYPNOSIS OF SIRHAN

DATE: JUNE 16, 1977

I. INTRODUCTION AND CONCLUSION

By telephonic request through Tom Mc Donald on June 8, 1977,
you asked the following questions:

   1. Was Sirhan hypnotized incident to his
       prosecution?

   2. Would there be any value in hypnotizing
       Sirhan at this time?

Though discussed extensively herein, supported by parenthetical
references to approximately 1000 pages of trial transcript
quickly reviewed since your request, my answers are:

   1. Both of the primary psychiatric experts who
       testified at trial, Dr. Bernard Diamond for
       the defense (6844 - 7211) and Dr. Seymour
       Pollack for the prosecution (7452 - 8032),
       extensively utilized hypnotic techniques
       with Sirhan.

   2. Recognizing that anything is possible,
       there nevertheless would be no value in
       any present hypnosis of Sirhan.

Admittedly, the following discussion of those questions is
lengthy. But I anticipate that recent developments will
probably generate pressures that Sirhan be hypnotized to
determine the "truth" or "whole story". Instead of waiting
for that to develop, plus I now had some time to summarize
my review of a substantial portion of the trial transcript,
this report, albeit lengthy, could prove to be a valuable
and often used internal tool with the passage of time.

An 18-page internal L.A. District Attorney's Office memo (pages 1 and
16 only are reproduced here and on following page) – released in the mid-
1980s – seeks to provide arguments and precedents for resisting any new
requests to hypnotize Sirhan and for squelching the "Manchurian
Candidate theory" (hypnotic programing of assassins), which the writer
of the memo fears might surface in the media (*SMURFK Archives*).

same scenario, solely because of hunches, speculation and conjecture, instead of some realistic and demonstrable evidence that "new" information might be revealed, would be totally worthless in any search for "truth".

Instead of achieving "truth", it appears that such a replay would only resurrect rejected notions of "truth" and thereby create controversy where no genuine or realistic dispute exists. Even worse is the specter of a "Manchurian Candidate" theory being revived and vigorously debated within the media, talk shows and other public forums.

Clearly, a decade ago, hypnosis of Sirhan was initiated by Diamond for reasons strikingly similar to those being advanced today - i.e., to get the "whole story" where others had failed. He was joined by Pollack in that endeavor. They arrived at sharply conflicting pictures of Sirhan, both as to his general mental status before and after the crime, as well as his mental state at commission.

Literally, two "giants" spent considerable time and effort to determine "truth" with whatever tools that psychiatry, medicine, and hypnosis had to offer. The result was a dispute as to virtually every significant issue. Fortunately, there was an opportunity to explore and resolve that conflict within the judicial process, with all of the vigor and tools inherent in the adversary process.

But there is no prospect of such exploration and resolution in any future hypnosis of Sirhan. Neither is it conceivable that the extent of energy expended by Diamond (over 100 hours) and Pollack (almost 200 hours) would be duplicated by any future "expert".

In fact, the lack of such prospects indicates why this office should consider opposing and resisting, if necessary, Sirhan's current suggestions to experiment with him by hypnosis. This position reflects the following considerations:

1. There is no sound basis for concluding that hypnosis is of any value in eliciting "truth" from Sirhan. Illustration - the split between Diamond and Pollack.

O   )

F B I

Date: 8/1/68

Transmit the following in _____
                                    (Type in plaintext or code)

Via _____ AIRTEL _____ AIR MAIL _____
                                         (Priority)

- -

TO: DIRECTOR, FBI (62-587)

FROM: SAC, LOS ANGELES (56-156)

SUBJECT: KENSALT

       Lieutenant MANUEL PENA, Los Angeles Police Depart-
ment (LAPD) today requested that the LAPD be advised in the
event the Bureau receives any information concerning potential publications with respect to the KENNEDY assassination.
PENA particularly concerned about any attemps to write stories
regarding the assassination which might tend to suggest a
conspiratorial aspect.

       The Bureau is requested to advise Los Angeles in
the event such information comes to its attention so that
any possible leads of interest can be thoroughly exhausted
by Los Angeles and the LAPD appropriately advised.

ALL
b7C

3 - Bureau
2 - Los Angeles
(5)

SEARCHED _____
INDEXED _____
SERIALIZED _____
FILED _____

56-156-1505

Approved: _____ Sent _____ M   OFFICE COPY
          Special Agent in Charge

In a memo dated August 1, 1968 – released by the Bureau in the mid-
1980s – LAPD Lt. Manuel Pena asks the FBI to help the department keep
tabs on "potential publications" and/or "attempts" to write about
conspiracy (*SMURFK Archives*).

POSSIBLE ASSOCIATION WITH COMMUNISTS

On the day following the assassination of Robert Kennedy,

(1+2)

-460-

LAPD censorship: Above, a page from the department's *Summary Report*, as released in March 1985, is totally expunged. Opposite page, the undeleted version of the page. The *Summary Report* was re-released in 1988 by the California State Archives; there was almost no censorship, and the LAPD deletions were restored (*SMURFK Archives*).

POSSIBLE ASSOCIATION WITH COMMUNISTS

On the day following the assassination of Robert Kennedy, information was received from a confidential and reliable source that a man named Walter S. Crowe, Jr. had been talking to people about his long-standing acquaintance with Sirhan Sirhan.

Crowe had told the informant that he had been with Sirhan a few weeks before the assassination and that the two had discussed Crowe's activities with the Communist Party. Walter Crowe subsequently told investigators that he feared that he might have influenced Sirhan's decision to kill Senator Kennedy because he attempted to interest Sirhan in the Communist movement.

The F.B.I. report of Crowe's remarks also described a 1961 Volkswagen sedan registered to Adel B. Sirhan, brother of Sirhan Sirhan, which was observed parked in the vicinity of Baces Hall, 1528 North Vermont, Los Angeles. The vehicle was observed on two occasions, December 5, 1963, and January 16, 1966, while meetings of the "Citizens Committee to Preserve American Freedoms" and the W.E.B. Du Bois Club were in progress at that location. The occupant of the vehicle was not seen on either occasion.

A confidential source also reported that members of the Southern California District Communist Party were greatly concerned that an association between Sirhan and the Communist Party might be created. This fear apparently developed after

TEST FIRINGS

Test firings were conducted on June 11, 1968, using a weapon and ammunition supplied by the Los Angeles Police Department as being of the most nearly identical manufacture possible to that of the fatal weapon. An area adjacent to the firing range on the Los Angeles Police Academy was utilized. Personnel consisted of Drs. Holloway and Noguchi, Mr. DeWayne Wolfer and Sgt. William J. Lee. Preliminary studies were with a target composed of a single layer of muslin over 3/8 inch (9 mm) gypsum board. The muzzle was perpendicular to the target unless otherwise noted.

A firm contact firing shows a circular defect about 3/8 inch (9 mm) in diameter, surrounded by a concentric zone of powder deposition about 7/8 inch (22 mm) in diameter and sometimes having a multi-laminar configuration at the periphery. These are on the outer surface of the muslin. Also evident on the under surface is a concentric zone of pale soot deposition about 3 inches (7.5 cm) in diameter.

At a 1/4 inch muzzle distance, there is a 5/16 by 1/4 inch (7.5 x 6 mm) defect with transverse ripping of the fabric over a zone 1-1/2 inches (3.8 cm) in length and about evenly divided bilaterally. Also present is a concentric zone of dense, dark gray discoloration one inch (2.5 cm) in diameter with irregular "clouding" within a zone up to 2-1/2 inches (6.3 cm) in diameter. Several faint radial smudges are identified as corresponding roughly with the known land-and-groove characteristics of the test weapon.

A firing at 1/2 inch muzzle distance is similar in configuration except for the absence of ripping of the target fabric and absence of land-and-groove "puffs." Visually detected powder residue is present in a zone having a maximum diameter of about 6 inches (15 cm).

At one inch distance there is the usual central defect and dense but comparatively homogeneous smudging up to a radius of 1-5/8 inches (4.2 mm).

A firing at 2 inch muzzle distance shows fairly homogeneous but comparatively lighter smudging up to a radius of 2-1/4 inches (5.6 cm). Discrete tattoo particles are now seen in a central zone up to 7/8 inch (2.2 cm) in radius.

The 3 inch distance firing shows pale mottling of powder residue within a radius up to 2-1/4 inches (5.6 cm), as well as finely dispersed powder granules up to a radius of about 1-3/4 inches (4.4 cm).

At 4 inches there is a pale smudging zone up to 1-3/4 inches (4.4 cm) in radius. In sharp contrast, discrete powder tattoo particles are identified out to a radius as much as 2 inches (5 cm).

Target configuration was then changed as follows. A single layer of muslin was placed over several crumpled thicknesses of the same fabric. Additional firings at close contact, loose contact, 1/8 inch (3 mm), 1/4 inch (6.5 mm), all show patterns similar to those on the original target.

A series of firings was then performed using geometry simulating that of the fatal gunshot wound to the head, as determined by previous studies. The post-auricular region was simulated by the padded muslin described above. The ear was simulated by an animal ear obtained from an abbatoir and with the hair removed.

With the test weapon at an angle of 15 degrees upward and 30 degrees forward (to correspond with goniometric data) and at a distance of one inch (2.5 cm) from the edge of the right "ear," the test pattern is most similar to the powder residue pattern noted on the Senator's right ear and on hair specimens studied. Similarity persists, on the 2 inch (5 cm) distance firing, with respect to the distribution of discrete powder granules.

Officially released in 1988 is this LAPD June 11, 1968, test-firing report demonstrating conclusively that the only way to replicate the powder burns on the Senator's head and clothing was to have held the gun nearly point-blank to the target. Virtually all of the witnesses placed Sirhan's gun 1½ to 6 feet away from Kennedy (*SMURFK Archives*).

Official evidence from the Robert F. Kennedy assassination which
is reportedly lost, missing or destroyed:

1. "Two boards from door frame" from the Ambassador Hotel pantry,
   booked into evidence, containing what are described in FBI
   reports as "bullet holes."

2. An object reported to be a bullet clearly embedded in a door
   frame in police evidence photographs.

3. Two ceiling tiles taken from the pantry, through which bullets
   fired in the shooting apparently passed. These are important
   to reconstructing bullet flight paths and the number of bullets
   fired in the shooting.

4. X-rays or specialized photographs of the above evidence.

5. A bullet reportedly recovered from Sirhan Sirhan's pocket following the shooting.

6. The results of spectrographic tests said to have been taken
   during evidence examinations.

7. Documentation from the test-firing of Sirhan's gun reportedly
   performed by DeWayne Wolfer, LAPD criminalist on the case.
   (Only one photomicrograph, misidentified by Wolfer in 1975,
   has ever come to light from the 1968 bullet comparisons. The
   1968 firearms panel was unable to substantiate the matches to
   Sirhan's gun asserted in 1968.)

8. The left sleeve of Senator Kennedy's suit coat and shirt.

9. The report of police sergeant Paul Sharaga regarding suspects
   seen leaving the Ambassador Hotel shortly following the shooting.

10. Iver Johnson Cadet revolver number H18602, reportedly used as
    a substitute for Sirhan's gun in disputed evidence tests in the
    case.

Researcher Gregory Stone issued this list, in December 1986, of RFK assassination evidence that was lost, is missing or has been destroyed. The
list has been distributed at press conferences (*Gregory Stone*).

May, 1990

Partial list of additional RFK assassination evidence determined
to be lost, missing or destroyed following the release of the
available LAPD case files by the California State Archives in
April 1988:

1. 2,410 unidentified case photographs burned by Special Unit
Senator personnel on August 21, 1968. (Special Unit Senator
was the L.A. Police Department task force created to investigate
the assassination.)

2. Photographs of the shooting as it occurred, taken by a student
photographer and confiscated by police in the following hours.
It is possible that these photographs have great evidence value.
The photographer is currently suing the LAPD for damages.

3. Unidentified "important papers" burned by two SUS student
workers, according to police documents, at General Hospital incinerator on July 18, 1968.

4. The first page of an FBI document from the week following the
shooting, concerning photographs and captions of the RFK crime
scene taken by the LAPD. This page contained the names of LAPD and
FBI personnel involved in the transfer and identification of these
photos, following the filing of an earlier FBI report identifying
"bullet holes" in wood at the crime scene.

5. The name and interview and investigative records of two witnesses at the Ambassador Hotel after the shooting who gave a report to the LAPD Command Post chief directly corroborating the testimony of witness Sandra Serrano concerning the "polka dot dress
girl."

6. Daily logs of investigators on the case, required to be submitted by the Special Unit Senator organizational manual.

7. Two numbered "critique of investigation" reports submitted by
Special Unit Senator investigators.

8. Numerous referenced attachments to the SUS case supervisors'
"Daily Summary of Activities" file.

9. The official log of the L.A. Sheriff's Department concerning
the activities of Sheriff's personnel at the crime scene during
the three hours after the shooting. Referenced as an attachment
to the report of an interview with a Sheriff's deputy.

10. Any mention or report of an interview with Deputy Sheriff
Walter Tew, who marked and identified the locations of four suspected bullet holes in door frames at the west end of the pantry
crime scene, the locations later identified as "bullet holes" by
the fbi.

Stone compiled this list of additional missing RFK assassination evidence
in May 1990, subsequent to the release, in 1988, of LAPD files on
Kennedy's death (*Gregory Stone*).

contention that she was taking her cues from Di Pierro. This is precisely the notion put forth in the June 20 interview in which Serrano finally retracted her story.

SERGEANT HERNANDEZ: And is that when you heard the kid [Di Pierro] say something?
SERRANO: Right.
HERNANDEZ: In a polka-dot dress?
SERRANO: Right.
HERNANDEZ: So that's where the thing about . . .
SERRANO: I guess. I don't know.
HERNANDEZ: The polka-dot dress, that's where it started.
SERRANO: I guess.

In a more orthodox investigation, doubts concerning Serrano's credibility would have been substantially diminished by her good fortune in selecting a Los Angeles law-enforcement official to spontaneously tell her story to, before she went on TV or to the witness room. If LAPD remained unimpressed by Sergeant Schraga and the other Ambassador witnesses, they could have interviewed Ambrose in minute detail, as they did Serrano and Di Pierro, by perhaps administering a polygraph. Supposedly, the polygraph was being administered on the basis of the importance of what the witness had to say, and Ambrose was crucial. Instead, he was virtually ignored in the department's intensive Serrano investigation.

LAPD's *Summary Report* dismisses Serrano on the basis of the polygraph, the sound test proving she could not have heard gunfire, and also an interview with Captain Cecil R. Lynch of the Los Angeles Fire Department: "During the time Senator Kennedy made his victory speech in the Embassy Room, Lynch began checking various stairways and exits for possible violations of fire regulations. Lynch stated that he checked the stairs Serrano alleged to have been seated on moments before Kennedy was shot, and at the time no one was on the stairs."

It seems odd that, moments before the speech, outside staircases that were considerably removed from the crowd's central focus would need checking. Unlike Serrano, who was overcome by the heat and the crowd, few people could be expected to be clogging the external stairways during the Senator's speech.*

Among the surviving tapes released 20 years after the crime is Sandra Serrano's final interview – her June 20 polygraph session and, a few minutes later, the retraction of her story. Perhaps it survived because Serrano was such a publicized witness, with her witness history detailed in Houghton's book *Special Unit Senator,* that its loss or disappearance would be too conspicuous. In any event, it has the singular distinction among 301 taped interviews of being the only one to be officially embargoed, both internally and externally. The log states: ''Do not play or have transcribed without written permission of Captain Brown [second in command].''

The interview was conducted by Lt. Enrique Hernandez, the investigation's polygraph operator, who also investigated conspiracy avenues and who worked very closely with Lt. Manuel Pena. Pena served as supervisor of day watch investigators and was a key member of the case preparation team that readied the case for trial. Hernandez was a 15-year veteran and was 37 years old.

The polygraph test and the key portions of the interview were conducted when Hernandez and Serrano were alone. She had phoned the FBI on June 12 stating that she should be contacted only through her lawyers. During the June 20 interview she brought up the subject of her lawyers and told Hernandez she had not yet met with them.

The polygraph tests were administered between approximately 9:00 and 10:00 p.m. Prior to the interview, according to Houghton's book,[6] Lt. Pena asked Hernandez what he was doing for dinner that night and ''suggested he might like to take Sandra Serrano out for an SUS [Special Unit Senator] bought steak.'' There is no known recording of the dinner, but one cannot help but wonder how much fun it was for Serrano and what was discussed. LAPD's Serrano investigation was surely the most imaginative of this case – firing guns in the pantry, buying steaks,

*For a detailed analysis of the problems with Lynch's account, see Appendix B.

assembling a polka-dot-dress fashion show.

During the first part of the interview Sandra's aunt was present (her parents lived in Ohio). Lt. Hernandez was very cordial and sympathetic. He credited her with being an "intelligent young woman" and invited her to tell her story "as best she can remember." He explained the workings and wonders of the polygraph, and how it was thoroughly reliable.

When her aunt departed and the grueling interview transpired, Sandra expressed her distrust several times. To the polygraph question, "Do you believe that I will be completely fair with you throughout this examination?" she answered, "No." Hernandez later inquired whether she believed what he was telling her. Again she said no.

LAPD's *Summary Report* tells us that after the June 10 polka-dot fashion show Serrano was asked if she would take a polygraph: "She answered affirmatively." FBI Agent Richard Burris says the same thing in his report of the June 10 session. But the audio tape contains no such question and answer. Perhaps it came off the record. However, a June 20, 1968, FBI memo from J. Edgar Hoover to his five top assistants, discovered by Greg Stone in FBI files, says something quite different. In the memo, marked "secret," Hoover reports on his briefing of Attorney General Ramsey Clark and states:

> I said we were checking various lines as to Ray [James Earl Ray] and Sirhan Sirhan in the Robert F. Kennedy case as to the mysterious woman in the pantry of the Ambassador Hotel and so far they have all fallen through. I said the girl in the Sirhan case has refused to take a lie detector test, but I thought the police were going to give her one although so far she has refused to take one. The Attorney General asked if this were the woman in the polka-dot dress and I told him it was the one who claimed she saw the woman in the polka-dot dress. The Attorney General said he had read the report on her and got the feeling she was unbalanced. I commented that she was seeking publicity.

Serrano's discrediters were in Washington, D.C., as well as Los Angeles. It would be instructive to know what "report" the Attorney General was referring to and what the foundation for Hoover's comment was, if any.

The interview on the night of June 20 will now be recounted in detail, for it provides a window onto LAPD's approach to the entire case. With Serrano's aunt present, Hernandez describes his long experience as a polygraph operator and describes, in technical specifics, the reliability of the machine. "No guess-work," he promises.

Serrano doesn't buy it. She mentions that the courts won't allow it, that a teacher once told her it was not reliable: "I don't trust the polygraph with what I've read and what people have told me."

Hernandez is audibly less patient when defending challenges to his machine. He reassures her, "That's why Maggie [Sandra's aunt] will be here" [but only for the pre-test, not for the actual tests or the interview].

Early on, Hernandez makes it clear that Serrano's polygraph has an official mandate: "There is a tremendous amount of turmoil, shootings, lack of respect for law and order, lack of respect for the decency of other people. And the Department of Justice and the country needs to know that what I believe you're telling me as the truth is in fact the truth, and that's why they have asked me to come down and talk to you and administer a polygraph."

Later, after her aunt departs, Sandra protests, "It was rotten in the beginning because you never mentioned to my aunt that we were gonna take a polygraph."*

---

* In his book *Special Unit Senator* (p. 120) Chief Robert Houghton told readers: "Hernandez called for Miss Serrano, and over dinner they talked about what she had seen and heard after the assassination at the hotel . . . Hernandez asked if she would be willing to undergo a polygraph examination. *She readily agreed* [emphasis added] . . .

A June 20 FBI memo from the Los Angeles field office to Director Hoover states: "LAPD attempting contact with Serrano for interview evening hours this date. Polygraph examination will be given if Serrano still consents. Bureau will be advised results."

HERNANDEZ: Oh yes, I did. I told her this morning.

SERRANO: She said you just wanted to talk to me, 'cause I asked her.

HERNANDEZ: She was here during the test [the preliminary control questions].

Serrano finally says, "We can't do anything about it so let's go [proceed]." After her first test he asks her if she is afraid. "Yes, I don't like this. I just don't like this," she says.

In 1978, the House of Representatives Select Committee on Assassinations (HSCA) employed a panel of polygraph experts in its re-investigation of the assassination of Dr. Martin Luther King, Jr. The panel assessed the validity of two tests administered to convicted assassin James Earl Ray in 1977 – one for *Playboy* magazine, the other for columnist Jack Anderson.[7] The panel concluded that the tests were seriously flawed. Some questions contained words that were too dramatic, and the tests were administered in close proximity and in the early morning hours, thus creating a "fatigue" factor.

Serrano's test, administered between 9:00 and 10:00 p.m., was surrounded by intense questioning that clearly upset her. During the first part of her test she was instructed to answer yes or no. She was asked, "When you told police that a girl in a polka-dot dress told you she had shot Kennedy were you telling the truth?" Serrano replied that the girl did not say *she* shot Kennedy but "we" shot Kennedy. Hernandez comes across patently during this interview as a proponent of the pronoun-confusion theory, proposing that the girl said *they* shot Kennedy, thus indicating the crucial importance of the pronoun. Thus, this was a sloppy question, confusing to the subject. He immediately rephrased it correctly, and she answered negatively.

After the first series of questions he reminds her to answer "yes or no." She counters that the questions could not be answered that way; he assures her that he'll rephrase them any way she wants.

To this researcher, Sergeant Hernandez' questioning, following the polygraph test, appears to be classic "good cop, bad cop," except that he plays both roles. He uses the allegedly negative polygraph results to further pressure her into withdrawing her story. What follows is a series of excerpts, not necessarily in chronological order, which capture the flavor of this emotionally charged session.

Hernandez tells Serrano that he wants to talk to her like a brother. He informs her – with considerable editorial license, according to this author's reading of the case – that "19 girls" have come forward with stories, but only two "really loved Kennedy as a person." The rest were gold diggers or publicity hounds. But, he says, Sandra is one of the two who loved RFK and she is honestly mistaken about what she saw: "You owe it to Senator Kennedy, the late Senator Kennedy, to come forward. Be a woman about this. You don't know if he's a witness right now in this room. Don't shame his death by keeping this up."

Later Serrano says, "I seen those people [the polka-dot girl, Sirhan, the other man].

Said Hernandez, "No. No. No. No, Sandy."

Hernandez invoked a wide range of themes for his game of "truth" and consequences: "You will live a life of shame knowing what you're doing right now is wrong."

He then tells her of his personal affection for Kennedy "the man," how Kennedy allegedly gave him a commendation that he greatly cherishes. He accuses Serrano of thwarting the investigation into the Senator's death by diverting it. "What you say you saw is not true. Tell me why you made up the story."

He repeatedly invoked Robert Kennedy or his family. . . .

"Please, in the name of Kennedy," says Hernandez.

"Don't use that name," Serrano protests.

"The Kennedys have had nothing but tragedy," says the sergeant (promoted to lieutenant a month later). "They must be satisfied. It [unintelligible] them to know the truth . . . And I'm sure – you mark my words – that one of these days, if you're woman enough, you will get a letter from Ethel Kennedy – personal – thanking you for at least letting her rest on these aspects of this investigation."

Serrano, occasionally feisty, made several attempts to hold her ground: "I'm not gonna say nobody told me ["We shot him."] just to satisfy anybody else."

But her interviewer would have none of it.

"This didn't happen," he states forcefully.

"It happened," she replies.

"No, it didn't happen."". . .

"Nobody told you 'We shot him,' " says Hernandez.

"Yes" (inaudible, her voice fading), she affirms.

"No," insists Hernandez.

"I'm sorry but that's true. That is true," states Serrano.

At another point, when he again states flatly that she did not hear this phrase, she again disagrees and laughs nervously (sounding on the verge of breaking into tears).

"Don't laugh it off," he says in a menacing tone.

"Don't shout at me," says Serrano.

"Well," says Hernandez, "I'm trying not to shout, but this is such an emotional thing with me. If you loved the man, the least you owe him is letting him rest in peace, and he can't."

At various times he expresses a paternalistic concern for her anguish and welfare. "Why are you making yourself suffer like this," he interrupts. He tells her that this stress is "bad for the heart. . . . This is gonna make an old woman out of you before your time." He implores her to "redeem something that's a deep wound that will grow with you like a disease – like cancer."

With all of the important points, such as history, the nation, the Kennedy family, the Senator's ghost, law and order, self-improvement, good health and redemption going for her, Sandra Serrano finally saw the light as LAPD wanted her to, and she recanted. She admitted, under guiding questioning, that her account was wrong. She had been confused and pressured by the expectations of the media and the investigators. She felt compelled to give more information than she actually had; she could not admit the lie for fear of appearing foolish.

In return for her confession of falsehood she was promised

confidentiality and freedom from further interrogation. Even before the polygraph test began, she asked Hernandez: "The results of this test – how far will they go?"

"Just between you and me," Hernandez answered.

"I don't want any of this stuff made public," said Serrano.

"We're not dealing with publicity," Hernandez insisted.

In 1970, Chief Robert Houghton would publicly reveal her alleged failure of the polygraph test in his book *Special Unit Senator*. In March 1986, when the Los Angeles Police Commission first released LAPD's 1,500-page *Summary Report*, the names of every witness in the case – including Serrano and the dozens of others discussed in Houghton's book – were deleted in order to protect "rights to privacy."

Hernandez offered her, "Tell me why you made up the story and no one else will talk to you." If she will tell him "the truth," he has the authority to prevent further investigation of her. Or: "The other way is for me to go out there [to the officers outside the interview room], hold up the paper [the polygraph test] and tell these people that she failed the polygraph test." Later he warns, "There's people out there waiting for you if you don't tell me the truth. They're gonna wanna talk to you again and again."

After the polygraph, Hernandez proposes that she make a statement to a stenographer, setting everything straight. But she doesn't want anyone else in the room. Serrano sounds fatigued and distraught.

SERRANO: Can't you use a tape recorder?
HERNANDEZ: Well, probably we can.
HERNANDEZ (later): Let me get a stenographer.
SERRANO: Can't you do a tape recording?
HERNANDEZ: Let me see if I can, O.K.? . . . I'm gonna go out there and just get a tape recorder, see if I can.

Under calm, sympathetic questioning by Hernandez, Serrano finally recants, admitting that "the whole thing was a lie." She admitted that the idea of polka dots came from Di Pierro.

The final phase of Serrano's certification as a failed witness was Hernandez' report of December 1968 to Captain Hugh Brown, entitled "Polygraph Examination of Sandra Serrano." It states:

> Miss Serrano was interrogated extensively and ultimately she admitted that the story about Sirhan Sirhan, the girl in the polka-dot dress and the gunshots was not true. She stated that she had been sitting on a stairway at the time that she had mentioned and that she did in fact hear a car backfire a couple of times, but she knew that the sounds did come from a car and were not gunshots.

During the interview in which Hernandez sought to expunge the "pack of mistruths," the only passage relevant to the above conclusion reads as follows:

HERNANDEZ: Well, also before, you had stated you heard some shots.
SERRANO: No, I never said I heard shots.
HERNANDEZ: You never said that? Well, now, somebody quoted you as saying that you had heard shots.
SERRANO: I never said I heard shots.
HERNANDEZ: O.K.
SERRANO: I heard backfires of a car . . . I know they weren't shots.
HERNANDEZ: You know, for a fact, that they were not gunshots.
SERRANO: I know it.

Hernandez' report on the polygraph interview asserted, "She said that while she was sitting on the stairway, approximately four to five people came running down the stairway screaming that Kennedy had been shot."

To the author's knowledge, Serrano never attributed "screaming" to the people she encountered. "Screaming" seems more compatible with the notion that the people in question were shocked Kennedy supporters (and thus more likely to say "they" shot him). During her numerous interviews Serrano typically described the polka-dot woman as "saying," "We shot him!" In one FBI interview she said the woman "yelled" the phrase.

In addition to keeping the polygraph results from public view and keeping the other investigators at bay, Hernandez raised another point of potential embarrassment for Serrano, and promised to take care of it too: "What we are going to do, Sandy, is I'm not going to tell your aunt anything. I think we should decide how we're going to handle it. . . . Do you want to tell her, unless you want me to? I don't want to tell her unless you want me to." Serrano does not want her aunt informed.

In order to understand the priorities and perspective operating within L.A. law on this case, one need only refer to two case studies in the treatment of key witnesses: Lisa Urso, by the District Attorney's Office, and Sandra Serrano, by LAPD.

Serrano's ordeal did not end in 1968. Twenty years later (April 19, 1988), when LAPD files were released for the first time by the California State Archives in Sacramento, media coverage was extensive. Press kits issued by the California Secretary of State's Office specifically mentioned Serrano's polka-dot-dress story, her lie detector test and her retraction. The press was hungry for substantive tidbits from the voluminous file, and reported that Serrano had told LAPD, "The whole thing was a lie."

Three days after the documents were released, then-40-year-old Sandra Serrano Sewell surfaced to tell radio interviewer Jack Thomas, "There was a lot of badgering that was going on. I was just 20 years old and I became unglued. . . . I said what they wanted me to say."

Despite the public disclosure of police and FBI files containing data that corroborated Serrano's original account, and that also revealed an effort by Los Angeles authorities to discredit her, and despite the availability of the audio tapes of her polygraph test and related interviews (publicly available since May 1988), the most recent press account still does not reflect any of this important evidence. In April 1990, a national wire service article repeated Serrano's 1968 polka-dot-dress story and her 1988 charge that she was pressured into changing her account. "Police dismiss the woman's badgering allegations," the article concluded. "Although she recanted her story it was often resurrected by conspiracy buffs who suggested the woman in the polka-dot dress was part of an assassination plot."

Thus, with the exception of Serrano's allegation of badgering and LAPD's dismissal of it, the Serrano story was reported essentially the same way in 1990 as it was 18 years earlier by Chief Robert Houghton in his book *Special Unit Senator*. The newly available data contradicting the official version regarding Serrano and the polka-dot-dress girl went unreported.

Chapter 15

GUNS AND GIRLS

"Actual Girl in the Polka-Dot Dress"
— Heading, p. 421, LAPD *Summary Report*

LAPD's polka-dot-dress investigation was clearly geared more toward making her disappear than to finding her. As previously discussed, virtually every witness who claimed to have seen the mystery woman, either at the Ambassador or at other Kennedy campaign locations, was consistently discredited or dismissed. Instead of pursuing the Schraga APB or the description provided by Serrano, the Bernsteins and others, police half-heartedly showed a few mug shots — mostly Kennedy campaign workers — to several witnesses who claimed to have seen the suspicious young woman. Investigators also pursued a series of dead-end leads in their "search" for the woman. Most were clearly frivolous from the outset.

In the first week or so following the crime, a plethora of eyewitness evidence pointed to a possible Sirhan accomplice. Several candidates for an innocent explanation arose, but none panned out. On June 5, police took into custody an attractive young woman named Cheryl Wessels, based on an informant's telephone call identifying her as the polka-dot girl. When she produced an alibi that placed her at home during the shooting she was released.

On June 7, a 19-year-old Kennedy volunteer came forward and identified herself as the innocent source of confusion that had spawned the search. Cathy Sue Fulmer told authorities she ran into the Embassy Room after the assassination, yelling "They shot him!" Serrano viewed Ms. Fulmer at police headquarters and rejected her candidacy as the polka-dot-dress girl. Not only was she not on the stairs where Serrano claimed to have seen the fleeing woman, but she was wearing a green dress that had no polka dots. She was, however, wearing an orange polka-dot scarf. This, she speculated, might have been the source of the sightings.

Another young woman came forward. She wanted the authorities to establish her alibi because her friends were accusing her of being the polka-dot girl.

A week later a woman named Muriel Lee turned herself in as another candidate for innocent sartorial confusion on the part of the witnesses. She had been in the pantry before the shooting wearing a black, long-sleeved dress and a large white hat. LAPD's *Summary Report* dutifully reports: "It was determined by investigators that she was not the woman that Serrano had allegedly seen due to the totally different description of her clothing and physical description."

After dismissing each and every witness to a sinister polka-dot girl, LAPD opted to produce its own benign polka-dot-dress girl. The department's *Summary Report* offers a section headlined "Actual Girl in the Polka-Dot Dress."[1] Those few witnesses who were not hallucinating or fabricating were, police claim, seeing coed Valeria Schulte and merely misperceiving her behavior. Valeria was certainly no threat to anyone, especially L.A. law. A "Kennedy Girl" campaign volunteer, the attractive blonde was allegedly wearing a polka-dot dress at the Ambassador the night of the shooting. Although Booker Griffin and Sandra Serrano would flatly reject her, that didn't matter to LAPD because these two witnesses were deemed to have been discredited anyway, relegated to the status of unreliable, and nothing they had to say would matter to officials in charge of the investigation. Since the witnesses with the best descriptions of the polka-dot-dress girl were "wrong," LAPD was free to nominate just about any female they chose. In contrast to what the witnesses described, Schulte wore an oversized Kennedy button at the crime scene, her dress was green with large yellow spots (not small dark ones), her leg was in a cast from hip to ankle, and she walked with a crutch (a rather distinctive trait that apparently somehow went unnoticed by all of the other polka-dot-girl witnesses).

Witnesses who claimed to see Sirhan and an attractive young woman, sometimes accompanied by another, taller man – at the Ambassador Hotel, at Robbie's Restaurant, at RFK campaign offices and appearances – were all wrong. But in the process of building an airtight case against Sirhan, authorities found that he was at a pistol range the day of the June 4 shooting with a young, attractive blonde and a taller man. The police handling of this complex incident reveals much about why the entire investigation of this case is in such disarray.

To the prosecutors' glee it was easy to place Sirhan at the San Gabriel Valley Gun Club in Duarte on the morning and afternoon before the post-midnight assassination. He was positively identified by numerous persons. He rapidly fired his .22 pistol for hours and was therefore very conspicuous. For the prosecution this showed premeditation of the first magnitude: The assassin spent hours perfecting his murderous skills. Sirhan had even signed the gun-club register. In the process of interviewing 37 witnesses to select the best ones to use at the trial, LAPD found that the specter of conspiracy had popped up again. Sirhan had been seen on the firing range in the company of an attractive, young blond female. Her account of the incident was fraught with unanswered questions and conflicted with those of other witnesses. Typically, LAPD half-heartedly investigated her story and succeeded only in raising more unanswered questions. Moreover, the woman would turn out to be a waitress at a topless bar near Santa Anita racetrack, where Sirhan had worked, a bar located eight miles from another topless bar Sirhan had frequented.

The first problem was Everett Buckner, the range master. He gave two lengthy interviews to the FBI on June 8 and 12 before LAPD had talked to him. His story was the same both times. He claimed that shortly after Sirhan checked in, a couple entered sometime between 10:00 and 10:30 a.m. They had a rifle and what Buckner believed to be a .22 pistol. The woman was young, blond and attractive. While the man fired the rifle on the rifle range, the woman was having difficulty firing the .22 pistol. Buckner claimed that when Sirhan offered to help, she blurted out loud enough for him to clearly hear, "God damn you, you son of a bitch, get out of here or they'll recognize us." Sirhan did not leave, but continued to instruct her, according to Buckner.

The FBI seemed to be taking Buckner seriously. On June 10 it dispatched two agents to the gun club to rake up expended shells at the position where Buckner said Sirhan was shooting and at several adjacent firing postions "[i]n view of the statements of range officer Buckner that Sirhan Sirhan was talking to a blond female who was shooting in the vicinity . . ."

LAPD would dismiss Buckner as not credible. He allegedly also failed the polygraph, as had several other undesirable witnesses in this investigation. Buckner's story was, in part, demonstrably garbled. There were two couples at the range that day, each with a blond woman. One couple did not interact with Sirhan. Buckner's story was partially a composite. He attributed to the couple that was with Sirhan an argument that the other couple had, even though the two couples were markedly different in appearance and in the number of persons in their party.

While it is not possible to discern from FBI and police files whether Buckner's unravelling as a witness was caused by his own confusion or by police pressure, the familiar trail is clear. An FBI report dated June 13 indicates that Lloyd Hager, the manager of the gun club and Buckner's boss, reported to the bureau that Buckner was "shooting his mouth off all over the place" and talking with the press, including a *Life* magazine reporter. The FBI memo then states that when Hager phoned this report to the Bureau, there were two LAPD intelligence officers in his office. The officers said they would talk with Buckner, and one asserted that he:

> personally was going to read to Buckner a copy of the court order restricting any comment concerning the Senator Robert F. Kennedy assassination, to be sure that Buckner understood its meaning, and if possible, get Buckner to sign a statement to the effect that he had read and understood its contents.

The question is whether LAPD personnel really understood the order, since the intelligence officer seemed to regard it as a blanket suspension of free speech regarding the Kennedy case.

On June 16, the day before his first recorded interview with LAPD but apparently after they had talked to him about not talking, Buckner phoned the FBI's Los Angeles office. According to the FBI report, he claimed he had more information that he had not told the Bureau because of pressure from his boss not to talk. He said he was scheduled to be interviewed by LAPD the next morning but also wanted to talk in person with FBI agents. Agent William Nolan decided that the Bureau should not recontact Buckner until LAPD had talked with him. The memo concludes that the FBI will inform LAPD of Buckner's call and will advise the department about any re-interview by Bureau agents.

Whether Buckner was exaggerating in order to enhance his status as a conspiracy witness or was trying to dupe the FBI into insulating him from being further pressured by LAPD is not clear. Buckner *was* recontacted by the FBI. A terse, one paragraph report dated June 23 states that "he actually had no additional information." Another FBI report recounts that Buckner's boss, Lloyd Hager, told interviewing agents on June 17 that he fired Buckner on June 16 because he was unreliable. In contrast, Hager's June 17 LAPD interview contains no mention of Buckner or the FBI agents's earlier June 16 allegation of Hager's reported firing of Buckner.

Finally, on July 2, Buckner was given a polygraph test by Sergeant Hernandez. This witness also allegedly failed. Hernandez' remarks included: "You know you did not hear this woman tell

Sirhan anything about someone recognizing them."

"We have to correct that."

"We don't want the name of Everett Buckner coming up and people saying he lied about that."

"I want you to tell me why you injected this statement."

"Was it publicity, was it money, what was the reason . . . ?"

"Because I think it's true," says Buckner. "I think she said it. I still think she said it."

Hernandez insists that Buckner fabricated and demands "man to man" to know why.

Among the gun-club witnesses were two very credible ones whose account must have seemed to them very simple and straightforward, but it presented a problem for LAPD. Roberta and Richard Grijalva, 19-year-old twins, had seen Sirhan firing a rifle at the rifle-range section of the gun club. Since Sirhan did not own a rifle, and since no other patrons reported innocently loaning him one that day, the question was, as defense investigator Robert Kaiser asked in his notebook, "Where did he get a rifle?"

According to Richard Grijalva, Sirhan was not just "trying the rifle for a couple of shots." He was firing it for about a half-hour. This would appear to argue against a brief, casual loan by a patron he did not know. The blond, attractive woman (whom we will discuss shortly) who was seen interacting with Sirhan on the pistol range was accompanied by her husband, who was seen with (and admits to bringing) a rifle. But the couple denies being at the club until just about closing time, when everyone but Sirhan had departed. The Grijalvas saw Sirhan firing a rifle at around 11:00 a.m. Thus the rifle could only have been obtained by Sirhan under circumstances LAPD could not account for.

The Grijalva twins were very good witnesses – clear, cautious, consistent. They accurately described Sirhan's attire (blue pants, sweater, sunglasses). Like other witnesses, they noted his rapid-fire technique with his .22 when he was on the pistol range instead of the rifle range. But their observation of Sirhan firing a rifle was obviously unwelcomed by LAPD.

Richard was given a polygraph test, as if he might be fabricating annoying loose ends to purposely impede LAPD's crafting of a streamlined official version of the case.* He passed. Of course, in LAPD's interpretation, this proved not that Sirhan was firing a rifle but that the witness was "honestly mistaken." Then the police decided to invent a mythical solution for this unexplained incident: "An unidentified person resembling Sirhan in general appearance was observed by witnesses firing on the rifle range."

None of the 37 witnesses at the gun club reported anyone remotely resembling the dark-featured, blue-clad, rapid-firing Sirhan (each witness was asked to describe everyone they saw at the gun club, and I have read the entire, voluminous file). The Grijalvas' identification of Sirhan was as good as the witnesses whom the prosecution would bring to the trial to establish his presence there. But for the twins who saw him fire a rifle, LAPD would invent a Sirhan lookalike,

Regarding the unidentified woman who had been with Sirhan on the pistol range, police received a dramatic call on June 6. According to LAPD's phone log, Deborah Jaimison[†] called to say that at the firing range, Sirhan "was next to her shooting . . . he asked her if she wanted to try his gun and shot several rounds. Could be gun that killed the Senator?" Her address and phone number were provided.

It is strange that with all the furor over Buckner's remarks about Sirhan and a woman who said, "Get out of here or they'll recognize us," the police did not interview Ms. Jaimison until June 19. She and her husband did not sign the gun club register. Even so, it would appear that LAPD wasn't following up on phone calls about the assassination with much investigative zeal. Deborah and her husband Arnold each told their story to the police and later to the FBI. Their account of their time and motion regarding the incident was at odds with data provided by other witnesses.

---

* It should be noted that such polygraph tests were reserved almost exclusively for witnesses whose stories suggested conspiracy rather than those whose stories – even if shaky or fraught with conflicts – were significant for the official conclusions.

† A pseudonym provided by the author.

The shapely, blond, long-haired Deborah claimed to have left home with her husband at 3:00 on the afternoon of June 4. They dropped the kids at a baby-sitter, then drove to the Briar Patch bar to get directions to the gun club. Arnold would fire his rifle; Deborah would learn to use the .22 pistol she received as a Christmas present in 1966 but had never used.

They arrived at the gun club at about 4:00 and got targets from the range master. Except for Sirhan and the range master, the place was deserted. Sirhan noticed that she was having trouble with her weapon. She initiated contact and asked for his help. He demonstrated how to fire her gun and shot approximately 18 rounds. He then offered to let her fire his weapon – the one that would soon become infamous. She fired it twice. Her husband came over from the rifle range and the three chatted briefly about guns before parting company. Mrs. Jaimison told LAPD that this encounter with Sirhan lasted about 20 minutes, "maybe a little more. He was very polite. Didn't make any advances or anything like that, even though there was only him and I out there."

The Jaimisons rendered very positive IDs of Sirhan. They placed the gun in his hand only hours before he would arrive at the Ambassador Hotel. The untidiness of the Buckner and Grijalva stories seemed incidental now that the gun-club mystery woman was known and the affair seemed to have an innocent explanation.

But was the explanation valid? The dogged attention to inconsistencies, to cross-checking and to background checks that LAPD mustered against troublesome witnesses and critics was absent from its investigation of the gun club couple who interacted with Sirhan. There were indeed conflicts in the data that needed to be resolved. But even with serious inconsistencies, for some unexplained reason this couple was not given a polygraph test.

The stories of several witnesses are at odds with the Jaimisons' assertion that they encountered Sirhan between four and five o'clock after everyone but range master Buckner had departed.* While it is an open question as to which elements of Buckner s story

* A December 16, 1968, FBI report entitled "Chronology of Events: Life of Sirhan Bishara Sirhan" states that on June 4 he was at "San Gabriel Valley Gun Glub from approximately 11:00 a.m. to 3:00 p.m. [p. 8]."

are accurate (since at least one is not), he places the interaction between Sirhan and the attractive blonde as occurring mid-morning. Two witnesses saw a woman fitting Mrs. Jaimison's general description, accompanied by a man, arriving at the target range in the morning rather than the late afternoon.

Harry Hicks, an employee who was painting the range, told the FBI that in late monring he saw a man and a woman arrive, and the woman was "quite shapely." Hicks joked about her good looks with co-worker Russell Doyle Weaver. Weaver told the Bureau that shortly after his 11:00 a.m. arrival, he saw a man and woman come in. The woman walked closely past him. He described her as 18 to 19 years old, 5-foot-2 to 5-foot-3, 100 pounds, with blond hair. She was still there when he left. Deborah Jaimison is described in her FBI interview as 26 years old, 5-foot-2, with green eyes and blond hair. Her LAPD photos clearly show that she is slim and attractive. The reader will also recall that the Grijalva twins saw Sirhan firing a rifle for about a half-hour around 11:00 a.m. The Jaimisons had a rifle as well as a pistol.

LAPD should have considered the possibility that these earlier sightings of an attractive blonde were of Deborah Jaimison. Moreover, this raised the possibility that both her presence at the range and her interaction with Sirhan were at a different time, and perhaps more extensive, than her story indicated. Consider that the author's analysis of all 37 gun-club witnesses found that none of these identifiable persons had physical descriptions (in their FBI and LAPD interviews) that should allow them to be confused with the attractive blonde and the man who were seen arriving in the morning.* Thus, if witnesses Weaver and Hicks are correct about such a couple arriving in the morning, either we have a completely unaccounted-for mystery couple who looked generally like the Jaimisons, or the Jaimisons, who did not sign the club register, were

---

* Though there were two couples each having a blond woman, whom Buckner seems to have confused regarding which couple had an argument, the couples were really quite different in appearance. The other couple besides the Jaimisons included a blonde who was described as "chunky" and was wearing attire of a different color. This couple had two teenaged children with them, and the man wore a distinctive hat. (Mr. Jaimison had no hat.)

there in the morning and their story is highly inaccurate. LAPD might have shed some light on this conflict by showing police photos of the Jaimisons (17 in all) to the gun-club witnesses. But there is no indication they did so.

There were also two witnesses whose brief accounts were buried in LAPD's rather voluminous gun-club investigative file, probably because these witnesses did not see Sirhan and were of no use to the prosecution. But it is what else they didn't see, and when, that appears to conflict sharply with the Jaimisons' story. Ben Trower and his friend Jim Langlois claim to have arrived at the range at approximately 3:45 and departed at 4:45 – 15 minutes before closing. Neither saw Sirhan or heard rapid firing. Trower was firing from about "the middle of the range" and heard occasional shots from the pistol range but did not recall seeing anyone in that area – not the rapid-firing Sirhan, not the attractive, blond Mrs. Jaimison – only the range master. Langlois did not see any females on the range. According to the Jaimisons, the range was deserted except for Sirhan and the range master during their entire time there (which they asserted to be around 4:00 until closing).

Police did investigate the Jaimisons' account, but very half-heartedly. An LAPD summary of Mrs. Jaimison's interview of June 19 gives the reader the false impression that the story had been thoroughly checked out. The summary accurately reports that the Jaimisons' baby-sitter vouched that they dropped their kids off at the time and day they had specified. Regarding the more crucial aspect of when and why they went to the Briar Patch bar, the summary simply invents data to corroborate the story. It asserts: "Mrs. Jaimison states that after leaving the baby-sitter's they drove to a local market and then to the Briar Patch bar to ask directions to the San Gabriel Valley Gun Club. Her boss, Mr. Robert White, was unable to give the exact directions . . . Mr. White verifies the time as approximately 4:00 p.m. when Mr. and Mrs. Jaimison left his bar."

Sergeant M. J. McGann, who wrote the police summary, also conducted the investigation. His handwritten report indicates that there were two Whites, a father and son, who operated The Briar Patch. The son was "very uncertain as to the exact time [of the Jaimisons' arrival]" because he was outside painting and did not have a watch." McGann reports: "He first told me the time they arrived was between 1:00 and 4:00. He then conferred with his father and his father told him it was about 4:00."

The report continues: "The father refused to speak to me or to identify himself. The son stated that they had a lot of trouble in the past as a result of bad publicity. The Whites operate a topless bar known as The Briar Patch."

McGann failed to press for an interview with the man who was corroborating the part of the story he had come to investigate. If the timing was important enough to ask about, it was important enough to pursue firsthand rather than simply taking a secondhand comment. Moreover, a central element in the story that appears in McGann's summary (that the Jaimisons went to the bar to get directions to the gun club and did not get complete directions) does not even appear in the field report of the officer's visit to The Briar Patch.

During her LAPD interview, Deborah Jaimison claimed that they stopped at the bar for directions "on way" to the gun club. The Jaimisons' home in Rowland Heights was 18 to 20 miles southeast of the Briar Patch bar in Arcadia. Duarte, where the gun club is located, is four miles east of Arcadia. It certainly appears that the couple would have to go out of their way to get to the bar. It would seem more logical to have asked for directions from someone in or near Duarte.

Deborah told police that she "knew quite a few sheriffs from the bar. They come in practically every day."

Besides the sheriffs, her LAPD interviewer asked, did she have "any particular type or descent that comes in mostly to The Briar Patch there?"

"What do you mean?"

"Well, such as Mexican or Italian or Greek or whatever?"

"We have a sort of mixture really. There's mostly white, you know . . . But coloreds . . . tend to stay away from there."

When asked if she told Sirhan to "get away or they'll recognize us," she said no; she did not know him previously.

"The place where I work is very strict. The hands-off business . . . [inaudible] we wear costumes down there."

"You wear . . ."

"We wear costumes down there. We change costumes."

"Do you think you might have made any comment to Sirhan to this effect?"

"You mean as far as where I worked?"

"Well . . . to the effect that your husband who is over on the firing range is a jealous man or . . ."

"No. I think I mentioned that my husband was over on the rifle range shooting, but I didn't mention anything about his being jealous."

LAPD asked her if she had a photo that they "might borrow for a little while." In released LAPD files there are no fewer than 17 police photos of the Jaimisons (five of Deborah, 12 of her husband). These mug-shot-type facial photos bear LAPD identification numbers and seem to have been taken at police headquarters. The tape-recorded interview of the Jaimisons was conducted at their home. It remains unclear as to when the photos were taken, why and to whom, if anyone, they were shown.

The investigation failed to probe effectively what the Jaimisons went to the bar for, what they did there, or how this might have related to the gun club. LAPD's tepid effort to check out their story, compared with its zeal for preventing Buckner from telling his story, is all the more inexcusable given the nature of The Briar Patch and the uncooperativeness of its law-enforcement-shy proprietor.

One would surmise that the attractive Ms. Jaimison, who worked as a "barmaid-waitress" (she told LAPD) at a topless bar near the racetrack, should have aroused some degree of investigative curiosity. This is especially the case because the massive background file on Sirhan Sirhan indicated that he seemed to gravitate toward waitresses, ponies and topless bars.

Robert Kaiser, who worked on Sirhan's legal defense team, described one of Sirhan's nights on the town with his friends. The four young men consumed four pitchers of beer while watching a series of three topless dancers parade across the stage to the strains of jukebox rock. They then adjourned to the more active Cat Patch bar, which featured three topless dancers simultaneously, on a runway that extended down the middle of the bar. Sirhan ordered more beer from the bikini-clad waitress.*

One might also surmise that LAPD would have had good cause to look into a possible Jaimison connection, because The Cat Patch is only eight miles from The Briar Patch. The latter is only three-quarters of a mile from Santa Anita Racetrack where Sirhan groomed horses from October 1965 to the spring of 1966. It is known that Sirhan did go to Arcadia, where The Briar Patch is located, during that period. Despite these proximities, there is no record of any LAPD investigation into his possible relationship with Ms. Jaimison.

Gwen Gum met Sirhan when they were both students at Pasadena City College in 1964. She was an object of his romantic interest. They never dated, but he asked her out on several occasions. Gum told the FBI that she lived in the Arcadia area, and had last seen him about a year and a half before the assassination, at Santa Anita Racetrack.

Gum's name appeared among the strangely repetitive writings in his notebook. On the first page, where her name is scrawled repeatedly, it is interspersed with (or beside) Sirhan's name. "Arcadia Calif." appears five times.

In a thorough background investigation, the possibility that the dregs of the pony crowd or Sirhan's other peers brought him to The Briar Patch is one that should have been checked out, obviously to determine if there was some sort of link between the bar and Sirhan.

An FBI report of June 28 indicates that a waitress from the Red Lion restaurant, at the corner of Foothill and North Garey in Pamona, phoned to inform the agent that she had secondhand information: Sirhan frequented the restaurant, was "well ac-

---

* Robert Blair Kaiser, *"RFK Must Die!"* (New York: Dutton & Co., 1970), p. 228.

quainted with several of the waitresses," and was friendly with one in particular. The caller named a fellow-waitress, whose name is deleted, who could verify this. The caller stated that she thought it her duty to report this information. The Red Lion was about 15 miles down the road from The Briar Patch, farther away from the city and from the Sirhan family home in Pasadena.

At the trial, Sirhan's presence at the gun club and his target practicing were stipulated by both sides, but none of the major questions and contradictions pertaining to this aspect of the investigation were addressed. As with other facets of this case, LAPD's inconsistent and sketchy treatment left unresolved some of the most troublesome matters: where Sirhan got the rifle from; the conflicting data provided by some of the gun club witnesses; whether Sirhan had ever been to the Briar Patch bar. Because of their biases and tunnel vision, Los Angeles authorities spared themselves from investigating the most troubling question of all. Since Sirhan Sirhan apparently genuinely cannot recall planning to shoot Kennedy on June 4, what was he doing rapid-firing hundreds of rounds for hours and hours, as if possessed by some all-consuming passion? Was this behavior conscious, subconscious – or somehow hypnotically programmed?

Chapter 16

IRANIAN ENIGMA

Ian Fleming in his most inventive moments never concocted a James Bond thriller to surpass the real-life drama that was taking place in the palace of the Shah of Iran . . . 1962. The action pivots about two principal protagonists, Shah Reza Pahlavi and the Khaiber Khan. Who is Khaiber Khan?
— Fred J. Cook, "The Billion-Dollar Mystery," *The Nation*, April 12, 1965

Within days after the assassination, police and FBI would interview a Kennedy campaign worker with an espionage background who had information concerning Sirhan and the polka-dot-dress girl. His name was Khaiber Khan, and he had worked at RFK headquarters on Wilshire Boulevard. Khan was a very provocative witness. He would be subjected to extensive investigation by both the FBI and LAPD, but neither would get to the bottom of this complex matter.

In FBI interviews on June 12, 14 and 20, Khan told the following story. While working at the headquarters on June 4, election day, he saw a man whom he would later recognize as Sirhan sometime between 5:00 and 5:30 p.m. Sirhan was standing near the water cooler, facing a young woman (about two feet apart). Khan did not see them converse, but his impression was that they were acquainted. A few minutes later he looked again to find them gone.

The girl wore a dress like one he had seen on the cover of *Vogue* – a light, short-sleeved dress with black or blue polka dots the size of a dime. She was Caucasian, in her early 20s, 120 to 125 pounds, with light brown or dark blond shoulder-length hair, large dark eyes, a round face and "a good figure and nice legs." He thought she was "American."

According to Khan, what caught his attention was that he had seen the girl twice before – once on June 3 sitting in a Volkswagen outside headquarters and earlier on June 4, perhaps mid-afternoon.

On June 3, when Khan walked past the parked Volkswagen, he noticed that the woman was sitting with another man who was Caucasian, 5-feet 8-inches to 5-feet 11-inches, had black hair and eyes, and was well dressed (not Sirhan). As he passed, Khan heard the man say, "I just spoke with Lilli Lawrence. But Lilli said it was impossible." Khan later told the FBI that he knew a Lilli Lawrence. She was an Iranian girl married to an American. The man in the VW somewhat resembled an acquaintance of hers that Kahn had met in New York. Khan also said Lilli "aided," but was not employed by, the U.S. Immigration Service.

After telling his story, Khan positively identified Sirhan from photos provided by the FBI. Now the case had not only another polka-dot-dress allegation but one with a Middle Eastern dimension, thus paralleling Sirhan's alleged motive.

By talking to other witnesses the FBI found some corroboration for a Sirhan appearance at the Wilshire Boulevard headquarters. The woman Khan described as his "half sister" Rose, also a Kennedy volunteer, identified Sirhan as having been there on June 2. She claimed to have seen him twice that afternoon, once outside the headquarters and once inside. She had noticed him because she was on crutches and he held the door for her. She did not see him on June 4 as her brother allegedly did.

Ellenor Severson, a Los Angeles housewife who worked at the headquarters, told the FBI on June 11 that a man she positively identified as Sirhan was there on the afternoon of June 2. "It was him," she told agents. She remembered a co-worker asking Sirhan if he needed help.

Severson also alleged something else. She told the Bureau that shortly after Sirhan was in the vicinity of her desk, she noticed that the Senator's daily schedule was missing from it. She made "considerable" inquiries among campaign workers, but it was never found. The schedule was not considered a public document, she said, and there were only a few copies printed for field personnel.

Yet another Sirhan appearance was reportedly made at Kennedy headquarters. Kennedy volunteer Larry Strick told the FBI that a man he identified as Sirhan was there at about 2:00 in the afternoon on June 2.

Khan was twice interviewed by the FBI before LAPD interviewed him almost a week later. His three FBI interviews were consistent and detailed. He had provided a possible conspiracy lead, but he surely did not appear to be a publicity hound. He claimed that he was an Iranian exile who had been harassed and attacked by the Shah's agents and that he feared more reprisals. Therefore, Kahn was reluctant to provide his address and brought a lawyer to his first two interviews. He stated that he did not want to testify in public or otherwise "get mixed up in an affair involving Arabian countries and the Jewish State as a result of the Kennedy assassination." In the interest of justice, however, he agreed to provide whatever help he could.

Khan claimed that the splint on his hand was the result of an attack by his enemies. He also indicated that he shortened his name from Khaiber Khan Goodarzian and was nicknamed "Goody." For *bona fides* he proffered a British visa showing that he entered the United States in 1963 and several letters written by U.S. officials relating to his testimony before a Congressional committee (charging the Shah with stealing U.S. foreign aid). There was even a brief 1965 letter from Robert Kennedy to Khan's attorney. It read:

Thank you for sending me the letter which you sent to Senator McClellan about the Khaiber Khan matter.

I am sure Senator McClellan has responded appropriately, but if you think that there is anything in particular that you think I should be doing about this matter, I would appreciate hearing from you further.

Khan also provided a copy of a U.S. House of Representatives bill filed to grant him political and economic relief from the oppression of the Iranian government.

From the FBI's RFK files emerges the image of an articulate, politically well-connected dissident who reluctantly provided provocative information and seemed to have nothing to gain (and much to lose) from publicity. As previously described, the Bureau found two other witnesses (besides the woman described by Khan and his half sister) who thought Sirhan *was* at the headquarters.

An FBI report dated June 28 describes photos received from CBS news relating to the "LAPD all points bulletin on the girl in the polka-dot-dress." The photographer, Chris Borgen, was a CBS reporter who thought the APB description fit a girl who had been photographed in street demonstrations near the United Nations building in New York. She was protesting on behalf of "Arab nations." This lead apparently produced nothing. Still, there is no indication that the Bureau was dismissing Khan's stories about Sirhan, the polka-dot girl and the "Lilli Lawrence"/New York angle. But it was clear that LAPD rejected all of it.

It should be recalled that at the time Khan was talking to the FBI (June 12-20) the police already had memos in their files stating that the polka-dot-dress girl had been found and Sandra Serrano's story was "phony." Other witnesses who alleged seeing the mystery woman were being rejected or discredited, culminating in Sandra Serrano's June 20 "failure" of the polygraph and her subsequent recanting. To LAPD, Khan was simply a foreign trouble-maker. If he was correct, or even credible, it would redound negatively on the department's preferred conclusion and on its handling of the many discredited witnesses.

LAPD files on Khan contrast sharply with FBI files. Khan's sighting of Sirhan is rejected by police. According to LAPD, Khan was interviewed no fewer that five times between June 18 and July 27. Only two interviews (June 18 and 19) are preserved on tape.

What of the other three alleged interviews? One (on June 24) is summarized in a couple of sentences; there is no record whatsoever of the other two. This is suspicious given Khan's story and the controversy surrounding his credibility.

Also odd is the fact that nowhere in LAPD files is there any report of the Lilli Lawrence/Iranian/New York dimension that is extensively reported in two of Khan's FBI interviews. He had offered Lawrence as a possible lead to the polka-dot-dress girl whom he had allegedly seen at RFK campaign headquarters on the afternoon of June 4.

A July 19 LAPD "case progress report" summarizes Khan's story in a way that directly conflicts with his consistent, detailed FBI interviews. LAPD states that the polka-dot-dress girl and the man alleged to be Sirhan, whom Khan claimed to have seen on June 4, were the same couple Khan saw in a VW outside the headquarters on June 3. There is no mention of the Lilli Lawrence angle, and the other man in the VW is out of the story. Khan is portrayed as claiming to have seen Sirhan twice (June 3 and 4) whereas his FBI interviews clearly state that he saw him only once. A hand-written LAPD report of the June 24 interview mistakenly says Khan "stated he saw Sirhan twice."

LAPD's *Summary Report* and its July 19 "progress report" assert that Khan refused to take a polygraph or to view a lineup to pick out Sirhan. Khan is also described as "unsure" of his identification. The progress report states that "he was always unsure." The handwritten summary of the June 24 interview says that the "subject is unsure of his previous ID of Sirhan." In a new twist on LAPD's report-writing procedures, this notation is written at the end of the report in a clearly different handwriting with a different writing instrument.

It seems logical that LAPD's hostility to polka-dot-dress witnesses would not be lost on Khan, who, unlike the young Kennedy volunteers, was politically savvy and seasoned in dealing with the law, especially after his experiences with the Shah's notorious secret police apparatus. After his first two interviews with police, Khan telephoned the FBI, which had already interviewed him twice. An FBI summary of his June 19 call says that he informed agents of LAPD's requests for a polygraph and a lineup and of his refusal "to go to jail" to conduct these tests without first consulting his attorney. The Bureau report in no way indicates that Khan had become less sure or "unsure" of the two positive identifications of Sirhan that Khan had given to FBI agents.

LAPD's Khan documents are replete with implicit and explicit challenges to his credibility, which was its modus operandi throughout the investigation when dealing with witnesses who possessed information that differed from LAPD's accepted version of the events. The summary of his June 19 interview alleges, "Officers found person interviewed to have a possible immigration arrest . . . Bail $50,000." The July 19 progress report says: "It was later found out by officers that Mr. Khan was arrested by immigration authorities and is presently on $4,000 bail pending a hearing."

The *Summary Report*[1] describes how interviewing officers had to meet Khan in "parks, coffee shops and various motels" and had to use code names, because he feared for his security. But the reader is encouraged to dismiss Khan's fears, along with his story, by a highly negative profile allegedly culled from interviews with people at Kennedy headquarters: Khan was "overdressed," a "phony," a "playboy," "appeared to do strange things," was "very overbearing."

Then there was the allegation that Sirhan had said he was "with" Khan. Ellenor Severson told the FBI that Sirhan came in on June 2 at about 2:00 p.m. It was shortly thereafter that the Senator's itinerary disappeared from her desk. She said that campaign volunteer Larry Strick asked Sirhan if he needed help, and Sirhan replied, "I'm with him," pointing to Khan. Strick positively identified Sirhan for both agencies and corroborated the time, place, the "I'm with him," and Sirhan's pointing to Khan.

Ellenor Severson's LAPD interview is not synopsized in the *Summary Report* nor does her name appear on the *Report*'s massive, supposedly complete, alphabetized list of witnesses. Her story about Sirhan and Khan is never mentioned in the 15 pages[2] dealing with Khan. In fact, the only LAPD reference to Severson's FBI story is in four lines of an undated, unsigned, single-page memo:

> Another one of these volunteers using a different name has been identified by witness Severson and another witness Strick . . . as Sirhan Sirhan. Strick spoke to Sirhan at the office when he was in the company of "Khan."

How LAPD determined that Severson saw a campaign worker and not Sirhan is nowhere described in the files. She positively identified Sirhan twice for the FBI. A subsequent but undated FBI report says that "she had not changed her mind." But her allegation about Sirhan and Khan did not exist so far as LAPD was concerned.

Instead, police worked on young Larry Strick, the 18-year-old high school student who claimed to have spoken to Sirhan and seen Sirhan point to Khan ("I'm with him"). Strick is summarized in the Khan section of the *Summary Report* as someone who "was not positive" that he saw Sirhan "in the company of Khan. When Strick was shown several mug shots, he was unable to identify Sirhan's photograph." An LAPD summary of Strick's August 19 interview goes even further: Strick "without hesitation retracted his former statement." Sirhan's mug shots suddenly "did not look familiar at all."*

This is indeed strange, and simply incredulous. On July 28, Strick had positively identified Sirhan for LAPD by picking three of his mug shots. He stated he was "positive" this was the man he saw on June 2. He also rendered a positive ID for the FBI on June 11, based on photos shown to him by agents. He told LAPD that at about 5:00 a.m. the morning of the assassination he first saw Sirhan's picture on TV and instantly recognized him as the man he had seen at the headquarters. He immediately tried to call Ellenor Severson, but her line was busy. When he hung up, the phone rang instantly. It was Mrs. Severson, who had had the same flash of recognition upon seeing the accused assassin on TV. Suddenly, however, LAPD managed to convince young Mr. Strick that

---

* There is no audio tape of this interview.

Sirhan's twice-identified face had absolutely no familiarity to him. It is amazing how effective police investigators were at getting to the "truth" after their repeated meetings with so many confused and mistaken witnessess, who finally realized what they had really seen only after being straightened out by these impartial public servants.

Exactly where was Sirhan when Severson and Strick claimed to see him at the Wilshire headquarters at 2:00 on the afternoon of June 2? Was he accounted for elsewhere? LAPD's hourly chronology of his movements for the 72 hours before the shooting list his "activity/location" as "unknown" from 11:15 a.m. to 5:00 p.m. on June 2. He *was* at a Kennedy rally at the Ambassador Hotel from 8:30 to 9:30 p.m. that same day. This lends circumstantial credence to the possibility that he was also at RFK headquarters, not far from the Ambassador. And what about Khaiber Khan? Was he somewhere else?

Police apparently never asked him (or never reported the inquiry). The FBI did. Khan told the Bureau he had no recollection of the "I'm with him" incident. He did not see Sirhan except on June 4. Khan hypothesized that since he recruited numerous Middle Eastern volunteers to the headquarters, someone might have thought Sirhan was part of his group. He asserted that he *was* at the headquarters on June 2 but at a later time than the 2:00 to 2:30 reported by Strick and Severson.

With Sirhan unaccounted for, and the enigmatic Khan's story (about never seeing Sirhan) directly challenged by two witnesses, one would think the police and FBI would attempt to sort out this potentially very serious matter. If they did, there is no record of it. LAPD spent its energies debunking Khan's polka-dot-dress story as well as Strick's ID of Sirhan.

What *did* the agencies find out about Khan? Neither file reflects the man described by Fred J. Cook in the *Nation* article quoted at the beginning of this chapter, even though Khan gave a copy to FBI agents and told police about it.[3] The lengthy piece is based on documents and interviews with sources in and out of government. It sympathetically details the spy saga of Khaiber Khan. More than a whistle-blowing dissident who embarrassed the Shah by documenting his theft of U.S. foreign aid, Khan was a skilled spy-master whose moles in Teheran obtained secret information, which Khan then brought to the attention of Congress and the Johnson administration.

Cook traces Khan's career from 1944 when, at the tender age of 20, he joined British intelligence and ran an Iranian spy ring during World War II. Then he served as liaison between the occupying allied forces and several Iranian tribes. He was rewarded with an aristocratic title.

Cook credits Khan with helping the CIA overthrow Premier Mohammed Mossadegh in 1953. The coup rid the U.S. of the left-leaning premier who had seized the Iranian government and nationalized a British oil company. It also put the Shah in power: "The Khaiber Khan's role in the counter-coup that toppled Mossadegh is not quite clear but indications are that he helped." One CIA insider described the coup as "a real James Bond operation."[4]

According to Cook, Khan achieved great power in Iran. He drove a customized Cadillac with secret compartments housing weapons and surveillance gear. His falling out with the Shah sent him into exile in London. From there he directed his spies to gather damaging evidence about the Shah's finances.

Cook quoted an intelligence report written by the Shah's agents in London saying that Khan spent 80 to 90 British pounds per day on hotel rooms for his entourage and 100 pounds per diem on nightclubs. Two Scotland Yard detectives provided security for him. He drove a Rolls Royce with Washington, D.C., plates.

If Cook is correct, then obviously Khan was doing something perceived as worthwhile by the British and U.S. governments. Far from being a lonely, struggling exile, he appeared to really be a well-heeled player in international espionage games.

By 1963, Khan and the Shah's agents were engaged in a deadly international game of hide and seek, which Cook described as "a cloak and dagger spiral." Each side had moles in the other's camp. Khan narrowly escaped abduction by Iranian agents in Switzerland.

He finally came to the U.S. Cook described him in 1965 as the "dapper Iranian exile now living in a plush New York apartment, a champion golfer, one of the world's best dressed men."

A 1963 *New York Times* article entitled "Khan Visits Paris with His Luggage" graphically described his opulent lifestyle, maintained even in the midst of his struggle with Iranian intelligence (about which the *Times* article manifested complete ignorance):

> The Khaiber Khan, a man whose life is devoted to sport and elegant dress, arrived here from Geneva. With him were his party of eight, including a private detective provided by the insurance companies to make sure none of the Khaiber Khan's possessions went astray. . . . The Khaiber Khan's possessions include, for example, 440 pairs of shoes, 55 evening jackets, 818 handkerchiefs, 180 sweaters, 714 neckties, 127 summer suits, 77 autumn suits, 154 pair of gloves, 12 watches and 165 watchbands.

Khan was quoted as saying, "I was fortunate to be born in the middle of an area where oil comes from."

His public discrediting of the Shah infuriated certain elements of the U.S. State Department and probably the intelligence community, which believed that His Despotic Majesty was an essential pillar of U.S. interests in the Persian Gulf. Given Khan's background, however, it is not unthinkable that his campaign had the blessing, if not backing, of some elements within the intelligence community who believed the Shah should be displaced or chastened, or who had some more convoluted agenda in which Khan's crusade was a working component.

Khan was in his early 40s when he surfaced in 1968 as a Kennedy volunteer with a potential conspiracy story. The incongruous nature of his RFK campaign activities apparently was not perceived by the investigating agencies – perhaps because they did not know, or care to acknowledge, his background. Could neither agency bring itself to read Cook's intriguing *Nation* article and follow up on it?

When a man with a resumé as a master spy and supreme clandestine-game-player proffers a story fraught with inconsistencies and gaps, it is surely worth probing. According to available case files, the police and the FBI never did.

Khan told the Bureau he came to Los Angeles "early in 1968." He said he "had personally spent considerable time at Senator Kennedy's Wilshire headquarters working on behalf of the Senator." Yet he worked there only four days (June 1-4).

Khan's self-described role was to bring in young volunteers to help Kennedy. According to the Wilshire staff, he did bring in about 20 people, all of whom seemed Middle Eastern in origin. Thus, according to his FBI statements, Khan was simply a local volunteer.

Khan portrayed himself to the FBI as someone with Kennedy contacts. He showed the brief letter from Kennedy reprinted earlier in this chapter. He told the Bureau that President John Kennedy and the Senator "understood and supported" his campaign against the Shah. Kahn said he had been allowed to use quotes from Senator Kennedy to support his cause. He claimed to have been introduced to Robert Kennedy in Washington. He said he had met Kennedy confidant Walter Sheridan at the Wilshire headquarters and had known Sheridan in Washington in 1963, when Sheridan served as an investigator for the Kennedy Justice Department.

There is no indication that the FBI checked any of this out. In LAPD files there is only a scant, one-phrase reference to Khan's putative Kennedy connections. If these elements of Khan's background are true, they raise the question of what a man with recent political visibility, Kennedy contacts and (as of 1965) considerable wealth was doing serving as a lowly procurer of leafleteers and doorbell ringers, a man whose only other contribution to the campaign was to work the phone bank. This was a presidential campaign potentially capable of turning Khan's political fortunes around, if not saving his country from a repressive regime. Whatever financial resources he had lost to the Shah, he did not have to work to support himself in 1968. He told the Bureau that he had sold property in Iran and lived off the proceeds. Given Khan's career, Swiss bank accounts might have been another source of support.

For someone with his supposed political position and goals, pressing the flesh with Kennedy notables would seem a very desirable activity. Yet Khan told the FBI he did not go to the Ambassador Hotel that night and knew nothing about the crime scene. According to FBI interviews given by Khan and a young man named Michael Wayne, Khan and his "half sister" Rose gave Wayne a ride and dropped him off "in the vicinity of Westwood Blvd. and Wilshire Blvd. in West Los Angeles shortly after 8:00 [p.m.]."

This is indeed curious. After faithfully working at the headquarters until the polls closed, Khan drove to within a half mile of the Ambassador Hotel, giving a ride to a young man who wanted to attend the party. Nevertheless Khan supposedly did not attend this star-studded political gala hosted by the Kennedy elite. Why? What *did* he do? His precise activities and whereabouts on the night of the assassination were not a subject of inquiry of LAPD or the FBI.

Rose Khan is described by Khan in his FBI interviews as his half sister. Her real name is Mariam Kouchan. Fred Cook offers a far richer description of her in his 1965 *Nation* article:

> She is the daughter of one of the Shah's most prominent retainers . . . educated in London where, in 1957, she first met K.K. . . . Then one night in late November or early December 1958 she and her parents happened to meet the Khaiber Khan in the Colbeh. During the conversation, he offered her a job as his private secretary . . . With her parents' consent she accepted the offer, and a year later, when the Khaiber Khan had to flee Iran, she went with him. She was to prove utterly loyal, withstanding family blandishments, attempted bribery and even a savage beating.

In 1968, Khan informed the Bureau that he had been interviewed on several occasions by the New York FBI office regarding his Iranian situation. He said that "John Stratton" was one of the agents. Released FBI files contain no reference to any background check on any of the claims put forth by Khan.

He also told the Bureau that he had recently been assaulted in West Los Angeles by the Shah's men and that a record of the incident would be in LAPD files. To the best of my ability to research LAPD's files, their documents do not reflect this.

During my 1986 interview with author Theodore Taylor (who co-wrote Chief Robert Houghton's account of the RFK case), he asserted that he had access not only to police and FBI files but to CIA documents as well. The agency was "looking into foreign aspects of it [the assassination]," he told me. It is difficult to imagine that Khan, who helped the CIA topple a government during the 1953 Iranian uprising, was unknown to the agency. Did the CIA reveal anything concerning Khan to the FBI and LAPD? Did the agency vouch for him as an asset or known commodity?

It is especially rather strange that Khan was not the subject of a more probing investigation, given Sirhan's supposed political motive. After all, here is a man alleged to have been seen with Sirhan, a man whose account of his activities is riddled with glaring incongruities, whose whereabouts during the crime was not established, and who was deeply enmeshed in the Byzantine politics of the Middle East. While none of these conditions render Khan guilty of anything, they should certainly have fueled LAPD's desire to do a thorough job of clearing up the case record, if that was indeed its goal. The question is whether the investigating agencies simply ignored Khan's background as a master of espionage and thus neglected to investigate him thoroughly, or whether it was precisely his espionage connections that exempted him from such scrutiny.

Chapter 17

THE WEB OF INTELLIGENCE

Since the 1950s the college and university campus had been the most important single concentration area of American intelligence units both federal and local.
      – Frank Donner, *The Age of Surveillance*

And he [Sirhan] never took part – other than in radical Arab Affairs – in campus politics.
      – Pasadena City College student and
      FBI informant William Divale

The shadowy but perceptible presence of federal intelligence is manifested in this case in some significant and intriguing ways – in LAPD's "emergency command post" the night of the shooting, in the connections of LAPD personnel, and in data on Sirhan gathered before the assassination. Two of LAPD's most pivotal officers in the RFK investigation clearly had important federal ties that apparently involved secret missions for the foreign-policy or intelligence bureaucracy in Washington, D.C.

Lieutenant Manuel Pena was a "supervisor" for Special Unit Senator, in charge of preparing the case for trial and supervising "day watch investigators."[1] Pena's signature of approval is on many of the case's most crucial witness interviews and reports. He played a major role in coordinating the incoming data and in the disposition of controversial witnesses such as Sandra Serrano.

The stocky, 49-year-old Pena was a 22-year veteran when he worked on the case. He had been given the LAPD Medal of Valor and had been decorated during his military service, which included one stint as a petty officer in the Naval Air Corps and another with the U.S. Army in France during the Korean War. There he served as "warrant officer-agent in charge of the 35th CID [civilian intelligence division]." He spoke fluent Spanish.

The most interesting of Pena's career involvements was not on his LAPD resume. According to a November 13, 1967, article in the *San Fernando Valley Times*, discovered by Floyd Nelson and reported by authors Christian and Turner,[2] Pena had "retired" from LAPD and was given a surprise testimonial dinner at the fashionable Sportsman's Lodge. Chief Tom Redden and a heavy contingent of department brass attended the festivities. The article stated that Pena was retiring "to advance his career." He had accepted a position with the International Development Office of the State Department, where he would serve as a "public safety advisor" and train foreign police forces. "After nine weeks of training and orientation," the article continued, "he will be appointed to his post, possibly a Latin American country, judged by the fact that he speaks Spanish fluently."

We now know that in the 1950s and '60s the U.S. State Department Office of Public Safety functioned as a front for CIA covert operations. Much of the training involved toughening the security forces of friendly dictatorships so they could more effectively crush leftist insurgents (and political dissidents). Whatever Pena's new career entailed, his full-time federal service was exceedingly brief; he was back with LAPD in April 1968, less than six months after retiring.

Chief Robert Houghton gave us a broad clue about Pena's contacts, stating in *Special Unit Senator*[3] that the lieutenant had "connections with intelligence agencies in several countries." In 1975, Pena's own brother was much more specific. While appearing on an L.A. television show, his brother, a principal at an East L.A. school, was chatting with host Stan Bohrman during a commercial break. The educator mentioned how proud he was of Manny's service to the CIA. "Nobody's supposed to know about that," he cautioned. "It's supposed to be a secret."[4]

In 1977, researcher Betsy Langman interviewed Pena, then retired from LAPD – this time, presumably for good. She attempted to question him about his intelligence ties. "I worked with the aid [or AID] program out of the Office of Public Safety" he confirmed. The phonetic reference could have been to general assistance (aid) or to the State Department's notorious AID (Agency for International Development), unmasked in the mid 1970s as one of the CIA's main covers for clandestine activity abroad (under the guise of foreign assistance).

Langman next asked, "Is AID not CIA?" Pena replied, "Ah, not to my knowledge." Later, when she asked Pena if his work away from LAPD in 1967 "was gonna be for AID," he replied, "Yeah." When queried about the nature of his work he frostily replied, "Ah, that I can't ah . . . I don't think that's anybody's business." He laughed briefly.

A second key investigator with some heavy federal connections was Sergeant Enrique "Hank" Hernandez. When he worked on the RFK case he was 37 years old, decorated (Medal of Valor, "military decorations"), with 15 years of police work behind him. Hernandez administered the polygraph exams that were so crucial in the handling of controversial witnesses like Serrano and DiPierro. He was assigned to "background investigation and conspiracy aspects of the case." Like Pena, Hernandez had served in the Army during the Korean War and was proficient in Spanish.

Unlike Pena, however, the idea that Hernandez worked for the federal government in a sensitive capacity comes not from newspaper clippings or the comments of relatives but from his own self-advertisement to Sandra Serrano. During the lengthy, intense

session in which he interrogated her and administered the polygraph, he began by attempting to convince his frightened, distrust-
ful subject that the test would be accurate because of his experience
and expertise as a polygraph operator.

> I have been called to South America, to Vietnam and
> Europe and I have administered tests. The last test that I
> administered was to the dictator in Caracas, Venezuela. He
> was a big man, a dictator. [Inaudible] was the man's name
> and this is when there was a transition in the government
> of Venezuela and that's when President Bettancourt came
> in . . . but this is all behind. But there was a great thing
> involved over there and I tested the gentleman.

During the 1960s and 1970s the CIA had extensive, secretive
ties to local police departments throughout the nation. In 1982,
under the Freedom of Information Act, I obtained from the agency
its "Domestic Police Training" file.[5] The documents revealed that,
during those decades, the CIA had a clandestine relationship with
numerous departments. The Agency provided largess for officers,
training, and gratis equipment (often of an exotic nature). Police
returned the favors by conducting surveillance and break-ins for the
Agency and providing police credentials to CIA operatives. Documents specifically mention Los Angeles as one of the cities that
received "training."

In a 1975 interview with Betsy Langman, ex-CIA officer Victor
Marchetti stated that while he was with the agency in 1967 he
became aware of two departments that received several days of
"training" – Chicago and Los Angeles. Marchetti was told that the
training was perfectly legal and aboveboard, but he discovered that
it was being run out of the Clandestine Services Division. When he
saw a dozen or so of L.A.'s finest at CIA headquarters, he inquired
about why they were there. Marchetti was told that it was a
"special," "sensitive" activity that had been directly approved by
the Director of the CIA.

It seems that another agency – Army Intelligence – had a behind-the-scenes role in the early stages of the RFK investigation. An LAPD chronology of law-enforcement activity states that at 5:00 p.m. on June 5 the "following persons were on duty in ECC [Emergency Command Center]: FBI agents Acott and LaJeunesse. U.S. Army Intelligence Timothy Richdale."

During a June 5 interview with police, eyewitness Vincent Di Pierro was asked to whom he had given his account (in the hours immediately following the shooting). He replied, "The police officers came in [at the crime scene] and they interviewed me and then the intelligence people came in [inaudible] the police."

The most intriguing item is the LAPD chronology's reference to data about Sirhan provided by Army Intelligence:

> Tim Richdale, Military Intelligence liaison, reports Terry Fall, Military Intelligence in San Francisco, 415-561-3242 or 415-561-2370, states that Sirhan was a student at 1. Pasadena CC 2. Longfellow Grammar School 3. Geo. Washington Jr. High 4. John Muir H.S. Sirhan active in gaining support for Shah of Iran's visit.

How did Military Intelligence in San Francisco come to have background data on the young man arrested for shooting Robert Kennedy? The answer is both simple and provocative: Sirhan Sirhan seems clearly to have been in federal intelligence files *before* the assassination, because of his association with a known communist.

Forty-eight hours after the shooting, Los Angeles Mayor Sam Yorty went before the press and described Sirhan as having been "influenced by contacts with the Communist party and contacts with communist-dominated or infiltrated organizations." Yorty had already gleefully noted the apparently leftist, pro-communist phrases in the assailant's notebook, but now he talked of "contacts." Where did the flamboyant, arch-conservative mayor come by such data? Surely, it came from intelligence files (federal or local); just as surely, William Tulio Divale was the primary source. Divale was an FBI informant who had knowledge of Sirhan.

Divale's 1970 book *I Lived Inside the Campus Revolution*[6] maintains on the jacket that he "organized and led campus revolts" for four and a half years and was the Bureau's "most valuable" undercover operative.

A July 1969 LAPD document confirms that "William T. Divale, a known Communist who was interviewed by SUS during the Walter Crowe investigation, has been an FBI informant since 1965. This fact was brought out at the Congressional hearings on the SDS [Students for a Democratic Society] and was verified by Bill Nolan [FBI, L.A. field office]."

Walter Crowe enters the story because he grew up with Sirhan in Pasadena. They first met in the sixth grade, were friends in junior high school and both attended Pasadena City College (PCC) in 1965 where they continued their association. The short, pudgy, bespectacled Crowe was enrolled in one of Sirhan's courses and lent Sirhan books (C. Wright Mills's *The Power Elite*, a book by Albert Camus and other works).[7]

Thomas D. Good had attended high school with Crowe and Sirhan. He too was at PCC and took the same course Crowe and Sirhan were in. Good told the FBI that at PCC Sirhan seemed "alienated" from people in general, even other Arabs. Walter Crowe appeared to be Sirhan's only friend, Good observed, but the friendship was not a close one.

Even so, anyone associated with Crowe would probably have been a subject of interest to LAPD and/or the FBI: Crowe was deeply enmeshed in radical politics with FBI snitch Divale. Divale would describe Crowe as "my closest friend."[8]

Crowe tried unsuccessfully to form an SDS chapter at PCC. He found nothing but apathy.[9] Good refused to help or even join. Crowe said that Sirhan knew of the effort to start a chapter but was "apathetic" and would not participate.

At the end of the 1965 academic year, Crowe transferred to UCLA. He allegedly didn't see Sirhan for nearly three years, until the two renewed their acquaintance on May 2, 1968.

In the interim Crowe was very active in leftist politics at UCLA. According to an LAPD intelligence report, he "had become a Communist."[10]

The LAPD *Summary Report*[11] tells us that Divale, whose status as an FBI informant is not revealed, met Crowe at PCC. Discovering that they shared an interest in "Marxist theory," they "became close friends." They enrolled at UCLA and shared an apartment there until July 1967. Furthermore, says the *Report*, "Divale stated to investigators that he was admittedly a communist and had recruited Crowe into the Communist Party." Crowe did not know that his recruiter was an FBI informant who was, without doubt, reporting on him while enlisting him.

Although disassociated from Sirhan from 1965-68, Crowe was a target of LAPD surveillance and, quite probably, was also a subject of FBI interest (thanks to Divale). Divale himself was, at minimum, aware of Sirhan Sirhan, as he describes in his book:[12] "Although Sirhan was attending Pasadena City College during most of the time I was there, I never met him. He never dropped over to the house when Doug Layfield and I lived there. And he never took any part – other than in radical Arab affairs – in campus politics. Somehow, during his first year or so at PCC, he'd changed. 'Kind of cracked up,' Walter had diagnosed on several occasions."

This alleged crack-up that supposedly troubled Crowe does not appear in any of his FBI or LAPD interviews or in any of the background reports on Sirhan. Divale's book presents further data on Sirhan that similarly does not appear anywhere else. Sirhan is described as participating in "radical Arab affairs."

LAPD's *Summary Report* indicates that he was a member of the Organization of Arab Students at PCC. The head of the group, Kanan Hamzek, told LAPD that Sirhan seemed very interested in school work but did not seem interested in politics. Another leader described the group as just "a social organization" for Arab students – a far cry from "radical Arab affairs."

Divale also describes an incident that fails to crop up in any of the voluminous official files on Sirhan's political background, including Crowe's interviews. Sirhan supposedly stormed back stage at PCC after a guest speaker from Saudi Arabia made disparaging remarks about Egyptian President Nasser.

"Instead of berating the speaker for his anti-Nasserism," wrote Divale, "Sirhan's attention had drifted to a couple of Arab students who were discussing the Koran. Sirhan burst suddenly into their conversation, cursing, 'To hell with the Koran.' There was no understanding Sirhan. But, then, Sirhan had never come close to understanding himself."[13]

Divale went on to describe a conversation between Crowe and Sirhan that occurred May 2, 1968, concerning politics and Sirhan's life. Divale's version is more substantive and detailed than what appears in Crowe's FBI interviews. For example, Divale alleges that Crowe found Sirhan "more distraught than usual," an observation not found in any of Crowe's descriptions of the May 2 meeting. In fact, Crowe offered nothing even approximating that description.

On the subject of Vietnam, Divale reports Sirhan's May 2 comments as follows:

> Others, Sirhan shrugged, might get their jollies just protesting. But not he. Bluntly, he told Walt if he ever "got political," got interested, say, in the anti-Vietnam movement, "I'd want to do the whole thing."
> Sirhan's concept of the "whole thing" was organizing a guerrilla band, holing up in the mountains somewhere and waging a shooting war against the establishment.

For someone who allegedly never met Sirhan, Divale certainly claimed to know a lot about him. Whatever Crowe told Divale, Divale's Sirhan was much more radical, hotheaded and mentally distressed than he appears in LAPD or FBI files or in Crowe's interviews. Divale fails to mention that on May 20, after an hour of conversation, Crowe and Sirhan were joined by two other former PCC students and the four young men went out for a night on the town drinking beer at two topless bars, then snacking at a Mexican restaurant.

Did Divale get more data from Crowe than LAPD or the FBI? Or was he gilding the lily to make Sirhan appear like the stereotypic

THE WEB OF INTELLIGENCE

American assassin – hotheaded, distraught, violence-prone (guerrilla warfare as opposition to the Vietnam War).

Surveillance on Crowe was sufficiently intense to raise the question of whether Sirhan could have escaped the intelligence net, his disassociation from Crowe notwithstanding. Crowe was put under surveillance by LAPD's intelligence unit, allegedly from November 25 to December 7, 1968. Police tried "to establish an undercover operator as a Crowe associate." The attempt failed and the surveillance supposedly ended.[14]

LAPD's *Summary Report* would have the reader believe that Crowe was surveilled only after he became separated from Sirhan in June of 1965:[15]

> Department Intelligence Division sources indicated an extensive record of Crowe's political activity from August 30, 1965, to June 1, 1968. Thirty-eight file cards from confidential sources showed a progression of association with Communist front organizations, such as the "Students for a Democratic Society" and the "W.E.B. Du Bois Club."

Yet, Crowe's failed effort to organize an SDS chapter at PCC had come while he and Sirhan were friends there (although Sirhan did not participate) and while Divale was living in a house near PCC that he described as a "hotbed" of political activity.

LAPD's file on Crowe contained "a total of 148 names of possible known associates, many with left-wing and Communist backgrounds." The department claims that after the assassination, it checked these names through local, state and federal intelligence files, searching for any association with Sirhan. Allegedly none was found. Despite the intensity of interest in Crowe, the *Summary Report* claims that, prior to the assassination, Sirhan's name "did not appear anywhere in the Department's Intelligence Division file."[16]

There are clear indications that Sirhan could have – even *should* have – been there. His older brother Adel worked periodically from 1962-67 as a musician at the Fez Restaurant in Pasadena. He parked his vehicle between the restaurant and Baces Hall, where the local branch of the left-leaning, mostly black W.E.B. Du Bois Club held its meetings. LAPD's Intelligence Division labeled the group a "Communist front organization." The head of the central Du Bois Club for the Los Angeles area was none other than William Divale.

According to LAPD, Adel Sirhan's car was "observed parked in front of Baces Hall on the same night that a Du Bois Club meeting was held at the same address."[17] The *Report* says that neither Sirhan nor his brother joined the Du Bois Club; it was all a mistake. "Intelligence reports noting Adel Sirhan's vehicle at that location did not take into account his employment at the restaurant. He was never seen entering or exiting the vehicle."[18]

LAPD interviewed the club's members and was satisfied that Adel had no links to it. But this occurred after the assassination. Prior to it, any license number noted in intelligence reports would surely be checked out. If the name "Sirhan" turned up, it might well have been cross-checked with data on Divale and Crowe (both Du Bois activists). With 148 associates of Crowe's in LAPD intelligence files, some of whom were not leftist activists, Sirhan's name could easily have popped up, rendering him a subject of interest to LAPD.

Another LAPD intelligence report exists that suggests Sirhan may indeed have been caught in the department's anti-war surveillance net. A June 12, 1968, memo from Lt. Clayton Anderson, Intelligence Detail, to George R. Stoner, Chief of the Bureau of Investigation, states that four months earlier (Feb. 1968) a "friend" of Anderson's was conducting an inquiry into the counseling provided by draft-resistance organizations. The friend "obtained a list of so-called draft counselors" and contacted one, a Du Bois Club member named Bob Dugan. The terse one-page memo concludes with the flatly stated but intriguing information that the "friend was told to go to 696 East Howard, Pasadena, for draft resistance information. This is the address of suspect Sirhan Sirhan."

This author could find no evidence of either follow-up or further explanation in released LAPD files. No dates for the "friend's" activities are provided. Again, however, if this data was in police files before the assassination, it further links Sirhan to the "red" arena inhabited by Crowe and informant Divale.

As mentioned previously, Crowe lost touch with Sirhan Sirhan from mid-1965 until May 2, 1968, when (at the urging of Sirhan's mother) Crowe contacted his childhood chum. According to Crowe, they met at Bob's Big Boy in Pasadena and discussed Crowe's leftist political activities and Sirhan's life, but not Kennedy.

A month later, William Divale, who claims he never met Sirhan, would suddenly appear and become knowledgeable about the May meeting – just 24 hours before the assassination. As Divale describes it, he had been out of Los Angeles for some time, participating in (and spying on) Communist party activities. He decided to return to the city to find a quiet place to type up his extensive reports to the Bureau. After spending all of June 2 typing, he contacted Crowe on June 3: "For some odd reason our conversation turned almost prophetically to Sirhan Sirhan, whom Walt had recently seen [May 2]."[19]

The morning after the assassination, Divale quickly contacted Crowe at his place of work. "My God, Walt, it was Sirhan."

"Why?" Crowe supposedly asked.[20]

Divale notified the FBI: "It [why Sirhan did it] was a question the Bureau (whom I'd alerted, thinking Walt's insight on Sirhan might be helpful) and the Los Angeles Police were to ask Walt time and time again . . . "

Thus, while working for the Bureau, Divale arrived back in L.A. 60 hours before the assassination, contacted Crowe, discussed Sirhan; then, after the assassination, immediately contacted Crowe to affirm Sirhan was the suspect, then informed the Bureau about Crowe (who was already writ large in Bureau files as a known Communist). No wonder L.A. Mayor Yorty was excited about the possibility of a Communist-inspired assassination. Was Sirhan being outfitted with a left-wing legend by unknown persons in the intelligence community?

A reddish tint to the assassination of Robert F. Kennedy – if not an outright Commie conspiracy theory – was given a fast start by the discovery of Sirhan's notebook (with its seemingly pro-communist rhetoric), by his previous association with a known communist, and by Divale's quick reporting of this association. According to the summary of Crowe's June 7 FBI interview, he was "told" by interviewing agents: "The question had now arisin [sic] as to whether there was any conspiracy to kill Senator Kennedy that might involve the CP [Communist Party]; that the public and Congress and the President was [sic] demanding and had a right to know the answer to that question."

Crowe himself was fearful that his May 2 meeting with Sirhan may somehow have spawned the attack on Kennedy. He expressed to the FBI his hope that the entry in Sirhan's "diary" that spoke of killing RFK was dated prior to their meeting.[21] It was dated May 18.

Sergeant Hank Hernandez polygraphed Crowe and concluded that he was deceptive on three "crucial questions."[22] Two of these involved whether he had foreknowledge of Sirhan's intent to shoot Kennedy.

Ultimately, of course, LAPD wasn't buying *any* conspiracy angle – even one with such an alluring red hue.

> The results of the [polygraph] test caused investigators to believe that Crowe had some knowledge of Sirhan's intention to kill Kennedy; however, it was considered improbable that Crowe could have influenced Sirhan, based on the conversation described by Crowe.[23]

Why should Crowe have been believed about the substance of the conversation when he was allegedly lying about his foreknowledge of the crime? Why wasn't this revelation of falsehood followed up by LAPD or the FBI? Neither agency has explained.

Sirhan, the wide-eyed young man with the smoking gun, had a brother who seemed to attend W.E.B. Du Bois Club meetings, an address that reportedly was used to counsel draft dodgers, a college best friend who was a known communist and a Du Bois member, a "diary" strewn with pro-communist, anti-American rhetoric, and an FBI informer who knew of him and who could immediately alert authorities to his leftist connections.

The fact that Sirhan's *tabula rasa* motive was eventually cartooned in by the defense and prosecution hypnotists and interrogators as geographic rather than ideological, Middle Eastern rather than Marxist, does not preclude the possibility that someone was choreographing a communist legend for Sirhan – either after the assassination or before, or both.

The web of intelligence seems to have spun itself around the young man who would become the convicted assassin, around two of the case's most important investigators – Pena and Hernandez – and around the police's Emergency Command Center (at which an army intelligence officer was present and actually provided data on Sirhan). The open question is what other elements it may have entangled, with what effects?

Chapter 18

RE-INVESTIGATION

> *It's commonly said there is no statute of limitations on murder. We of course abide by that. From that standpoint, it's always possible to re-open a case on credible evidence. After all these inquiries and reviews, we never found any credible evidence that could warrant a re-opening of the case. It doesn't mean that we don't have an open mind and on credible evidence, we'd certainly review it and see if it's worth pursuing.*

> — Los Angeles District Attorney
> Curt Livesay to journalist Andy Boehm, 1988[1]

Despite such pious rhetoric, Los Angeles law enforcement has worked ceaselessly to exercise spin control on the failings of the official conclusions rather than dealing with the glaring conflicts and burning questions I have documented in the previous chapters. After more than two decades of tortured evidentiary logic, secrecy and deception, the official version of the RFK assassination has been so discredited that it collapsed like a house of cards. A second gunman, a female accomplice, a hypno-programmed assailant — all have been obscured by what is surely one of the most concerted, longest-running, best documented cover-ups in the history of U.S. law enforcement.

The argument against re-opening the case is a pat one, articulated by LAPD Commander William Booth in 1988:[2]

> Through the criminal justice process, a person was apprehended, a trial was held and there was a conviction. And that conviction has been supported by the state Supreme Court. And so it's our view that the person who is responsible, the person who did in fact kill Senator Kennedy, has been arrested, prosecuted, convicted and is still serving time. And that person himself says that he and he alone was the one who killed Senator Kennedy. That is the position of the department.

This argument seems compelling only to those who are unfamiliar with the realities of this case – evidence was repeatedly ignored, altered, destroyed or covered up; the trial neglected the evidentiary issues; Sirhan's admission of lone guilt is an artificial product of his programming and his desire for parole.

The massive effort put forth by L.A. law for 23 years was primarily concerned with defensive propaganda rather than thorough, competent investigation. The official pronouncements were often so transparently erroneous that it is a woeful commentary on the effectiveness of the media that such blatant fallacies were not effectively exposed early on.

There were plenty of motives for a cover-up extending beyond an inherent desire to conceal an assassination conspiracy. There were policemen afraid for their careers, a department that wanted to protect its chief criminologist from further challenges to his professional competence, and a DA's office that wanted a smooth working relationship with LAPD. Thus the DA's office would tiptoe around the police department when dealing with the question of extra bullets. Carpenters were deposed in detail; the great pantry raid was orchestrated. But investigators would never take what was clearly the most obvious, necessary and productive step – re-questioning under oath those policemen who searched the crime scene for evidence.

With the controversies shrouded by the open-and-shut mythology, those who handled the case took credit for their work and moved onward and upward. Police sergeants became captains. Assistant Chief Gates took command of the department and is, at this writing, in the media spotlight for the brutality witnessed by the American public in the video-taped beating by his officers of an L.A. robbery suspect. A series of DAs and their assistants became successful politicians or were appointed to the federal bureaucracy or the bench. John Van de Kamp went from the great pantry raid and leaving "no stone unturned" in the RFK case to becoming California Attorney General (with designs on the governor's mansion). Those whose careers and professional credibility were, and are, inextricably entwined with the official version of the RFK case were not a small clique of police officers but a fraternity of powerful and successful men positioned within the elite structures of California politics and law enforcement.

To criticize the official findings was not simply to challenge LAPD's competence in its biggest case, but also to challenge the competence (and, inexorably, the integrity) of the Los Angeles law enforcement and political establishment over a period of two decades.

Still, the question is asked: Why bother to re-investigate this case? It's been so long; why stir up painful memories?* Robert F. Kennedy cannot be brought back, no matter how many commissions

---

* Regarding the obvious, oft-mentioned matter of subjecting the Kennedy family to further distress, Senator Edward M. Kennedy made an important distinction. In a January 22, 1980, letter to a researcher concerned about the RFK case, Kennedy wrote:

> I am sure that it is understood that the continual speculation is painful for members of my family. Our feeling is that, if there is sufficient evidence to re-examine the circumstances concerning the deaths of President Kennedy and Robert Kennedy, this judgment would have to be made by the legal authorities responsible for such further examination. I do not believe that their judgment should be influenced by any feelings or discomfort by any member of my family.

While the assassination of Robert F. Kennedy is a deeply personal matter for the Kennedy family, it is also a national political tragedy and a matter of criminal justice in which the search for the truth must be the overriding concern.

or committees look into his assassination. Why expend scarce resources when some people will never be satisfied with the resulting conclusions, when we've already had enough bad news about the troubled 1960s?

The arguments for re-investigation are numerous and compelling. Historically, we need to understand root causes of the violence that threatens our democratic system, the violence that substitutes bullets for ballots and robs us of some of our most visionary and irreplaceable political leaders. If for no other reason, such understanding is essential so that we can avoid a repetition of such tragedies. It is important to know whether Robert F. Kennedy was lost because of a psychically muddled young Palestinian with a political grudge or because powerful interests in America could not abide the possibility of an RFK presidency. Sirhan Sirhan can be incarcerated or rehabilitated so that he will not strike again; but such powerful interests can indeed strike again, should they feel threatened. And wouldn't they be emboldened to act again, given that such compelling evidence of a conspiracy existed yet was somehow ignored or purposely not investigated by the authorities?

Then there is criminal justice. The murderers of Robert F. Kennedy (who hatched this bizarre, complex plot) got away. This case should never be closed while perpetrators have not been brought to justice, no matter how "old" the case is. Nazis who committed war crimes are still being pursued after half a century. TV news periodically brings to public attention murder cases – some, decades old – in which new evidence (or "old," suppressed evidence) indicates that the crime is unsolved or the convicted person is innocent. If a regular homicide is worthy of *60 Minutes* treatment and public outrage, then surely we must pursue the unsolved case of an American leader whose death profoundly affected our political system. It is both ironic and tragic that numerous homicides in which there was, for example, a front-back problem (assailant's position versus the location of the victim's wounds) have been re-investigated simply because of this single, glaring conflict in the evidence. Yet the RFK case, which manifests not only this problem but other, equally severe ones, has never been reopened beyond the shallow cosmetic exercises conducted by L.A. law.

Public accountability of law enforcement (of agencies and officials) is an essential ingredient in a healthy democracy. Los Angeles authorities should be held accountable, not given a free ride because they successfully buried, suppressed and manipulated evidence that was contrary to their official, convenient version of events. This is the only one of the three major assassination cases of the 1960s that has never been reviewed or re-investigated by anyone beyond local jurisdicition (except for the FBI's role in assisting during the original investigation of what was then not a federal crime). *What should now be done?*

Clearly, this case must be pursued by an official body with subpoena power and investigative resources, not from Los Angeles or Sacramento, but from Washington, D.C. – perhaps a commission – whose members have no ties to Los Angeles politics or law enforcement. A special prosecutor would be ideal, if the right person were appointed. A Congressional committee might be too vulnerable to the influence of the California political establishment, but it is still a viable possibility.

There are pitfalls and problems inherent in any Washington re-investigation option. But our government owes the American people a competent probe of the assassination conspiracy that so violently distorted the politics and policy debates of the turbulent 1968 presidential race and negatively influenced politics for many years – by generating further alienation and division that caused many Americans to drop out of the political process, by changing the succession of leadership within the Democratic Party and perhaps the nation and by altering the issue agenda of the Democratic Party for years to come.

The passage of time and the destruction of evidence notwithstanding, there are fruitful avenues by which to pursue historical understanding and justice. Establishing the location of extra bullets through photos and testimony can provide clues to the position and possible identity of the second gunman. Leads to the polka-dot-dress girl might be developed by questioning witnesses in depth (without harassment) and by systematically collating old and new information. It is disgraceful that so many key witnesses were consistently ignored, mishandled or manipulated by Los Angeles law enforcement. My documentation of this pattern is surely only the tip of the iceberg and represents the results of the investigative work of only a few dedicated private individuals. Imagine what a *formal, serious* re-investigation could uncover, given subpoena power to determine what really happened in this labyrinthine case!

Furthermore, Sirhan's mind still harbors data on the assassination that could be elicited through skillful deprogramming. Numerous witnesses retain vivid recollections, in all facets of the case, that were never pursued, discovered or assimilated by the original investigation. Computer simulations of bullet trajectories, techniques of photo analysis and enhancement, and other high-tech expertise can mine the data much more effectively than was possible in 1968.

Even if it proves to be too late to bring the conspirators to justice, our democratic system will be strengthened by arriving at a more truthful version of this national tragedy. The Hollywood myth of the RFK case – lone assassin, open-and-shut, thorough investigation – that presently dominates our political culture is a costly deception. It hides an even worse threat to our democracy than that of the lone, alienated, violence-prone psychopath. That threat is the violent manipulation of the American political process by powerful interests who feel threatened by its legitimate outcomes.

A Possible Follow-Up for Readers

Citizens concerned about official accountability and historical truth in this unsolved assassination conspiracy can contact the following entities in ways that would be useful to re-opening the case:

The Inquiry and Accountability Foundation is a non-profit, tax-exempt organization, chartered in Los Angeles and Washington, D.C., founded by the late Greg Stone. It has served as a vehicle for re-investigation and re-opening by funding: investigation and research, legal challenges, and efforts to provide information to the public and the media. Those interested in contributing to the foundation and/or receiving information concerning ongoing development and activities can contact:

The Inquiry and Accountability Foundation
P.O. Box 85065
Los Angeles, CA 90027

Los Angeles Mayor Tom Bradley should be contacted about the importance of a re-investigation of this case, to be conducted by authorities outside the Los Angeles Police and District Atttorney's Office (as well as the State of California Attorney General's Office, now headed by John Van de Kamp, who was Los Angeles District Attorney during the mid- to late 1970s, when some of the most shocking manipulations and cover-ups occurred). Mayor Bradley should be urged to facilitate, and not impede, such an outside re-investigation, given the decades of secrecy and the deplorable performance by his city's law-enforcement agencies in the RFK case.

Mayor Tom Bradley
City Hall, Room 305
200 N. Spring Street
Los Angeles, CA 90012

Los Angeles District Attorney Ira Reiner should be persuaded not to stand in the way of an outside re-investigation of the case, even in the event that he should conduct his own review. A competent, open-minded review of the evidence by Mr. Reiner's office – as already requested by the author and other signators – would be an important first step. But final disposition should be handled by authorities outside Los Angeles – given the dismal record of this office's past mishandling of the case.

Congressmen and senators in the U.S. Congress – whether from California or elsewhere – need to be made aware of the lingering injustice, and the blot on American democracy, that this national tragedy presents. They should be urged to seek a federal probe of the case (via a special prosecutor or an appointed independent commission, or even a congressional committee with jurisdiction over the FBI that could look into the extra-bullets issue). You can write to the local offices of your congressmen or senators or to their Washington, D.C., offices.

(Your Congressman)
U.S. House of Representatives
Washington, DC 20515

(Your Senators)
U.S. Senate
Washington, DC 20510

The media – print and electronic – should be urged to actively and responsibly focus some in-depth attention on the issues and problems surrounding this case. Media coverage over the past 23 years has all too often been absent, biased toward official sources, sensationalized or geared exclusively toward human-interest stories (that is, who is still interested in the case and what makes them tick). Unwittingly, with the rare exception of occasional coverage that has perceptively probed the controversies, the effect of this deficient attention has been to make it easier for the investigating authorities to shield themselves from accountability as well as to perpetuate myths and disinformation supportive of the official version of the assassination.

Appendix A: Excerpts from Dan Moldea's 1987 Interview with Thane Eugene Cesar

Below are selected extracts – some of them previously unpublished – of investigative journalist Dan Moldea's March 27, 1987, interview with Thane Eugene Cesar.* I have inserted italic headings throughout as a topical aid to the reader.

Cesar's Proximity to RFK

MOLDEA: O.K., now, do you have ahold of Kennedy's arm?
CESAR: At one time, yeah, I had his arm. [Cesar takes my right arm above the elbow with his left hand.]
MOLDEA: You had his arm.

*My thanks to Dan Moldea for generously allowing publication of this interview data.

CESAR and MOLDEA (in unison): Just like this.

MOLDEA: You're holding his arm. Wow! Jesus! Okay, so you're holding his arm.

CESAR: Yeah.

MOLDEA: Now, what about Karl Uecker. He says that he has ahold of Kennedy's [right] hand.

CESAR: Yeah, he did.

MOLDEA: You had ahold of his [right] arm, and Uecker had ahold of his [right] hand?

CESAR: Right.

MOLDEA: Simultaneously?

CESAR: Yeah.

. . . . .

MOLDEA: And you were pushing people away with your right hand. Okay. Now, Uecker was holding his hand, too. He had [Kennedy's] right hand in his [left] hand . . . And then Kennedy pulled away, but then Uecker says that he grabbed him by the hand again. And, in an interview you did [with the LAPD], you said that you grabbed him again by the arm.

CESAR: I could have.

Cesar Looks at His Watch Just Before the Shooting

MOLDEA: Like I said, it's impossible to remember. From what I understand, you looked at your watch just before everything started to pop.

CESAR: Right.

MOLDEA: And it was at exactly . . .

CESAR: And you want to know why I looked at my watch?

MOLDEA: Why?

CESAR: Because I knew that I was supposed to, I could leave at 12:00. And I was tired, and I wanted to get out of there.

MOLDEA: But you were in the midst of meeting . . .

CESAR: It didn't matter.

MOLDEA: . . . a very important person, and . . .

CESAR: I didn't care. This kid's sleep is more important. [He laughs.] And that's exactly why I looked at my watch. I wanted to see if it was 12:00, because I was going to leave.

MOLDEA: O.K., so it was exactly 12:15 [a.m.] at that point.

CESAR: Uh-huh.

Did Cesar See Sirhan Before the Shooting?

MOLDEA: Sirhan emerges. Do you see Sirhan?

CESAR: No.

MOLDEA: O.K. Did you see Sirhan in the pantry when you were either guarding the east or the west door?

CESAR: No.

MOLDEA: You never saw him?

CESAR: No.

MOLDEA: O.K. He was by the – where was he? – he was by the tray stacker. I guess he was by the tray stacker [at the east end of the ice machine].

CESAR: Right.

MOLDEA: And he emerged from there. But you never saw him.

CESAR: Never. Mainly because of the lights being in your eyes, you couldn't see nothing back there.

Cesar's Reaction to the Shooting

MOLDEA: Because you had said to the police that you thought that Sirhan was actually firing at you. You thought that the shots were actually . . .

CESAR: Well, that's what it looked like.

MOLDEA: . . . It looked like the shots were coming right at you.

CESAR: Oh, yeah.

MOLDEA: So you were right up on Kennedy.

CESAR: That's right.

MOLDEA: O.K. Now the, O.K., on this thing [the *Stern* magazine drawing], this is where you are. You guys are very, very close together. O.K., now, you must have been terrified. I mean, you got a gun firing at you. Was there any security guards, were there any other security guards in that area at all? Was there, did you see . . .

CESAR: I didn't see any of that.

MOLDEA: . . . any other guns in that area?

CESAR: No.

MOLDEA: Did you see a person reach into his pocket? Did you see a person with a fast motion around you or anything like that?

CESAR: No.

MOLDEA: You didn't see anything like that?

CESAR: No.

MOLDEA: You're up against the ice machine; Kennedy's directly in front of you.

CESAR: Right.

. . . . .

MOLDEA: Now, you see the red flash. O.K., now, let me ask you a series of questions here. How does Kennedy fall? Do you recall?

CESAR: No, because when the flashes went off, I hit the deck. [He laughs.]

MOLDEA: O.K., now . . .

WEBER (Garland Weber, Cesar's lawyer, who was also present at the interview): Did you know what they were?

CESAR: Oh, sure.

MOLDEA: You ducked, right? You ducked?

CESAR: Oh, sure. I went down, went down.

MOLDEA: O.K., did you duck and then stumble and fall?

CESAR: Yeah, and when I did I had a breakaway tie and it landed on the floor. And if you can ever get the photograph by *Time/Life* magazine, you'll see my tie laying there.

MOLDEA: Yeah, I've seen it. Right next to Kennedy's body.

CESAR: Right.

MOLDEA: Did Kennedy grab your tie?

CESAR: Not that I know of. Somebody picked it up. I don't know who. I went back to get it, and it was gone.

MOLDEA: No, did Kennedy grab your tie when he fell?

CESAR: Not that I know of. . . . All I seen was the flash, the gunshots go off. And the first thing in my mind was that I thought it was firecrackers. Then I realized what it was, and I ducked. I went down. But, when I got back up on my feet, Kennedy was laying on the, was on the floor already. So, basically, I didn't . . .

MOLDEA: So, when you ducked, you stumbled and fell.

CESAR: That's right.

MOLDEA: O.K. No one fell into you or anything like that.

CESAR: Not that I know of.

Powder Burns in Cesar's Eyes

MOLDEA: Right. Now, powder burns in your eyes. You had powder burns in your eyes?

CESAR: Yeah, I got particles, you know . . .

MOLDEA: Okay, you know a lot about guns, don't you? And you know something about .22s and how they . . .

CESAR: Well, I'm not an expert on guns, but I've been a sportsman.

. . . . .

I'm not an expert.

MOLDEA: O.K., how do you think you got the powder burns in your eyes? Just from Sirhan's gun?

CESAR: I know that anytime you fire a gun at as close a range as he did, whether it be a .22 or anything else, it puts out minute particles in a spray. And it can be dust in the air, or it can be particles from the powder. But I was close enough that I got sprayed with it.

MOLDEA: You got sprayed with it. Did it blind you momentarily or anything?

CESAR: No, no. I just felt it in my eyes.

MOLDEA: It was itchy? How did it feel? It was just . . .

CESAR and MOLDEA (in unison): An irritation.

CESAR: Yeah.

Appendix B: Analysis of LAPD Interviews with Capt. Cecil R. Lynch

The Lynch interview is dated June 19, 1968; at that approximate time (June 19 and 20), LAPD was gathering a good deal of information that allegedly discredited Serrano (sound test, polygraph).

Lynch's LAPD interview summary is indeed a strange document, even within the context of the department's anomalous file on the Kennedy assassination. The summary is dated June 18 but it claims to cover two interviews (one on June 18, another on June 19). This alone is very unusual. Consistent with the now-familiar pattern of selective documentation, the first interview was taped while the second, more important one was allegedly not taped.

The two interviews seem to contradict each other in ways that would cause a polka-dot-dress witness to be savaged by police interrogators. The first states that Lynch "was stationed at the west end of the Embassy Room during the Senator's speech. A woman approached him and asked if it was true that Senator Kennedy had been shot.'' The sentence stating Lynch's Embassy Room location is crossed out in pencil.

The very next paragraph contains a phrase so unusual that nothing even approximating it has been encountered in the hundreds of LAPD interviews I've read: "*A more detailed and exacting interview was conducted* [emphasis added] and it was determined that the informant had been on, and inspected, the outside fire escape [the stairs referred to in Serrano's testimony] on the southwest corner of the Embassy Room, at least 10 times during the course of the evening,'' including one inspection "ten minutes prior to Kennedy starting his speech.'' The report said there was no woman seated on the stairs.

During the second, more thorough interview, Lynch allegedly stated "that a woman approached him just prior to his arrival at the top of the stairs and said, 'Is it true the Senator has been shot?' '' Lynch allegedly surveyed the parking lot and noticed a nearby security guard: "There was not unusual activity . . . the guard did not appear excited or busy.''

These are unusual, marked changes from Lynch's simply being "stationed at the west end of the Embassy Room during the Kennedy speech'' to his inspecting an outside staircase just before, and seemingly just after, the speech. In the first interview, the encounter with the woman would appear to have occurred inside the hotel (it was mentioned in the next sentence after Lynch's location at the "west end of the Embassy Room'' was described). Now the encounter was placed outside at the top of the stairs.

A handwritten note in the margin of the Lynch summary says "not Sandy,'' with an arrow pointing to the sentence about the woman. Serrano's story is that she came inside and asked "a guard'' whether Kennedy had been shot. Several witnesses mistook uniformed firefighters for police officers or security guards, but Serrano claims to have seen no one but the fleeing couple until she went back inside the hotel. Lynch's first location (at the west end of the Embassy Room) is more compatible with the possibility that he encountered Serrano.

Lynch described the woman he encountered on the stairs as 30 to 35 years old and wearing a light-colored coat. This description does not fit Serrano. If it wasn't Serrano, then who was it? By Lynch's own account, he was not yet aware that Kennedy had been shot. He looked around and observed that everything seemed normal after the woman asked the question. Was this a second woman who, like Serrano, knew about the tragedy before the news reached the fringes of the Embassy Room and beyond? Despite the supposedly "detailed and exacting" nature of the second interview, which included a visit to the Ambassador and a time-and-motion reconstruction by Captain Lynch, key elements of his story remain sketchy or confusing. The audio tape also discloses some very leading questioning by LAPD.

Notes

Chapter 1

1. KPIX-TV San Francisco, "People Are Talking," July 11, 1986. Paul Schrade and the author were guests.
2. Author's interview of Lisa Urso, October 30, 1987, San Diego, CA.
3. KPIX-TV, "People Are Talking," July 11, 1986.
4. Jack Newfield, *Robert F. Kennedy: A Memoir* (New York: Bantam Books, 1969), p. 348.

Chapter 2

1. Telephone conversation with William R. Burnett, L.A. District Attorney's investigator.

Chapter 3

1. Interview with Ted Charach for his 1971 documentary film *The Second Gun*.
2. Di Pierro's account concerning the polka-dot-dress girl (a possible female accomplice) and distance changed during the course of his various interviews. Subsequently, he would place the gun closer than his original estimate.
3. Charach, *The Second Gun*.

Chapter 4

1. The series of Bugliosi-obtained affidavits discussed in this chapter was first described and published by William Turner and Jonn Christian in *The Assassination of Robert F. Kennedy: A Searching Look at the Conspiracy and Cover-Up 1968-78* (New York: Random House, 1979), Appendix.
2. Ibid., pp. 179-81.
3. Private letter from Van de Kamp to a journalist, January 12, 1979.

Chapter 5

1. Data on Schulman's handling by LAPD was provided to the author by Carolyn M. Smith, "Don Schulman: A Key Witness," paper presented in Political Science 444, Southeastern Massachusetts University, Fall 1988.

Chapter 6

1. The author gratefully acknowledges the excellent research done by Steve Kissell in "L.A. Law vs. Thane Eugene Cesar," seminar paper, Political Science 444, Southeastern Massachusetts University, April 1989. Kissell's paper has provided a valuable contribution to this chapter.
2. Ted Charach, documentary film *The Second Gun*, 1971.
3. Charach, *The Second Gun.*
4. In 1987 Cesar alleged to investigative journalist Dan Moldea that Ted Charach had manipulated the content of the interview to make him appear to be a violence-prone extremist: Dan E. Moldea, "Who Really Killed Bobby Kennedy?" *Regardies*, June 1987, p. 73.
5. Ibid., pp. 74-75.
6. Charach's film *The Second Gun* was re-released as a video in 1988 by MPI Home Video, American Films Ltd., under the title *The Plot to Kill Robert Kennedy.*
7. Robert Houghton and Theodore Taylor, *Special Unit Senator* (New York: Random House, 1970), p. 223.

8. This is discussed by Robert B. Kaiser in *"RFK Must Die!"* (New York: Grove Press, 1970), pp. 349-51.
9. "Investigator Convinced There Was No Second Gun in Kennedy Assassination," *Los Angeles Times*, March 1, 1976, p. 3.
10. Moldea, "Who Really Killed Bobby Kennedy?" p. 77.
11. Moldea, "Who Really Killed Bobby Kennedy?" p. 73.
12. I also discovered that Spangler was an ex-policeman and one of Ace's few full-time employees. Among other duties, he provided brief training in firearms and procedure to novice guards.
13. Moldea, "Who Really Killed Bobby Kennedy?" p. 74.

Chapter 7
1. 1971 interview of Enyart by Ted Charach in the film *The Second Gun*.
2. Journalist Jonn Christian first discovered this incident in newly released police files. See Christian and William Turner, "California Assassination Archives – Robert F. Kennedy, A Special Report,"*Easy Reader*, November 17, 1988.
3. Schraga interview with Jack Thomas, KUOP Radio, Modesto, CA, May 18, 1988.
4. Turner and Christian "California Assassination Archives – Special Report," p. 5.

Chapter 9
1. Los Angeles Police Department *Summary Report* of investigation into the Robert F. Kennedy assassination; 1,500 pages (at pp. 1,423-33).
2. Turner and Christian, *The Assassination of Robert F. Kennedy*. Chapter 15 contains some of these allegations.

Chapter 10
1. Sirhan's background is described in James W. Clarke, *American Assassins* (Princeton: Princeton University Press, 1982), pp. 79-85. It is also dealt with extensively in both FBI and LAPD

files.

2. Trial transcript, *People of the State of California v. Sirhan Bishara Sirhan*, 1969, Superior Court Criminal Case #14062, pp. 4,975-6.

3. Kaiser, *"RFK Must Die!"*, pp. 219-20, 270.

4. In 1985 I wrote to Dr. Diamond seeking access to the audio tapes of his sessions with Sirhan. He wrote that he had donated them to the Cornell University/New York Hospital Medical Library with the condition that "they not be made publicly available." Robert Blair Kaiser participated in the sessions and quoted the tapes extensively in his book *"RFK Must Die!"* See pp. 302-3 and 305.

5. U.S. Justice Department, *Research Brief*, "Forensic Uses of Hypnosis," December 1984, by Martin T. Orne, David F. Dingess and Emily Carota Orne.

6. Kaiser, *"RFK Must Die!"*, p. 151.

7. Turner and Christian, *The Assassination of Robert F. Kennedy*, p. 113.

8. Clarke, *American Assassins*, p. 90. The actual phrase in the notebook is "We believe Kennedy must be sacrificed for the cause of poor exploited people."

9. *San Francisco Examiner*, June 6, 1968, p. 1.

10. Kaiser, *"RFK Must Die!"*, p. 227; also on Crowe, pp. 111-13, 163-5.

11. There are numerous references to "Jet Spec," but this turns out to be a race horse at one of the tracks where Sirhan worked as an exercise boy.

12. Kaiser, *"RFK Must Die!"*, p. 337.

13. Kaiser, *"RFK Must Die!"*, p. 339-40.

14. Kaiser, *"RFK Must Die!"*, p. 340, taken verbatim.

15. Kaiser, *"RFK Must Die!"*, pp. 264-65.

16. Turner and Christian, *The Assassination of Robert F. Kennedy*, p. 194.

17. Turner and Christian, *The Assassination of Robert F. Kennedy*, p. 111.

18. Kaiser, *"RFK Must Die!"*, pp. 352-55.
19. The descriptions of these sessions are based on Kaiser, *"RFK Must Die!"*, pp. 303, 348, 352-5.
20. Kaiser, *"RFK Must Die!"*, p. 354.

Chapter 11

1. Taped interview with researcher Betsy Langman, 1974.
2. Ibid.
3. Turner and Christian, *The Assassination of Robert F. Kennedy*.
4. Alan W. Scheflin and Edward M. Opton, Jr., *The Mind Manipulators* (New York: Paddington Press, 1978), p. 447.
5. John D. Marks, *The Search for the "Manchurian Candidate,"* (New York: McGraw-Hill, 1980), pp. 182,   190 note.
6. Martin A. Lee and Bruce Schlain, *Acid Dreams: The CIA, LSD and the Sixties Rebellion* (New York: Grove Press, 1985). This interview was not included in the book but was conducted as part of Lee's in-depth research, portions of which he generously provided to the author.
7. This description is taken from Marks, *The Search for the "Manchurian Candidate,"* Chapter 11. He obtained 1,600 pages of CIA documents on mind-control research by using the Freedom of Information Act.
8. Marks, *"Manchurian Candidate,"* p. 183.
9. Marks, *"Manchurian Candidate,"* p. 183.
10. Marks, *"Manchurian Candidate,"* p. 187.
11. Marks, *"Manchurian Candidate,"* pp. 186-87.
12. Donald Bain, *The Control of Candy Jones* (Chicago: Playboy Press, 1976).
13. Scheflin and Opton, *Mind Manipulation*, pp. 446-67.
14. Kaiser, *"RFK Must Die!"*, p. 374.
15. FBI interviews of Patricia Strathman, July 16 and September 8, 1968.
16. Kaiser, *"RFK Must Die!"*, p. 213.
17. Kaiser, *"RFK Must Die!"*, pp. 207-8.
18. LAPD interview September 11, 1968.

19. Kaiser, *"RFK Must Die!"*, pp. 531-32.
20. CIA researchers experimented with mixing drugs and hypnosis in order to enhance programming (Marks, *"Manchurian Candidate,"* p. 41). CIA experimenters also had a penchant for spiking the drinks consumed by unwitting subjects, often in public settings. The liquid refreshment would be laced with LSD or other drugs.
21. This estimate comes from timing the audio-taped description of the struggle narrated by Andrew West of Mutual News Radio.
22. Kaiser, *"RFK Must Die!"*, p. 26.
23. Kaiser, *"RFK Must Die!"*, p. 38.
24. Turner and Christian, *The Assassination of Robert F. Kennedy*, p. 197.
25. Plimpton's June 5 interview, LAPD (audio tape).
26. Kaiser, *"RFK Must Die!"*, p. 41.
27. Taped interview with researcher Betsy Langman, 1973.
28. LAPD *Summary Report*, p. 625.
29. Ibid., p. 426.
30. Kaiser, *"RFK Must Die!"*, p. 296.
31. Kaiser, *"RFK Must Die!"*, p. 297.
32. Kaiser, *"RFK Must Die!"*, p. 89.
33. Kaiser, *"RFK Must Die!"*, pp. 302-3.
34. Kaiser, *"RFK Must Die!"*, p. 295.
35. Pamela J. Puputti, "Did the Rosicrucians Influence the Behavior of Sirhan Sirhan to Participate in the Assassination of Robert F. Kennedy?" Southeastern Massachusetts University, Seminar on Political Assassinations, Fall 1988.
36. Kaiser, *"RFK Must Die!"*, p. 367.
37. Kaiser, *"RFK Must Die!"*, p. 339.
38. Kaiser, *"RFK Must Die!"*, p. 273.
39. Kaiser, *"RFK Must Die!"*, p. 343.
40. Simpson and Schorr interviews conducted by Betsy Langman, 1974.
41. Marks, *"Manchurian Candidate,"* p. 191.

Chapter 12

1. Kaiser, *"RFK Must Die!"*, pp. 133-34.
2. Turner and Christian, *The Assassination of Robert F. Kennedy*, p. 224.
3. Turner and Christian, *The Assassination of Robert F. Kennedy*, p. 225.
4. Turner and Christian, *The Assassination of Robert F. Kennedy*, p. 228.
5. Turner and Christian, *The Assassination of Robert F. Kennedy*, p. 226.
6. The Committee ultimately decided not to re-investigate Senator Kennedy's assassination but only the cases of President John F. Kennedy and Dr.Martin Luther King, Jr.: Greg Roberts, "RFK Assassination Conspiracy Theory Hypnotist Found Dead in Las Vegas," *Hollywood Reporter*, March 21, 1977, p. 2.
7. F. Lee Bailey with Harvey Aronson, *The Defense Never Rests* (New York: Stein and Day, 1971), pp. 159-61.
8. Ibid., p. 165.
9. Ibid., pp. 239-304.
10. Turner and Christian, *The Assassination of Robert F. Kennedy*, p. 227.
11. Pamela J. Puputti, "Did the Rosicrucians Influence the Behavior of Sirhan Sirhan to Participate in the Assassination of Robert F. Kennedy?" p. 3.
12. Lee and Schlain, *Acid Dreams*, p. 90.
13. See Turner and Christian, *The Assassination of Robert F. Kennedy*, p. 206.

Chapter 13

1. From Kaiser, *"RFK Must Die!"*, p. 366.
2. Green was interviewed twice by the Bureau, on June 7   and 16.
3. As previously described, Robert Blair Kaiser sat in on Sirhan's questioning and the hypnotic sessions. The above description of Sirhan's recollection of "the girl" is taken from Kaiser's

book (*"RFK Must Die!"*, pp. 304, 350-51, 366, 368) and from his personal notebooks that reside in the Southeastern Massachusetts University Robert F. Kennedy Assassination Archives.

Chapter 14

1. Houghton and Taylor, *Special Unit Senator*, pp. 119-20.
2. See William Turner and Jonn Christian, "California Assassination Archives – Robert F. Kennedy," "Polka-Dots and Police Perfidy," *Easy Reader*, November 17, 1988.
3. The author has read the vast majority of interviews in all three files.
4. LAPD *Summary Report*, p. 413.
5. David Kal Haines, a 19-year-old co-worker of Serrano's in the Pasadena Youth for Kennedy group, told the FBI on June 12 that he encountered her after the shooting. He recalled that she said, "Oh, David, you don't know what I've seen. What should I do?" She was extremely upset. Haines said Serrano told him "other things" too, but he was so upset over the shooting he could not recall what they were.
6. Houghton and Taylor, *Special Unit Senator*, pp. 119-20.
7. U.S House of Representatives Select Committee on Assassinations, vol. 13, pp. 145-9 (Washington, D.C.: U.S. Government Printing Office, 1978). An in-depth analysis of LAPD's use of the polygraph in the RFK case was done in October 1990 by Lisa Perfetuo, an intern at the Southeastern Massachusetts University Robert F. Kennedy Assassination Archives.

Chapter 15

1. LAPD *Summary Report*, pp. 408-12.

Chapter 16

1. LAPD *Summary Report*, pp. 425-39.
2. Ibid.
3. Fred J. Cook, "The Billion-Dollar Mystery," *The Nation*, April 12, 1965.

4. David Wise and Thomas Ross, *Invisible Government* (New York: Vintage, 1964), p. 110.

Chapter 17

1. This information is taken from resumés of LAPD officers who worked on the case, contained in police files released in 1988.
2. Turner and Christian, *The Assassination of Robert F. Kennedy*, pp. 64-65.
3. Houghton and Taylor, *Special Unit Senator*, p. 103.
4. Audio tape, Betsy Langman conversation with Stan Bohrman, 1977.
5. See Philip H. Melanson, ''CIA's Secret Ties to Local Police,'' *The Nation*, March 26, 1983.
6. William T. Divale with James Joseph, *I Lived Inside the Campus Revolution* (New York: College Notes & Texts, Inc., 1970).
7. Kaiser, *''RFK Must Die!''*, p. 198.
8. Divale with Joseph, *Campus Revolution*, p. 147.
9. Crowe's FBI interview of June 7, 1968.
10. LAPD *Summary Report*, ''Possible Association with Communists,'' pp. 69-72, at p. 71.
11. Ibid., pp. 471-72.
12. Divale with Joseph, *Campus Revolution*, p. 52.
13. Divale with Joseph, *Campus Revolution*, p. 138.
14. LAPD *Summary Report*, p. 472.
15. Ibid., pp. 71-72, 472-73.
16. Ibid., p. 473.
17. Ibid., p. 474.
18. Ibid., p. 72.
19. Divale with Joseph, *Campus Revolution*, p. 136.
20. Divale with Joseph, *Campus Revolution*, p. 113.
21. Kaiser, *''RFK Must Die!''*, p. 113.
22. LAPD *Summary Report*, p. 71.
23. Ibid., p. 71.

Chapter 18

1. Taped interview with journalist Andy Boehm, 1988 (precise date is not marked on the author's copy of the tape).
2. KQED Radio, San Francisco, June 9, 1988.

A Selected Chronology of the Robert F. Kennedy Assassination

December 14, 1956 / After nine years as refugees from their home in Jerusalem, the Sirhan family and four-year-old Sirhan Bishara Sirhan come to the United States with help provided by Lutheran missionaries and the United Nations.

Fall 1963 / Sirhan enters Pasadena City College.

October 1965 / Sirhan takes a job as a stable boy at Santa Anita Racetrack. Quits March 31, 1966.

September 25, 1966 / Sirhan's ambition to become a jockey is ended by a bad fall from a horse during a workout on a fog-shrouded track.

September 24, 1967 / Commences employment at Organic Pasadena Health Food Store. Employment ended March 7, 1968.

March 16, 1968 / Senator Robert F. Kennedy (Dem., New York) announces his candidacy for the presidency of the United States.

The chronology was compiled by Lisa Perfetuo with assistance from Christopher D'Arcy.

March 27, 1968 / Sirhan is paid $2,000 by the Argonaut Insurance Company for injuries sustained when he fell from a horse.

Early 1968 / Sirhan manifests a fixation for mysticism and joins the Ancient Mystical Order of the Rosicrucians (AMORC).

May 18, 1968 / An entry in Sirhan's notebook, dated this date but not verified as this date, reads: "My determination to eliminate RFK is becoming more the more [sic] an unshakable obsession . . . RFK must die."

June 1, 1968 / Sirhan purchases two boxes of .22-caliber hollow-point bullets from the Lock, Stock and Barrel gun shop in San Gabriel, California.

June 2, 1968 / Sirhan goes to the Ambassador Hotel in Los Angeles, where a Kennedy rally is being held.

June 4, 1968 / Sirhan rapid-fires his .22 pistol at the San Gabriel Valley gun club for several hours from mid-morning to late afternoon, and is seen in the company of an attractive young, blond woman.

June 5, 1968, approximately 12:10 a.m. / Senator Kennedy and five others are shot at the Ambassador Hotel in Los Angeles, in a food-service pantry.

June 6, 1968, 1:44 a.m. / Robert F. Kennedy dies at age 42.

June 8, 1968, 10:30 p.m. / Robert F. Kennedy is buried at Arlington National Cemetery after a 21-car funeral train made an eight-hour journey from New York City to Washington, D.C.

June 9, 1968 / A decision is made by the Los Angeles Police Department to form a special task force to investigate the assassination: Special Unit Senator (SUS).

April 17, 1969 / Sirhan is convicted of killing Robert F. Kennedy. He will be sentenced to death in the gas chamber, but the Supreme Court will subsequently declare the death penalty unconstitutional. As of this writing, California authorities continue to deny his requests for parole.

June 27, 1969 / Crucial crime-scene evidence relating to a second gun – wood from the pantry doorframe and several ceiling tiles – is destroyed by LAPD while Sirhan's case is still being appealed.

1971 / Los Angeles authorities conduct a series of videotaped re-enactments of the crime, said to attempt to demonstrate that Sirhan could have inflicted Senator Kennedy's wounds. The videos are suppressed until 1986.

February 20, 1973 / Sirhan's conviction is upheld on appeal.

September 18, 1975 / Superior Court Judge Robert Wenke orders a retesting and examination of ballistics evidence. Ultimately, a panel of court-appointed firearms experts will conclude that the available bullets cannot positively be linked to Sirhan's gun, nor can they be excluded from Sirhan's gun.

December 10, 1975 / Los Angeles Police and the L.A. District Attorney's Office conduct a re-examination of the Ambassador Hotel's pantry, searching for second-gun bullets. Officials inform the media that none were found.

1975 / Special Counsel Thomas Kranz reinvestigates the assassination for the District Attorney's Office and issues the *Kranz Report*, reaffirming the official conclusions of 1968-69.

1975 / A group of petitioners, including *CBS News* and assassination shooting victim Paul Shrade, request that the California Superior Court order the release of Los Angeles Police case files, arguing in part that the files were previously disclosed to an author collaborating with Chief Robert Houghton on his book *Special Unit Senator*. The petition is denied.

1976 / the FBI releases three photos in response to a Freedom of Information Act request. They are labeled as "two bullet holes." If correct, the photos show too many bullets for Sirhan's gun and contradict the official record.

1977 / The Los Angeles District Attorney's Office conducts further re-investigation by interviewing witnesses, law officers, and informants and by staging a re-enactment of the crime. The results would remain largely secret until 1986, when they were released with the general case file.

December 1984 / Greg Stone and Philip Melanson use the Freedom of Information Act to request the release of FBI files related to the RFK case. Thirty-two thousand pages of previously unreleased documents begin to be processed for disclosure.

1985 / The Los Angeles District Attorney's Office processes its case file for release with a minimum of censorship, in response to requests from Greg Stone and others.

March 4, 1986 / The Los Angeles Police Commission releases, with some deletions, the 1,500-page *Summary Report* of the department's assassination investigation. The report was prepared by LAPD in 1969 and is analogous to the *Warren Commission Report* released the year following President John F. Kennedy's assassination.

April 19, 1988 / After 20 years of total official secrecy, the Los Angeles Police's 50,000-page case file is released by the California State Archives in Sacramento, following a four-year campaign by journalists, researchers and concerned citizens.

January 1989 / Federal Judge Charles Richey rules against Stone and Melanson and for the FBI, allowing the Bureau to delete the names of FBI agents from released documents on the grounds of privacy. Witness names are released. Judge Richey's decision is upheld by a federal appeals court in Washington, D.C.

May 15, 1990 / At a Los Angeles Press Conference, Greg Stone, ex-FBI agent William Bailey, journalist Dan Moldea, producer David Mendelsohn and the author present new evidence of a second gun and demand a re-opening of the case.

November 27, 1990 / A letter is sent to Los Angeles District Attorney Ira Reiner detailing the unresolved controversies and the new evidence of a second gun, and formally requesting a review of the case. Signators are Greg Stone, Paul Schrade, Paul Le Mat, Jack Gordon and the author. The official response is pending.

Dramatis Personae

For the reader's convenience in keeping track of the vast array of individuals who are in various ways significant in the Robert F. Kennedy case, the following glossary was prepared by the author.

Abo, Dr. Stanley / Physician who first came to RFK's aid after the shooting

Allen, Morse / Head of research for CIA project to produce hypnoprogrammed operatives and assassins

Allen, Ron / Investigator for Sirhan's defense team

Ambrose, John / Deputy DA who heard Sandra Serrano's polka-dot-dress account just after the shooting, before she talked to police

Bailey, F. Lee / Prominent attorney who used Dr. William Joseph Bryan, Jr., as a consultant

Bailey, William / FBI agent who examined the crime scene

Barry, Bill / RFK bodyguard and ex-FBI agent

Botting, Laverne / RFK campaign worker with allegation implying Sirhan stalked Kennedy in the company of others

Bradford, Lowell / Firearms expert who served on 1975 panel that re-examined the assassination bullets

Brent, Jeff / Continental News Service radio reporter who interviewed Don Schulman just after the shooting

Brown, Hugh / LAPD captain, second in command to Chief Houghton in Special Unit Senator

Bryan, William Joseph, Jr. / Hypnotherapist who worked on government mind-control research, suspected of being Sirhan's programmer

Buckner, Everett / Alleged Sirhan was with an attractive woman at his gun club hours before the shooting

Bugliosi, Vincent / Former L.A. prosecutor who conducted a private investigation of case evidence

Burnett, William R. / L.A. District Attorney's Office chief investigator on RFK case during the 1970s

Burns, Frank / Crime-scene witness and political assistant to Jesse Unruh

Burns, John / Head of California State Archives who processed LAPD files for public disclosure in 1988-89

Bush, Joseph P. / Los Angeles District Attorney

Castellano, Lillian / Private researcher and founder of Kennedy Assassination Truth Committee

Cesar, Thane Eugene / Security guard who stood next to RFK and drew his gun during the assassination

Cetina, Cavilo / Ambassador Hotel waiter who encountered Sirhan earlier on the night of the shooting

Charach, Ted / Investigative journalist who produced the RFK-case film *The Second Gun*

Christian, Jonn / Investigative journalist who worked on the RFK case and co-authored (1978), with William Turner, *The Assassination of Robert F. Kennedy*

Clemente, John R. / Amateur photographer who took pictures of pantry doorframe

Collier, Charles / LAPD photographer who took pictures of the crime scene

Compton, Lynn / Prosecutor at Sirhan's trial

Cook, Fred / Wrote an extensive article in *The Nation* on Khaiber Khan's espionage activities.

Cooper, Grant / Sirhan's lawyer in 1968

Creehan, Ethel / Campaign worker who supported Laverne Botting's account of Sirhan apparently stalking RFK

Crowe, Walter / College friend of Sirhan's and an avowed communist

Davis, Chief Ed / LAPD police chief; he succeeded Thomas Reddin

Diamond, Dr. Bernard / Psychiatrist on Sirhan's defense team

Di Pierro, Angelo / Crime-scene witness, hotel waiter and father of witness Vincent DiPiero

Di Pierro, Vincent / Crime-scene witness and controversial polka-dot-dress girl witness

Divale, William T. / FBI informant who knew Sirhan at Pasadena City College

Estrada, Daniel / Fellow prisoner of Sirhan's who brought a conspiracy allegation to the DA's office in 1977

Evans, Elizabeth / Shot in the head during the assassination and recovered

Falzone, Carmen /Fellow prisoner of Sirhan's who, upon release in 1977, worked for the DA's office to surveil the Sirhan family

Faura, Fernando / Journalist who worked on polka-dot-dress story

Gardner, William / Now-deceased chief of security at Ambassador Hotel during the assassination

Gates, Chief Daryl / LAPD assistant chief during destruction of the key evidence, and, at this writing (1991), on suspension from his post as LAPD chief

Goldstein, Ira / Crime-scene witness wounded during the assassination

Green, George / Alleged he saw polka-dot-dress girl flee pantry during the struggle to disarm Sirhan

Grier, Roosevelt / Ex-football star, RFK supporter, crime-scene witness, who struggled to disarm Sirhan

Griffin, Booker / Saw Sirhan and attractive girl together at the crime scene twice before the shooting and saw the girl fleeing the pantry after the shooting

Grijalva, Roberta and Richard / Saw Sirhan firing a rifle at the gun club just hours before the shooting. Sirhan did not own a rifle and there is no explanation of where the rifle came from

Grohs, Mary / Teletype operator who noticed Sirhan's strange behavior at the hotel, before the shooting

Harper, William / Renowned criminologist who challenged LAPD's ballistics findings and the work of LAPD criminologist DeWayne Wolfer

Harrington, Wesley / Hotel carpenter who saw what appeared to be a bullet in the pantry doorway

Hernandez, Enrique / LAPD lieutenant who administered all of the polygraph tests, mostly to conspiracy-related witnesses

Hoover, J. Edgar / Head of FBI during RFK investigation

Houghton, Robert / Deputy chief who headed Special Unit Senator (SUS), special LAPD unit set up to investigate the assassination

Howard, John / Assistant DA who played a major role in the prosecution of Sirhan

Isaacs, Godfrey / A Sirhan attorney in the post-trial era

Jaimison, Arnold (pseudonym) / Deborah Jaimison's husband

Jaimison, Deborah (pseudonym) / Woman who was with Sirhan at the gun club the afternoon before the midnight assassination

Johnson, Rafer / RFK supporter and crime-scene witness; Olympic champion

Joling, Robert / Former head of National Academy of Forensic Sciences, who challenged official evidentiary conclusions

Jones, Candy / Claimed to have been fitted with a second personality and hypnotized to perform work for the CIA

Jordan, William / LAPD sergeant who interrogated and dealt with Sirhan when he was first brought into custody

Khan, Khaiber / CIA-linked Iranian espionage master working in the RFK campaign in Los Angeles

Khan, Rose (real name Miriam Kouchan) / Allegedly Khaiber Khan's half sister, who was actually his trusted secretary

Kaiser, Robert Blair / Journalist and investigator on Sirhan's defense team; wrote *"RFK Must Die!"*

Kline, Milton / Psychologist who consulted with CIA mind-control researchers

Kranz, Thomas / L.A. District Attorney's Office Special Council who conducted a re-investigation in 1977

LaJeunesse, Roger / FBI agent who served as liaison with LAPD during RFK investigation

Langman, Betsy / Researcher who conducted dozens of taped interviews with case principals in the 1970s

LeBeau, Albert / Witness who alleged to have seen Sirhan and a young woman acting suspiciously at an RFK event the month before the shooting

Lee, Martin A. / Investigative journalist who studied CIA research on robot assassins

Lowenstein, Allard K. / Former Congressman who pressed for resolution of case controversies; murdered in 1980

Lubic, Richard / Crime-scene witness and TV producer

Lynch, Cecil / L.A. fire department captain whose testimony was used by authorities to impeach the credibility of Sandra Serrano

Macarthur, James / LAPD officer who was in the pantry during the search for evidence

MacDonnell, Herbert / Independent criminologist who challenged the official version

Manasian, Edward / Crime-scene witness and assistant maître d' at Ambassador Hotel

Mankiewicz, Frank / RFK's press secretary

Marks, John / Wrote *The Search for the "Manchurian Candidate,"* documenting CIA efforts to produce a robot assassin

McBroom, Marcus / Crime-scene witness who saw polka-dot-dress girl exiting the ballroom after the shooting

McKissak, Luke / Sirhan's attorney as of this writing

Mendelsohn, David / TV and radio producer who worked for public disclosure and re-opening of the case

Moldea, Dan / Investigative journalist who discovered major new evidence during the 1980s

Nelson, Floyd / Private researcher and founder of the Kennedy Assassination Truth Committee

Noguchi, Thomas / L.A. coroner who performed RFK autopsy

Noyes, Peter / Investigative journalist who brought conspiracy allegations to LAPD

Parsons, Russell / Sirhan's attorney in 1968

Patruski, Martin / Crime-scene witness and hotel waiter

Pena, Manuel / LAPD lieutenant who played a pivotal role in the investigation of conspiracy

Perez, Jesus / Crime-scene witness and Ambassador Hotel busboy

Pickard, Robert / FBI agent who worked the crime scene with agent William Bailey

Placencia, Arthur / LAPD officer who tested Sirhan's eyes for evidence of drugs or alcohol en route to jail

Pollack, Seymour / Psychiatrist on the prosecution team

Poore, Dale / Hotel carpenter who saw what appeared to be a bullet in the pantry doorframe

Raines, Martha (pseudonym) / Key crime-scene witness who saw a second gun fired

Rathke, Tom / Co-worker of Sirhan's at the racetrack

Reddin, Chief Thomas / LAPD chief at the time of the assassination

Reisner, Johathan (pseudonym) / Mysterious hypnotherapist (interviewed by the author) who allegedly had connections with Dr. William Joseph Bryan, Jr.

Richards, Amadee O. / FBI agent who was case superviser for RFK investigation

Romero, Juan / Crime-scene witness and Ambassador Hotel busboy

Royer, Judy / Kennedy press aide and crime-scene witness, who encountered Sirhan

Rozzi, Robert / LAPD officer seen AP photo apparently pointing to a bullet hole at the crime scene

Sartuche, Phil / LAPD sergeant who dealt with some key witnesses while working for Special Unit Senator

Schoor, Martin / Psychiatrist consulted by Sirhan's defense team

Schrade, Paul / Assassination shooting victim and RFK friend and colleague

Schraga, Paul / LAPD sergeant who put out an APB for two escaping suspects at the crime scene – which was later canceled

Schulman, Don / Controversial crime-scene witness who alleges that a security guard fired a gun during the assassination

Schulte, Valeria / Crime-scene witness alleged by LAPD to be the polka-dot-dress girl – not verifiable by several eyewitnesses

Serrano, Sandra / The key polka-dot-dress witness, who saw Sirhan and the girl together prior to the shooting, then saw the girl rushing out of the hotel after the shooting

Severson, Ellenor / Saw Sirhan at RFK headquarters where Khaiber Khan worked

Shirley, John / Amateur photographer who took pictures of pantry and saw holes in wooden doorframe

Simpson, Eduard / San Quentin prison psychologist who worked extensively with Sirhan to try to restore his memory of the crime

Sirhan, Adel / Sirhan Sirhan's brother

Sirhan, Mary / Sirhan Sirhan's mother

Sirhan, Sharif / Sirhan Sirhan's brother

Sirhan, Sirhan / Alleged and convicted assassin of Robert F. Kennedy

Slitsky, Irv / Ace Guard Service executive interviewed by the author

Spangler, Tom / Ace Guard Service employee who allegedly assigned Cesar to the Ambassador Hotel on the night of the assassination

Spiegal, Herbert, Sr. / Expert hypnotherapist who believes Sirhan was a programmed assassin

Stone, Gregory / Leading private researcher on the RFK case, who led the fight for public disclosure and re-opening of the investigation; recently deceased

Strathman, John / Friend of Sirhan's who witnessed personality change in Sirhan after he was injured at the racetrack

Strick, Larry / Witness who saw Sirhan at RFK headquarters where Khaiber Khan worked

Talcott, Robert / President of Los Angeles Police Commission during some of the public disclosure battles of the 1980s

Taylor, Theodore / Author who worked with Chief Robert Houghton on his book *Special Unit Senator,* the "authorized" story of LAPD's RFK investigation

Tew, Walter / Los Angeles Deputy Sheriff, now deceased, who circled what appeared to be bullet holes in pantry door frame

Turner, William / Investigative journalist who worked on the case and co-authored (1978) a book with Jonn Christian called *The Assassination of Robert F. Kennedy*

Uecker, Karl / Led RFK through pantry, grabbed Sirhan's gun; Ambassador Hotel maître d'

Unruh, Jess / Speaker of California Assembly and crime-scene witness

Urso, Lisa / Crime-scene witness and centerpiece of the District Attorney's official re-investigation in 1977

Van de Kamp, John / L.A. District Attorney during re-investigations and controversies in the late 1970s; subsequently became State Attorney General and unsuccesssful gubernatorial candidate

Ward, Baxter / L.A. County Supervisor who pursued evidence questions

Weidrich, Robert / *Chicago Tribune* reporter who wrote about bullets being removed from the pantry doorframe

Weisel, William / Shot in the stomach during the assassination

West, Andrew / Radio reporter who captured on audio tape the unfolding shooting and the struggle to disarm Sirhan

Wolfer, DeWayne / LAPD criminologist who handled the RFK case

Wright, Charles / LAPD officer in AP photo apparently pointing to a bullet hole at the crime scene

Yaro, Boris / *Los Angeles Times* photographer and crime-scene witness

Yoder, Jim / Co-worker of Thane Cesar, to whom Cesar sold his .22 pistol – allegedly before the assassination

Yorty, Sam / Mayor of Los Angeles at the time of the assassination

Younger, Evelle / Los Angeles District Attorney at the time of the assassination

Acknowledgments

More than any other project I have undertaken, this one has depended upon the cumulative efforts of a group of researchers, investigators, concerned citizens, and friends and colleagues too numerous to mention here. Without their efforts, this book would not have been possible. While not implying anyone's agreement with the analyses and conclusions I've presented, I wish to acknowledge a large and diverse group whose contributions were important.

First, there are the researchers, whose work on this case created such a rich body of data. The late Lillian Castellano was the driving force behind the Kennedy Assassination Truth Committee, a small band of Los Angeles citizens who sought to establish a complete and accurate case record. Her tenacious but analytical pursuit of the evidence, the documents and the truth in the face of official recalcitrance and disinformation was a model of citizenship activism in a democracy. The late Congressman Allard K. Lowenstein was the only elected official with the courage to pursue energetically the unanswered questions while keeping an open mind about the answers – with little or no help (and considerable resistance) from the establishment – until his tragic murder in 1980.

Floyd Nelson, also a founder of the Truth Committee, continued Lillian Castellano's work after her death. He has researched the case from its inception, and he preserved the committee's 30 boxes of files and tapes (with the help of Lillian's research associate, Jan Diaz) and donated them to the Robert F. Kennedy Assassination Archives at Southeastern Massachusetts University. From 1968 to the present, Floyd has selflessly shared his findings, thoughts and data with numerous researchers and journalists (some of whom don't speak to each other) and has never stopped caring about the pursuit of historical truth, even during the case's numerous crises and dark moments that continue today in the form of official resistance and continued cover-up. Floyd has been a source of intellectual and philosophical guidance for several prominent researchers, and especially for the author. He has been my mentor on the case, as well as my friend, generously serving as everything from investigative strategist and participant to expert reader of the manuscript.

It was in 1983 that my role in this case turned from interest to involvement, when Larry Schlossman linked me up with the late Greg Stone. Greg was a political scientist who had worked on this assassination in his capacity as administrative assistant to Congressman Lowenstein. He continued the work, selflessly giving his time, resources and energy to the pursuit of truth and the re-opening of the case. He personally conducted or sponsored the most groundbreaking research and investigation. He organized and led the tough fight for public disclosure (Los Angeles Police, District Attorney's Office and FBI files). He founded and directed the Inquiry and Accountability Foundation, which has funded research and intervened legally to preserve the case evidence (my thanks to Los Angeles attorney Marilyn Barrett for giving her time and expertise to handle the foundation's legal affairs).

Greg was the most intellectually skillful, honest and dedicated researcher I have encountered in any field. His leadership, activism and effective efforts were the core of progress in the Robert F. Kennedy case. More than any individual, and more than most of us combined, he has changed the history of this case for the better, even though the main goals of his life's work – to discover the truth, whatever it was, and to force officials and institutions to do what they should be doing – were not attained in his lifetime. The ethical and intellectual standards with which he pursued these goals were truly inspiring. Greg's death has left a tremendous void in the pursuit of truth and justice and in the lives of those of us privileged to work with him as a colleague and friend. Without appropriating his assent to my work, much of what I know about this case came directly or indirectly from his sharing of insights and data. I should add that Greg insisted that "books do not re-open cases." Without Floyd and Greg, I would not have been so intimately involved in this case and this book would not have been possible.

Paul Schrade was a friend of Senator Kennedy and served as labor coordinator for the California primary campaign. He was seriously wounded during the assassination. Despite the physical and emotional pain this tragedy visited upon him, Paul has been a beacon of courage to all of us who have fought along with him for disclosure, re-opening and a resolution of the issues. His political acumen, leadership and friendship were crucial elements in the successes, such as disclosure, and in our not giving up in the face of official stonewalling. Paul's overcoming his personal trauma to vigorously pursue the truth regarding Kennedy's death while constantly championing the Senator's living political legacy is indeed a profile in courage.

Without the concerted efforts of numerous persons to end two decades of official secrecy, the case would still be in the dark ages and this book could not have been written. The citizens, scholars, journalist and politicians (too numerous to mention) who supported disclosure of the LAPD, FBI and DA files helped make victory possible by creating enough moral and political pressure to overcome official disinterest or opposition. Larry Teeter was Los Angeles counsel for Greg Stone and myself in our efforts to obtain FBI files. Washington Attorney Jim Lesar fought brilliantly in his time-consuming effort to achieve release of the full FBI file, and to resist the Bureau's censorship. Jack Gordon served on Mayor Bradley's committee that set up the disclosure process for LAPD files, worked in the campaign for release, and developed important new evidence. Monica Weil gave encouragement and advice. Carol Moss of Los Angeles and Morris Polan, then chief librarian at California State University, were also important participants. The Southern California chapter of the American Civil Liberties Union provided strategic legal assistance in surmounting the barriers to disclosure erected by the Los Angeles Police Department and by some members of the Los Angeles Police Commission and its staff. Congressman Barney Frank (Dem., Mass.) was instrumental in obtaining a public-interest fee waiver from the FBI so that the Bureau's massive file could be obtained at affordable cost. Radio and television producer David Mendelsohn served skillfully as our press person and media advisor for the major events geared to disclosure and re-opening an investigation. David gave generously of his time, resources, friendship and advice to enhance the success of the campaign for valid conclusions.

John Burns, head of the California State Archives in Sacramento, and his staff, performed an exemplary national service in processing the LAPD files for public release – with practically no censorship and with a knowledgeable understanding of the case's issues, problems and controversies. This processing for disclosure was a model effort in the public right to know. Mr. Burns's assistant, Nancy Zimmelman, was very helpful to the author in fulfilling requests for numerous audio tapes of witness interviews, despite the heavy workload and technical problems regarding duplication faced by the Archives. Diane Nixon, then head of the Laguna Niguel, California, branch of the National Archives, and her staff, were very courteous and helpful during my visits there to obtain copies of the LADA's files and trial exhibits; they allowed Floyd Nelson, Greg Stone and me to obtain copies of fragile but crucial audio tapes. Ian Shapolsky and Todd Bludeau provided editing expertise that was extremely helpful.

The late Bud Fensterwald obtained the first release of FBI

documents (approximately 3,000 pages), including key evidentiary photographs. As a researcher-investigator and, later, as Director of the Assassination Archives and Research Center, Washington, D.C., Bud generously made available to researchers, including the author and Greg Stone, files and photographs on the RFK case. Bud and his Archives also pressed for release of LAPD files.

The Robert F. Kennedy Assassination Archives at Southeastern Massachusetts University has been a major resource for the advancement of knowledge in the case and has been a crucial resource for this project. Thanks go to Dean Janet Freedman and her staff at the library. Dean Freedman has been a strong supporter of the Archives and of disclosure, as has Associate Librarian Bruce Barnes. Maeve Hickok, University Director of News and Public Information, has done an excellent and energetic job of communicating to the public and the media the significance of the Archives and the questions and controversies in the assassination. My university colleague Jenny Howard played a key role in establishing the Archives and in acquiring its first material (Lillian Castellano and Floyd Nelson's collection). Jenny also worked with me in getting political support for public disclosure of official files and obtaining a fee waiver from the FBI. All of these persons, as private citizens, also share an understanding of the case's importance and its controversies.

I am especially indebted to Helen Koss, our archivist. She effectively organized the massive files and collections and made them user-friendly for everyone, including the author. She has always lent her expertise when I needed to find data. Her knowledge of the case and her excitement about its issues and problems have made my research easier and more enjoyable. I also want to recognize the outstanding work of her staff and interns, too numerous to mention, who have helped organize the wealth of documents, audio tapes, photos and exhibits that comprise this vast collection – especially Shelly Braga and Kim Slusarski.

My university community has given very significant support to the Archives and to the public disclosure process – faculty, students, administrators, President John R. Brazil and persons from the local-regional community (including some journalists and public officials). My colleagues in the Political Science Department have been supportive of these efforts as well as of my research and writing. The Library Associates and the Southeastern Massachusetts University Alumni Association provided financial support to the Archives for acquisition and collection development when there was no money available in the state budget. I received two research grants from the Southeastern Massachusetts University Foundation (awarded by the Faculty Research Committee) for travel to Los Angeles to do research and acquire documents. Our department secretary, Liz Tucker, provided invaluable help in typing and editing the voluminous correspondence (and some of the investigative-research memos) that my work produced. My students, in my course in Political Assassinations in America and especially in my research seminar, have been a source of encouragement and intellectual stimulation for my work. Their curiosity about, and frustration with, the state of knowledge in this case has had an energizing impact on me. Their specific, substantive insights are footnoted in numerous chapters.

The author wishes to acknowledge the contributions made by other authors and researchers from whose work this project benefited. The late Bill Harper, a courageous criminologist who brought his integrity and expertise to ballistics analysis concerning a second gun, raised questions and confronted the official version in the early 1970s. Jonn Christian and William Turner's landmark 1978 book was my first orientation (as a reviewer) to the mysteries and controversies of the case. Christian has continued to research disclosed files and to enhance the collective understanding of the case. Robert Blair Kaiser's 1970 *"RFK Must Die!"* is the most vivid account of the trial, the defense strategy and Sirhan's behavior. This and his private papers, donated to the Archives, have been very useful. Also, Ted Charach's 1971 film *The Second Gun* raised important evidentiary questions.

Dan Moldea is one of the few journalists to tackle this case with courage and conviction and make significant progress. He worked very closely with Greg Stone (and also with me) and pushed for disclosure and re-opening while energetically generating new evidence. His landmark articles (1987-90) and the new data he gathered represented important advances in understanding. Dan's unwavering commitment to finding the truth about the death of his political hero has been a boon to the case and to the friends and colleagues he works with.

Betsy Langman's numerous and detailed audio-taped interviews with principal figures in the case, conducted during the 1970s and culminating in her co-authored article in *Harper's*, are a valuable resource for the Archives (to which she donated them) and for this book. Marty Lee's generous sharing of interviews and data gathered while researching his book *Acid Dreams* was a cornerstone of my probe into the complex dimensions of CIA mind-control research.

Thanks also go to John Davis, Anthony Summers and David Sheim for their support and assistance.

I owe special thanks to the select group of energetic and perceptive students whom I was fortunate to recruit as my research assistants during the peak periods of research and writing. Dianna Perry and Alyson Wihry Shaw helped to organize the Archives and to develop its computerized data base and indices, as well as to administer to the logistics and media relations for its public opening. They worked with me as colleagues in researching the newly released LAPD files, and they made significant discoveries. Their effectiveness and good humor are much appreciated.

Bill Letendra contributed not only his excellent research skills but his perceptive skepticism concerning both official and unofficial conclusions. Ron Quintin and Jennifer Tavares did outstanding research on the case and also functioned as a team in challenging my assumptions concerning case strategy. Ron's work at the Archives was also outstanding. Lisa Perfetuo provided invaluable research assistance and findings (on such key matters as polygraph tests) and helped fact-check and coordinate the final phase of the book while simultaneously assisting Helen Koss in organizing archival data and public events. Steve Kissell played a special role as editorial consultant, bringing his insightful intellect to bear on the substance and logic of the manuscript. Cheryl Carvalho systematized the original FBI releases and provided helpful insights. Christopher D'Arcy developed useful data with his research projects.

Many thanks go to my friend Larry Schlossman for his encouragement and support, his sound advice on investigative strategy and media relations, and for introducing me to Greg Stone and urging that Dan Moldea be encouraged to investigate the case. Thanks, too, to Paul Le Mat for his firm commitment to historical truth and his support for finding it. David Cross conducted significant research and worked closely with Greg Stone. He and Greg performed the formidable task of copying the District Attorney's Office audio and video tapes while under official supervision. Zeta Cross helped the causes of disclosure and re-opening both on and off the air.

A salute is due to those law-enforcement personnel, both active and retired, who were willing to talk about this case when their peers would not – especially those who talked candidly and, to the best of my knowledge, truthfully. Most notable among these is retired FBI agent William Bailey, who, upon realizing that he had observed what turned out to be too many bullets for Sirhan's gun, placed his obligation of citizenship ahead of all else and courageously engaged in what he humorously describes as "a conspiracy to tell the truth." I appreciate those cooperative and civil Los Angeles officials with whom I dealt during the disclosure process: Steve Sowders of the District Attorney's office and Sheldon Brown; Barbara Schlei, then serving on the Police Commission.

Both the author and the nation owe a large debt to the key witnesses who provided detailed, thoughtful accounts despite the pain of reliving the tragedy and, in some cases, the uneasiness (or fear) created by their previous dealings with Los Angeles law enforcement.

This book owes its inception to my literary agent, Frank

Weimann. It was his idea, and he stuck with it through some tough times to bring it to fruition. Frank shared my goal of getting closer to resolving the case and would not sacrifice this goal to commercial pressures. His good humor and hard-nosed professionalism were sustaining resources for me.

As always, my extended family and friends have been wonderfully supportive during this long and complex project (especially my mother). My sons, Brett and Jess, have listened to my discussions concerning the substance and problems of the case – and my frustrations with it – and have been interested as well as supportive. I thank them and my wife, Judith, for putting up with my absence during literally hundreds of hours of case-related phone sessions and during the numerous weeks in Los Angeles.

I owe my largest personal debt to Judith. She provided the moral and emotional support that sustained me during the difficulties encountered in various phases of this project. She not only listened but gave me sound and much-needed advice that improved the political, colleaguial and investigative dimensions of my involvement. She also skillfully edited and typed the various drafts of the manuscript and the numerous and lengthy letters and research memos that preceded it. Again, I could not have completed this project and achieved whatever success it may have, were it not for the extraordinary quality and quantity of her support and her efforts.

For all this varied assistance I am extremely greatful.

Philip H. Melanson
Marion, Massachusetts
1991

Index